HOLTEN HIGH
DANVERS MASS.
SCHOOL

Richard V. Ellery

DEDICATED TO

The Alumni of Holten High School

For All They Have Accomplished

The Students of Danvers High School

For All They Will Accomplish

An Excellent Teacher, Friend, and Editor

Our Son, Peter N. Zollo

THE
DONNING COMPANY
PUBLISHERS
20TH
ANNIVERSARY

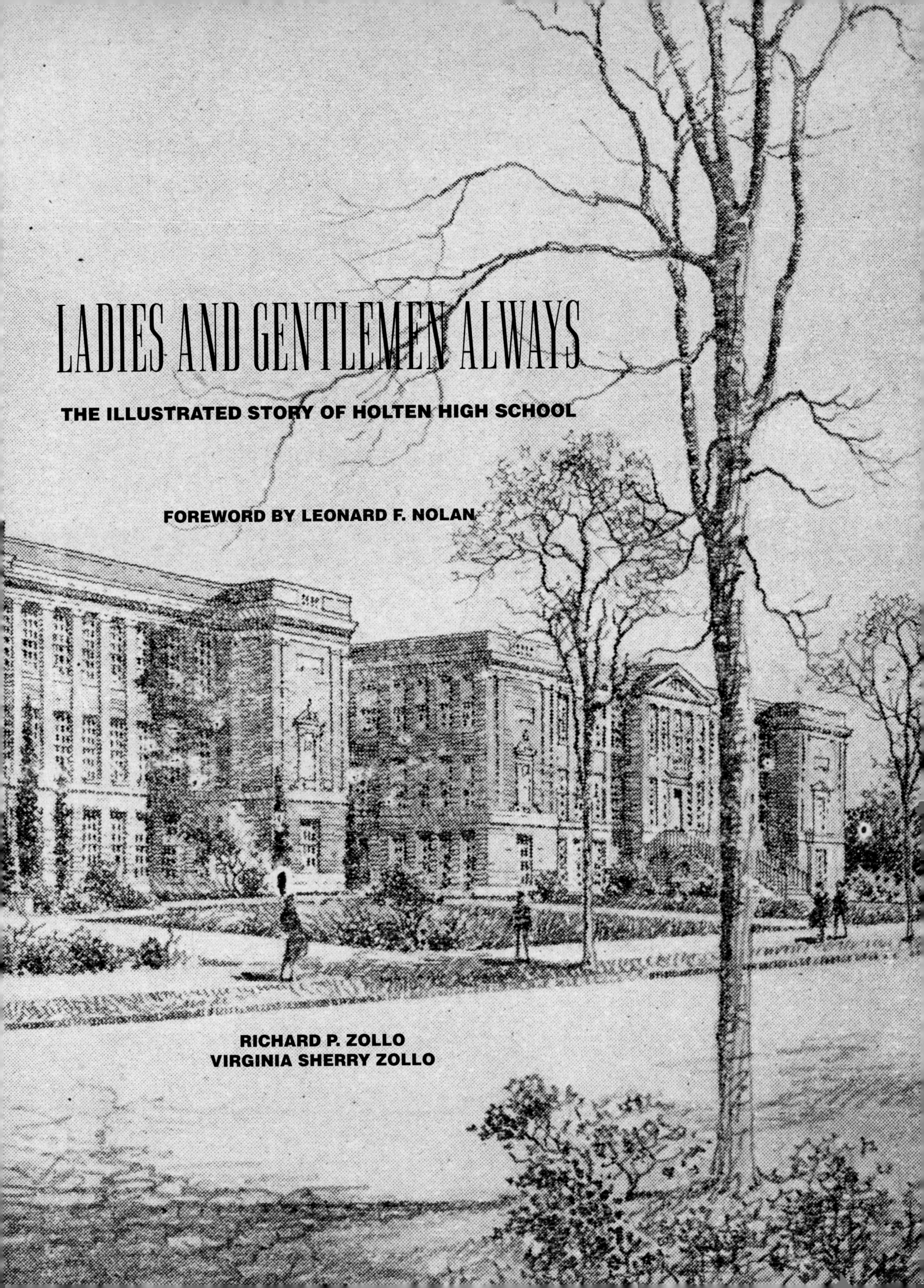

LADIES AND GENTLEMEN ALWAYS

THE ILLUSTRATED STORY OF HOLTEN HIGH SCHOOL

FOREWORD BY LEONARD F. NOLAN

RICHARD P. ZOLLO
VIRGINIA SHERRY ZOLLO

Danvers Town Hall/Holten High School circa 1900

Endsheet photo: The new Holten High School Band in 1929

For information, write:

The Donning Company/Publishers
184 Business Park Drive, Suite 106
Virginia Beach, Virginia 23462

Steve Mull, General Manager
Mary Jo Kurten, Editor
L. J. Wiley, Art Director, Designer
Debra Y. Quesnel, Project Director
Tracey Emmons-Schneider, Project Research Coordinator
Elizabeth B. Bobbitt, Production Editor
Tony Lillis, Director of Marketing

Library of Congress Cataloging in Publication Data:
Zollo, Richard P., 1926–
Ladies and gentlemen always: the illustrated story of Holten High School/
by Richard P. Zollo, Virginia Sherry Zollo; foreword by Leonard F. Nolan.
p. cm.
Includes bibliographical references and index.
ISBN 0-89865-927-2 (alk. paper)
1. Holten High School (Danvers, Mass.)—History. I. Zollo, Virginia Sherry. II. Title.
LD7501.D1695Z65 1994
373.9744—dc20 94-29213
CIP
Printed in the United States of America

TABLE OF CONTENTS

Philip Hopkins (top), Donald Horgan, and Carmine Bianco become a human totem pole in 1947 for Ann McNamara, at Canobie Lake for their class picnic.

Patricia Reynolds and Jayne O'Rourke point their new saddle shoes toward photographer and classmate Jane Porter on June 5, 1940, at Canobie Lake.

The Holten High School Orchestra in 1920–1921.

PREFACE

This is a description of Holten High School, its people and the events that made it unique. What began as a short appreciation of a beloved principal, Cornelius F. Dunn, grew to include all secondary schools that Danvers students could have attended up to 1962 when Danvers High School came into being.

The book has been written for the enjoyment of the alumni and their families. Each chapter begins with an overview setting Holten High School in the context of what was going on nationally in education. These opening segments can be omitted. The "I" in the narrative is the undersigned. As the months and months of writing passed, more anecdotes and a great many constructive criticisms were supplied by the former Miss Sherry. Wink with her keen recollections even recalled dialog, a great asset in any narrative. For these and other reasons, it is right that her name also appear on the cover.

This project eventually evolved into a family one when our son, Peter, volunteered to read and edit the text. At that point I became not only professor emeritus but also composition pupil. The situation reminded me of Wordsworth's, "The child is father of the man." I understand better now why his students appreciate him so much.

Our family circle, like the relationship of those who went to Holten High School, became an extended one after I asked Leonard Nolan to write the Foreword, which you are about to read. Then his son, Leonard Jr., loaned me the photograph of his parents. I first knew his mother as Miss McDewell, my fifth grade teacher at Danversport. She was one of the best teachers I ever had—and that includes a lot of teachers and a lot of schools.

I apologize to all those who do not appear in these pages. I've tried to include as many as I can (nearly eight hundred) and still have a readable text. I'm sure there are other more important people and events that I omitted. While I contacted many former teachers and students, that number is small compared to the number of living graduates. Please accept those who are here as representative of you all.

In these pages I've attempted to maintain a balance between matters academic and extracurricular, between sciences and humanities, and between college, commercial, and general students. There is a good deal here on authors who are also alumni. That represents my bias, but they have given me another voice and oftentimes a different point of view of teachers and school. I could

During a lunch break in 1946, Edith Turenne (left), Geraldine Tremblay, and Ruth Townsend mug for photographer Stacia Zuk. The girls behind them are practicing baton twirling. The open land abutting Conant Street was soon to be developed by Clyde Hennigar.

have included others like Helen Miller Swift, a writer of books for girls, and novelist Ardele Cogswell.

I wish I had written about Charles and George Abbe, the sons of a former Congregational minister in Middleton, but that material came too late. Both young men wrote up sports for *The Holten*. George, who was editor of his older brother Charles's *Hill Wind* (New York, 1936), a collection of letters and poems, is a writer of many books. His *Voices In the Square* (New York, 1938) is a first novel of quality for which Stephen Vincent Benet wrote an appreciation. People of Middleton, however, found it a little too autobiographical and too

critical of them, especially one nice young lady whose unusual first name was given to a much less-than-nice character.

Well, be that as it may, here is your opportunity to grade an old Holten High English teacher. I hope you enjoy the volume, for it has been written for you for all the pleasant memories you have given both Wink and me. Hey, you're history now!

Richard Zollo, Boothbay Harbor, Maine, March 28, 1994

A field hockey team in 1938. In the back row, left to right, are girls' physical education instructor Edith Dixie, Rose Ann Baker, Marilyn Kent, Mary Shabowich, Rita Cameron, Henrietta Newbegin, Lois Smith, Eva LeBlanc, Hazel Mello, and Jean Eisenhauer. Those kneeling are Dorothy Eastman, Ruth Burnham, Barbara Hammond, Elena DiPaolo, Malvina DeCotis, and Catherine Romeos.

FOREWORD

For a period of fifty years I was associated with two Holten High Schools and the current Danvers High School as a student and later as a teacher. Multitudinous changes occurred during this period both in the schools and in society.

The Holten High School in the Danvers town hall now arouses the curiosity of present high school students. How could that building house four grades of secondary school students in the upper two floors? What progress could one make with such limited facilities? What could hold your interest in a building lacking a gymnasium, cafeteria, library, and exterior playing areas? However, from this fine old building emerged many noteworthy students due to the excellent education they received. It enabled them tó make their mark in society not only locally but nationally and internationally.

The handicaps of the building's facilities were overcome in various ways. Life in those days was vastly different from life today. Phonographs and the new invention of radio provided some means of entertainment. Students devised their own games and out-of-school activities such as sandlot football and baseball. Thus, they accepted in the 1920s a high school as an institution for acquiring learning in their preparation for life. The school day ended at 1:15 P.M. as only sandwiches and soup were available during the recess period. The town library was in close proximity to the high school so students could easily obtain research material for their reports. The town park was located some distance away, but it was the site for football practices and games, for outdoor track, and the town diamond which was utilized for baseball games. Like a humble home for a family there was an innate feeling among the classes in the institution that this was their home for learning, which molded them into one organization. Facets in these bonds were class activities, George Peabody scholarship drives, athletics, and a respect for members of the staff who would be the instruments to assist them in their preparation for life. The Holten High song written in the late 1920s seems to state the epitome of this bond:

We will be true, oh Holten High,
In your defeat or victory.
Through all the years to come we pledge
Our unswerving fealty.
If in some future hour of need,
You should call us once again,
We would stand true,
Loyal to you,
Oh Holten High.

Holten High School cafeteria on Conant Street in 1961.

In 1931 the building inadequacies of the high school at the town hall were resolved with the opening of the new Holten High School on Conant Street. It was adjacent to the town park and connected to the Richmond Junior High School, which provided shared facilities. The new building had spacious classrooms on three floors. It included science, physics, and chemistry laboratories, a music department, a study hall library, and a beautiful cafeteria with ample chairs and tables for the students. It also had a gymnasium, which was the finest on the North Shore at that time. In 1932, this facility was utilized as the site for the North Shore Interscholastic Basketball Tournament. The event pitted basketball teams from area schools in Divisions A and B. There was intense excitement during these contests and large crowds attended for the five or six nights needed to determine a champion in each division.

Miss Lee Page, the girls' physical education instructor, organized the Blue and White Club. At the end of the basketball season, she initiated an intramural basketball tournament involving blue and white teams in each of the four grades. This organization continued to grow and offered competition in other seasonal sports. The outgrowth of the program was the development of interscholastic competition with area schools.

Under the leadership of the boys' physical education director, Charles Vye, with the cooperation of Principal Dunn and Faculty Manager Lewis Crosby, the Northeastern Conference was organized in 1931. It arranged competition for Holten High to play area teams in basketball and baseball. Football competition was added in 1934. The number of sports engaged in, by boys and girls in the conference, embraces twenty sports today.The new school, like the previous one, had a staff of devoted teachers who earned the respect of their students. Their leader, Principal Cornelius Dunn, had an aptness for selecting qualified teaching personnel and then molding them to instruct their students with compassion and understanding. He was extremely proud of his school and obtained the cooperation of the staff to serve the students proficiently and with propriety. Each year he was the senior class advisor to assist students planning to matriculate to college.

A young teacher joining the Holten High staff enjoyed a close association with older teachers who willingly shared their experiences and advice with a newcomer. This amicable affiliation was very conspicuous at the social gatherings of the faculty. Moreover, a well-mannered student body was a pleasure to instruct. It enabled a teacher to enjoy a fine rapport with his pupils. Their sharing with you their experiences, activities, and even their romances was conducive to developing a happy relationship. One looks back fondly on those joyous days and delights in reading or hearing of the successes of former students.

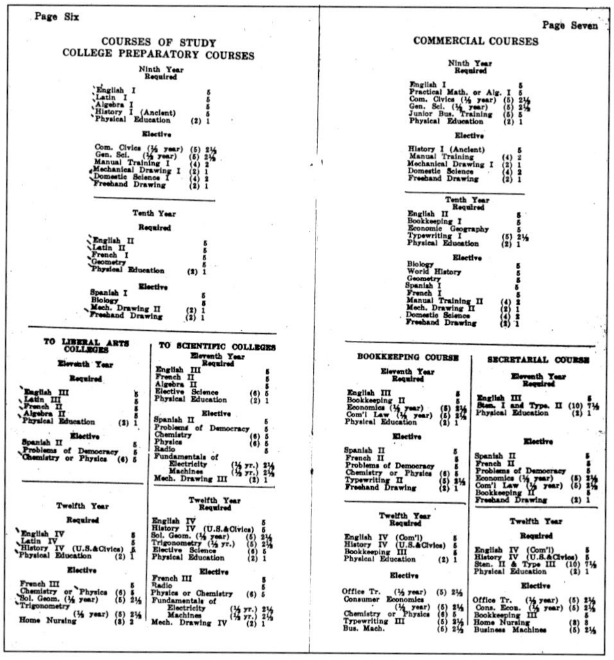

Page Six

COURSES OF STUDY
COLLEGE PREPARATORY COURSES

Ninth Year
Required

English I 5
Latin I 5
Algebra I 5
History I (Ancient) 5
Physical Education (2) 1

Elective

Com. Civics (½ year) (5) 2½
Gen. Sci. (½ year) (5) 2½
Manual Training I (4) 2
Mechanical Drawing I (2) 1
Domestic Science I (4) 2
Freehand Drawing (2) 1

Tenth Year

Required

English II 5
Latin II 5
French I 5
Geometry 5
Physical Education (2) 1

Elective

Spanish I 5
Biology 5
Mech. Drawing II (2) 1
Freehand Drawing (2) 1

TO LIBERAL ARTS COLLEGES

Eleventh Year

Required

English III 5
Latin III 5
French II 5
Algebra II 5
Physical Education (2) 1

Elective

Spanish II 5
Problems of Democracy 5
Chemistry or Physics (6) 5

Twelfth Year

Required

English IV 5
Latin IV 5
History IV (U.S.&Civics) 5
Physical Education (2) 1

Elective

French III 5
Chemistry or Physics (6) 5
Sol. Geom. (½ year) (5) 2½
Trigonometry (½ year) (5) 2½
Home Nursing (3) 2

TO SCIENTIFIC COLLEGES

Eleventh Year
Required

English III 5
French II 5
Algebra II 5
Elective Science (6) 5
Physical Education (2) 1

Elective

Spanish II 5
Problems of Democracy 5
Chemistry (6) 5
Physics (6) 5
Radio 5
Fundamentals of
Electricity (½ yr.) 2½
Machines (½ yr.) 2½
Mech. Drawing III (2) 1

Twelfth Year
Required

English IV 5
History IV (U.S.&Civics) 5
Sol. Geom. (½ year) (5) 2½
Trigonometry (½ yr.) (5) 2½
Elective Science (6) 5
Physical Education (2) 1

Elective

French III 5
Radio 5
Physics or Chemistry (6) 5
Fundamentals of
Electricity (½ yr.) 2½
Machines (½ yr.) 2½
Mech. Drawing IV (2) 1

Page Seven

COMMERCIAL COURSES

Ninth Year
Required

English I 5
Practical Math. or Alg. I 5
Com. Civics (½ year) (5) 2½
Gen. Sci. (½ year) (5) 2½
Junior Bus. Training (5) 5
Physical Education (2) 1

Elective

History I (Ancient) 5
Manual Training (4) 2
Mechanical Drawing I (2) 1
Domestic Science (4) 2
Freehand Drawing (2) 1

Tenth Year
Required

English II 5
Bookkeeping I 5
Economic Geography 5
Typewriting I (5) 2½
Physical Education (2) 1

Elective

Biology 5
World History 5
Geometry 5
Spanish I 5
French I 5
Manual Training II (4) 2
Mech. Drawing II (2) 1
Domestic Science (4) 2
Freehand Drawing (2) 1

BOOKKEEPING COURSE

Eleventh Year
Required

English III 5
Bookkeeping II 5
Economics (½ year) (5) 2½
Com'l Law (½ year) (5) 2½
Physical Education (2) 1

Elective

Spanish II 5
French II 5
Problems of Democracy 5
Chemistry or Physics (6) 5
Typewriting II (5) 2½
Freehand Drawing (2) 1

Twelfth Year
Required

English IV (Com'l) 5
History IV (U.S.&Civics) 5
Bookkeeping III 5
Physical Education (2) 1

Elective

Office Tr. (½ year) (5) 2½
Consumer Economics (½ year) (5) 2½
Chemistry or Physics (6) 5
Typewriting III (5) 2½
Bus. Mach. (5) 2½

SECRETARIAL COURSE

Eleventh Year
Required

English III 5
Sten. I and Type. II (10) 7½
Physical Education (2) 1

Elective

Spanish II 5
French II 5
Problems of Democracy 5
Economics (½ year) (5) 2½
Com'l Law (½ year) (5) 2½
Bookkeeping II 5
Freehand Drawing (2) 1

Twelfth Year

Required

English IV (Com'l) 5
History IV (U.S.&Civics) 5
Sten. II & Type III (10) 7½
Physical Education (2) 1

Elective

Office Tr. (½ year) (5) 2½
Cons. Econ. (½ year) (5) 2½
Bookkeeping III 5
Home Nursing (3) 3
Business Machines (5) 2½

Required and elective courses for four out of the five academic tracks for 1946–1947 are represented here. The fifth was the general course for those completing their educations when they received their diplomas. Students were required to take at least twenty credits per year, and not more than twenty-five without the principal's permission. Outside credits could be earned in certain areas of music.

The administration expanded the curriculum to include tracking programs for students in the college scientific, college preparatory, business education, and general courses. Homeroom teachers served as guidance counselors to assist in selecting their courses for the next school year. The school day was extended from 1:15 to 2:00 so class periods could be lengthened and additional activities were included to fulfill the interests and needs of the student body. *The Holten* magazine increased in staff and more students became involved in its contents. A student council was organized with representatives elected from each class. Now students could express their opinions, which could be commendable or otherwise. Pep rallies were held in the gymnasium before important athletic contests, adding immensely to the school spirit. The band represented the school at football games and town parades. Students were now able to enjoy weekly assemblies. Teachers were assigned dates to direct assembly programs, which usually featured the talents of their pupils, or they directed programs commemorating historic holidays. Each year a special assembly was held to raise funds through the sale of magazines for a number of projects that were not financed in the school budget. From these funds the football players who earned a letter in this sport were awarded beautiful sweaters at the Christmas assembly.

A Gladys Damon photograph of a 1941 basketball game between Holten and Peabody high schools.

These extracurricular festivities enriched the lives of the students. The pleasures which they enjoyed were a distinct contrast to the few activities in the previous Holten High School. They were also a reflection of the changes in society between the 1920s and the 1950s.

As the 1960s approached, the Danvers School Committee informed the citizens of Danvers that a new high school had to be built. The existing high school would require expenditures in the millions to enlarge and rebuild or refurbish existing areas and equipment to provide the mandatory requirements of the state School Building Commission. Consultants hired by the school committee recommended building a new structure that would be large enough to house the increasing high school population. It would also include modern laboratories, research centers, language audio rooms, enlarged gymnasium, library, cafeteria, and assembly room. Moreover, it would satisfy all the safety requirements mandated by the state. The townspeople supported the report of the school committee, and the new structure was opened in 1962.

Former students of Holten High at their reunions still cherish their days spent at the last two schools, the town hall/high school and the Conant Street facility, and reflect on the educational training they received and the extra-curricular activities they enjoyed. The years spent in the high schools of Danvers represent a lifetime of teaching and guiding young lives that gives one immense satisfaction with their accomplishments. The pleasure of their friendships and being a part of their lives are cherished memories.

Leonard F. Nolan, chairman of the History Department, and his wife, Ellen.

Leonard F. Nolan

Grand March for the Senior Snowball Dance in 1953. Shirley Oldson, Eugene Kimball, Sandra Masi, Chester French, Barbara White, Fred La Montagne, Priscilla Wheeler, and William Faust are in the front row.

ACKNOWLEDGMENTS

This work has taken many years to complete; therefore, the list of those I have to thank is long—and should be longer. Unfortunately, I have lived in three different houses since its commencement. If in the enumerations that follow I have omitted anyone, I ask indulgence as age has dulled my memory and hasn't done too much for my knees either.

Among those who helped in this project are Roger Barry, Jacqueline Brooks, Roger Budgell, Bessie Bliven, Attilio Capra, Earl and Betty Clay, Helen Cook, Paul and Barbara Cotoia, Carl Crossman, Elinor Cullen, Ernest DiPaolo, Olive Durkee, Victor Elmere, James Gaffney, Jr., Marjorie Giles, Roger Hansen, Dorothy Hart, Stephen and Merle Hawkes, Doris Robinson, Sally Ann Jackson, Elizabeth Kennedy, Evelyn King, Joanne Klosowski, Yvonne Kendley, Robert Leach, Ray LeColst, Albert Lyons, William Lyons, Elizabeth McCarthy, Ann McNamara, David and Joyce Ouimette, Charlotte Parrott, John Peterson, Shirley Raynard, Peter and Edith Riso, Helen Seeley, Thomas Shehan, Jane and Robert Southworth, Cory Staid, Sally Symmes, Toni Theriault, Daniel Toomey, Frank Tyrrell, Harry Ventre, Ruth Weeks, Beatrice Welch, and Lucy Young.

Others gave more time and effort than requested for the success of this volume. They are Thurl D. Brown, Mingo Citroni, Priscilla Curda, Robert Deering, Bruce and Martha Eaton, Faye Gardner, Virginia Hayward, Roger Hubbard, Jean Pedrick Kefferstan, Rita and Ruth Kirby, David Knowlton, Dorothy Kraft, Sandra Masi, Cynthia Meehan, Marguerite Morris, Newell Moore, Elizabeth Morrison, Richard Morrissey, Frederick Usher, Fred and Helen Vaillancourt, Vasilea Varoutsos, Priscilla Watson, and Allen R. Wylie.

Finally, there were those who not only provided extra assistance, but much encouragement as well: Dr. Walter L. Creese, Eileen Lynch, Marie Lynch, Audrey Meyer, Leonard Nolan, Jr. and Leonard Nolan, Sr., Jane Potter, Henrietta Sears, and Jack Zollo. Librarians who always do far more than is requested were Barbara Harvey of the Boothbay Harbor Memorial Library, Paige Lilly of the Penobscot Marine Museum of Searsport, two wonderful but anonymous researchers at the Maine State Library in Augusta for all the material they located on Holten High School authors, Suzanne McLeod of the Peabody Institute Library, and especially to Richard B. Trask, the Danvers Archivist, without whose help no volume on the history of Danvers can be written.

The home of Daniel Epes, third headmaster of Salem Latin School, corner of Church and Washington streets. This cut appears in Sidney Perley's History of Salem, *volume 1.*

CHAPTER I

Educating for God—The 1600s

The instruction of Puritan children in the seventeenth century represents one of the great achievements in the history of American education. Our founding fathers honored learning as no other colonies would. Their system was not perfect. The recitation method they employed was stultifying; their discipline, harsh. The education of girls was oppressively inadequate.

But the Puritans brought into the New World's wilderness an Elizabethan respect for the ancient classics upon which Western thought is based. And with a magnanimity unknown in the Old World, they established a remarkable precedent, universal free education. Amazingly, in view of the extreme hardships they were experiencing, they did their most effective and innovative work during the first forty years of the colony's existence before large-scale immigration and a British mandate forcing them to accept the Anglican religion and its adherents within their borders dissipated the cohesiveness of their small Bible Commonwealth.

Whenever our colonial forebears had a choice between the practical and the ideal, they opted for the latter as long as ideal equated with accepted doctrine. For that reason Harvard College was founded in 1636 to insure that future generations of ministers would be learned men. One statistic has it that 95 percent of seventeenth century New England clergymen held college degrees. The maritime historian Samuel Eliot Morison makes the point in *The Building of the Bay Colony* that it would be the duty of these American-educated divines to insist "on giving the people education to receive the Word, and understand the minister."

To insure fulfillment of that goal, the General Court enacted a statute in 1647 stipulating that communities of one hundred households had to keep a grammar or boys' secondary school. Also called a Latin school, its main purpose was to train boys destined for the ministry. Towns of fifty families had to provide a teacher for boys and girls who applied to them to learn to read, write, and cipher. Both reading and arithmetic were necessary for Bible study since, as Paul Leicester Ford explains in *The New England Primer*, the latter was offered so that children could locate chapter and verse.

So strongly did the Puritan theocracy feel about everyone's being educated that in 1673 the General Court passed a law requiring youngsters to be "brought up in some honest calling and to be taught to read perfectly the English tongue." Five fathers in Salem in November of that year, according to Perley's *History of Salem*, had their children taken from them for neglecting their family responsibilities in this regard.

Beyond the primary level, girls had no further schooling unless they had affluent parents who hired tutors. The seventeenth century concern about educating girls beyond the rudiments was that advanced study would addle their minds and make them unsuited for motherhood. In his 1640 *History of New England*, for example, Governor John Winthrop related the sad tale of "a goodly woman of special parts (talents), who was fallen into a sad infirmity, the loss of her understanding and reason which had been growing upon her divers years by the occasion of giving herself wholly to reading and writing and had written many books." And so women were taught to weave and sew and cook, bear children, and not to be actively engaged in the affairs of the world.

A year previous to Harvard's opening, Boston Latin School held classes for its initial scholars. And nearer to home in 1637, Salem also voted to have a town grammar school. Because Salem Village (Danvers) and Middle Precinct (Peabody) were then part of Salem, although settled later in the century, their young men could attend this school.

In a limited way, Salem's grammar school can be said to have been free. Schoolmasters were guaranteed a set wage each year. This money was raised from three sources: private endowment from wealthy citizens, the ratepayers of the parish, and tuition. When the matter of tuition was considered, it was voted, "If any poor body hath children or child to be put in school, and not able to pay this schooling . . . the Town will pay it by vote." In this 1644 decision is the origin of local free education.

Church and school acted as one in saving souls. Second only to the minister, a town regarded its schoolmaster as its most respected citizen. Both men shared the same education, and teachers were generally ordained. For over two hundred years, it was the practice that religious leaders in New England serve on school boards. In Danvers right through the nineteenth century, ministers were either appointed or elected to school committees. First Church pastors from Benjamin Wadsworth, who served his church from 1772 to 1826, to Milton Braman, 1826–1861, and then to Charles B. Rice, 1863–1894, evaluated both pupils and teachers. The Reverend James Fletcher of the Maple Street Church, 1849–1871, was the fifth principal of Holten High School before he became headmaster of Lawrence Academy. What should be kept in mind is that since the towns paid the schoolmasters and supported the schools they were essentially civic institutions.

Ministers were frequently present in the classroom in the seventeenth and eighteenth centuries to catechize scholars. They were always there on the final day of school for the same reason. No matter how successfully a master taught academic subjects, wrote Morison, if one asked him why he taught, he would answer, "For Godliness." The Puritans believed children were born tainted by Adam's original sin and therefore, innately evil. Education might not save them, but without it there was no hope of salvation.

Evidence of how basic the primary education was that Puritan youngsters received in those early years can be found in the entrance requirements for the Latin schools. A boy of six or seven had to read a few passages from the Bible, show evidence of good spelling, and understand the rudiments of arithmetic. Once into the school, however, he found the generally seven-year course of study rigorous. Among those Latin texts to be mastered would be several grammars, Aesop's *Fables*, Cicero, Caesar, Ovid, Virgil, Horace, Juvenile, and other classical authors. In addition, he had to have a basic knowledge of Greek for entrance into Harvard. If he was a particularly apt scholar, he might even embark on the study of Hebrew.

Of the Bay Colony's most prominent schoolmasters in the seventeenth century, two had close Danvers connections. One was Ezekiel Cheever, Sr., Boston Latin's first headmaster, who had an extraordinarily long career as an educator, seventy years in all, including thirty-eight of them in Boston and eleven previous to that in Ipswich.

Born in England in 1615 and educated at Cambridge University as so many of the original Puritan religious leaders were, he assumed his position in the Boston grammar school in 1670. His *Accidence, A Short Introduction to the Latin Tongue* (1671) was used for almost two hundred years in American Latin schools. The year Holten High School was founded in 1850, the eighteenth edition of *The Accidence* was printed. Harriet Webster Marr, in researching her *New England Academies Founded before 1826*, tells us that scholars had to memorize all eighty-two pages of Cheever's text. This included fourteen pages of verbs and the rest of the pages of rules and paradigms.

Cheever had a reputation for not sparing the rod. *Social Life in Old New England*, by Mary Caroline Crawford, preserves for us the Reverend Samuel Maxwell's word portrait of Headmaster Cheever: "He wore a long white beard, terminating in a point, and when he stroked his beard to the point it was a sign for the boys to stand clear."

In his eulogy of Cheever, Cotton Mather in *Corderius Americanus* had the Boston master address New England teachers in these ironic words:

> TUTORS, Be Strict, But yet be gentle too:
> Don't by fierce Cruelties fair Hopes undo.
> Dream not that they who are to Learning slow,
> Will mend by Arguments in Ferio.

In other words, use the rod judiciously.

Cheever educated two sons, Thomas and Samuel, to be ministers. To a third, his namesake who had become a Salem tailor, he and his wife deeded the farm in Salem Village, near the Middleton line in Hathorne, that she had inherited from her uncle, Capt. Thomas Lothrop, killed along with seventy-one of his men, the Flower of Essex County, during the Indian Wars at the Battle of Bloody Brook. This was in Deerfield in 1675.

Ezekiel Cheever, Jr., and his family moved to the Village in 1684. If this Cheever had not the erudition of his brothers, he had been given a good education. In recognition of that attainment, he was appointed by the magistrates to record the first witchcraft hearing on March 1, 1692, at the Village meetinghouse. In all, he wrote up the examinations of Sarah Osburn, Sarah Good, and Tituba.

Through the Salem grammar school's third master, Daniel Epes, who had even closer Salem Village associations than the senior Cheever, we learn much about local seventeenth century education. Born on March 24, 1649, and taught by Thomas Andrews in Ipswich, Epes graduated second in his class from Harvard in 1669. First in order was his older brother Samuel. While the younger man was an excellent student, his class standing was not due to his scholastic achievements. It was based on the wealth and social standing of his family.

Following graduation, Daniel Epes taught in Salem in 1671. Then he left for a few years, probably to occupy a pulpit in some other township since he often preached in nearby parishes like Topsfield. In the 1650s, he was invited to minister at Salem Village on a visiting basis between the pastorates of George Burroughs and Deodat Lawson. Teaching, however, was his preference. He returned to Salem in 1677 and taught there until 1699. Long before his retirement, he was referred to affectionately as "the old schoolmaster."

At the beginning of his career, Epes had been hired to teach English, Latin, Greek, the principles of the Christian religion, and good habits. His course of study was directed toward preparing his charges for entrance into Harvard, where the first statutes, laws, and privileges of the college stated young men had to demonstrate the ability to read "Cicero and any other classic author presented to them." Latin was still the universal language of diplomacy, scholarship, and religion. These students of Epes had also to show that they could write and speak both Latin prose and poetry. Because the quality of Puritan verse was not especially high, with the exception of the lyric poetry of Anne Bradstreet, the latter was perhaps not so difficult as it might seem. "God's altar needs not our polishings," explained the Reverend Richard Mather, Cotton Mather's grandfather, in his preface to the *Bay Psalm Book* of his committee's literal translation of the sacred songs from the Hebrew.

Finally, these prospective freshmen had to demonstrate their proficiency in Greek grammar. Their intense study of the classics did not inspire heretical thoughts in the minds of young Puritan scholars because, Edmund Morgan notes in *The Puritan Family*, "They were taught to look at the classics as simply other sourcebooks of the laws of nature, inferior to but not in conflict with the greatest sourcebook, the Bible."

In his 1702 history of the colony, *Magnalia Christi Americana*, Cotton Mather asked, "May not schoolmasters do much to instill the principles of religion and civility, as well as other good points of good education, into the children of the Towne [Boston] Only let the Town well encourage its well deserving schoolmasters." For more than two centuries in American education, *good* meant almost invariably *moral*, not *effective*.

Daniel Epes was certainly well encouraged. Like all masters he was given the title "Mister" rather than the common man's "Goodman." When tuitions and endowment did not completely compensate him for his annual salary in 1678–1679, he received the rent for the commonlands at Royall (Rial) Side and Baker's and Misery Islands. Lease money from the ferryboat operators between Salem and Beverly and between Salem and Marblehead and even the haying rights over the cemetery at Burial Point were also at various times paid him and other schoolmasters.

In a sense there was even a merit raise possibility for Epes because if what he collected exceeded his salary, he was to have the tuitions of out-of-town scholars. His also was the right to graze his cow on Salem Common free of charge. Privileges he and other masters were granted were exemption from taxes, militia drill, and service in the town's censoring and security provisions called "watching and warding." In regard to the last, on November 3, 1675, the General Court sent out a warning against men wearing long hair "like a woman's," women immodestly "laying out their hair, . . . new strange fashions . . . with naked breasts and arms," and the wearing of "superstitious ribbons." This intrusiveness into private lives many years later caused much resentment and led to the satirical definition of a Puritan as "A person who stays awake nights worrying that somewhere, someone may be having a good time."

Such was the importance of schoolmasters in the seventeenth century that they received the second highest salaries in town; ministers, not surprisingly, were first. There were also other encouragements to make the master's job more pleasant. In the 1670s on School House Lane, where the Masonic Temple is located today in Salem, a new two-story townhouse was constructed with Daniel Epes's classroom on the first floor and a courtroom on the second. The shingles for this building were given by Francis Nurse of Salem Village to settle a debt he owed the town. Ironically, in late June, 1692, in the courtroom, his wife Rebecca was declared guilty of witchcraft and sentenced to be hanged. In January 1695, a belfry was mounted on the roof. Beginning in 1700, the selectmen ordered the bell to be rung for the start and closing of the school day, i.e., at 7:00 A.M. and 5:00 P.M. from the first of November to the first of March. For the balance of the year the schools hours were from 8:00 A.M. to 4:00 P.M.

There was a generous lunch break, and wisely, the final hour of the long day was given over to the practice of handwriting and the sharpening of quill pens for the next day's lessons. Epes's classroom was a rather bare space. There were two platforms—one for the master's desk and the other for student recitations.

There were also a few rows of hard benches on which the scholars sat according to year or form, the latter being the retention of the English public school term. When the boys of one form had repeated their lessons, which they had memorized, they were given another assignment, with little instruction, and sent back to their benches to study. In the meantime, Epes was hearing the lesson from another form. As classroom size increased in the next century and the waiting periods between recitations grew longer, students became increasingly restless and resentful.

But in Epes's century, before what became traditional and tedious to later generations of American scholars, memorization and recitation were also encouraged in the home by parents and guardians and even entered into voluntarily by both girls and boys. Children often chose verses from the Reverend Michael Wiggleworth's 1622 bestseller, *The Day of Doom*, to commit to memory.

From several seventeenth century sources, we can picture Epes ("the most eminent schoolmaster in New England," English traveler John Dunton called him) as a heavyset man, seated in his parlor in one of his "Russion leathern chairs," his silver-headed cane leaning against one knee. As a well-educated colonial with close ties to his brother Samuel living in England, he could have spoken knowledgeably on a variety of subjects of particular interest to a visitor from London: the latest religious controversies being argued here and abroad; farm management and horticultural concerns; attempts to develop New England industries, especially iron foundries, by John Winthrop, Jr., and others; the effect on the local economy of the seizures of coastal vessels by French warships; or the enslavement of prisoners of war taken by the colony's militia as based on Biblical example.

In his autobiography, *Life and Errors,* Dunton tells of his 1686 visit to Salem, where he met Epes. With unintended humor, Dunton described Epes as a "Gentleman; yet he has not humbled his meditations to the industry of compliments, nor afflicted his brain in an elaborate leg (he cannot kiss his hand, and cry, 'Madam, your humble servant'; nor talk idle enough to bear her company). But though a School, and the Hermitage of his Study, has made [him] uncourtly, yet (which is a finer accomplishment) he is a person of solid learning; and does not, like some Authors, lose his time by being busy about nothing, nor make so poor a shew of the World, as to hug and embrace it."

Made welcome in Epes's house with its several gables, overhanging second and third stories, and small diamond-paned windows, Dunton further tells us, "By frequent conferences I had with him, I found him to be a person of great worth; he is free from vice, if ever any man was, for he hath no occasion to use it; and being a good man, is above those ends that make men wicked. I shall only add, I lately received a letter from Mr. Epes for two hundred pounds worth of Books. . . ."

Among those books he listed may well have been several on horticulture since Epes is credited with developing the Epes or Danvers sweeting apple on the large farm he purchased from Col. Thomas Reed's son Samuel in 1701 in that section of Salem's North Fields that became Middle Precinct.

The will Epes made out in 1722 reflects fairness and close attention to details like the listing of his chairs. Phrases like "good young fat pork" and the unnecessary enumeration of the types of "small meat" like veal, lamb, and mutton bespeak a man of generous appetite. To Daniel, his elder son and executor, went the 1636, 300-acre Reed farm, near the present-day North Shore Shopping Center, together with house, barns, fields, and orchards, tools of husbandry, flocks and herds of "Cattell and Sheep," etc. Ever the Latin scholar, at the bottom of page one of his will he directs the reader to "Verte folium" rather than "Turn the page." Apparently he was so thoroughly steeped in a language that he had studied and taught for more than sixty-five years that he thought in both English and Latin. Certainly "Verte folium" was an instruction he used thousands of times in the classroom.

Compared to the era in which Epes taught, the succeeding century seemed one of stagnation, more accurately, one of very slow transition in an attempt to fulfill the different values of the eighteenth and early nineteenth centuries. It is a necessary consequence of religion and education that they must alter slowly or else Truth, as a society perceives it, has no validity. A question historians disagree on today is this: Was the education young people received in the nineteenth century the legacy of the seventeenth century?

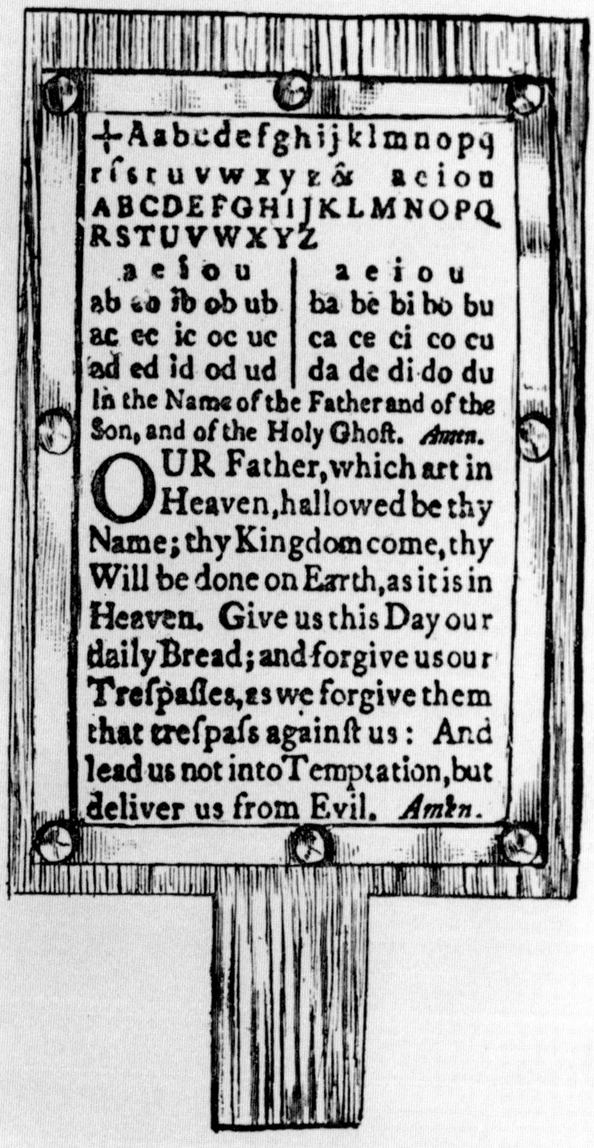

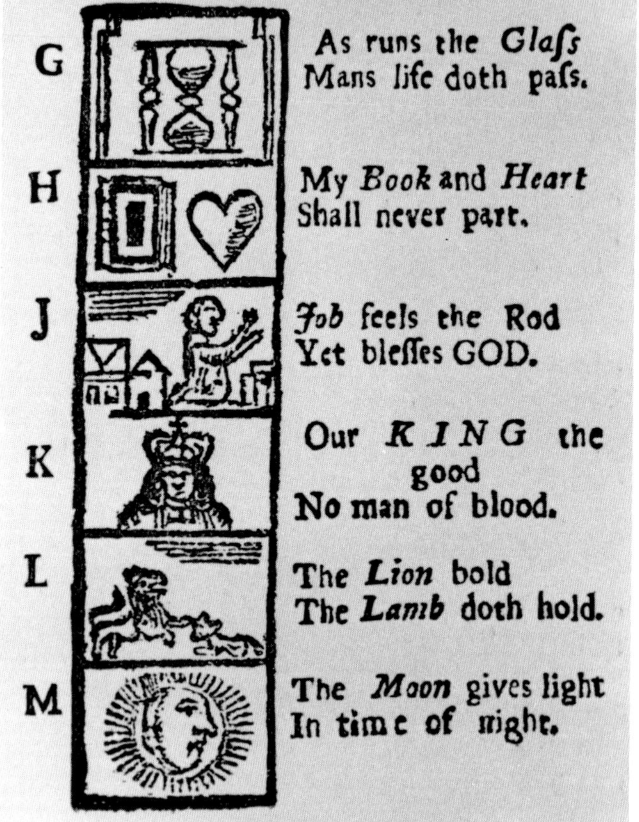

A page from the rhyming alphabet in The New England Primer. *Both illustrations in Chapter Two were taken from Paul Leicester Ford's 1899* The New England Primer.

A horn book. Note the shorter version of the Lord's Prayer and also the two forms for the letter S.

CHAPTER II

Educating in Chaos—The 1700s

The absence of detailed records on education in the eighteenth century frustrates the researcher. One thing is certain. This period was not the best of times, but one of continual and sometimes violent change. Almost every aspect of life in the colonies was in the process of becoming. Education, society, government, and even religion would be decidedly modified by century's end.

The 1700s began with an interval of inflation. In 1714 a Salem Village committee was empowered to find a schoolmaster "and to get him as cheap as they can for the pepell." As long as America was a possession, Great Britain restricted its manufacturing and maritime ambitions. For years Salem Village men fought in wars that were essentially spill-overs from armed struggles on the Continent. In mid-century, the village became a town, Danvers, with the responsibility of setting and collecting its own taxes. Lacking from its revenue were endowments from wealthy citizens like those in Salem willing to supplement school expenses. Finally, the best minds in Essex County were preoccupied with the evolving political controversy, and by the 1770s with training militia companies to take part in the Revolution.

In a sense, Danvers was less a united community than a cluster of individual settlements of which Salem Village was just one section. Education was the loser. In the 1760s to bring business to their river port, the inhabitants of New Mills (Danversport), laid out segments of a road to connect Porter's Plains, the crossroads known today as the Square, with the road to Salem and thence to Lynn and Boston. Those other sections of town bordering on the Ipswich Road feared (and correctly as it transpired) losing the trade this winding old highway brought to them if much of its traffic were siphoned off by a more direct route to the farmers' markets in those large communities.

Since education's benefits are obviously less immediate and tangible than those that highways bring, small wonder it was neglected as long as it was. However, one's duties to others were much on the minds of these people. By the end of the century, they realized they were remiss in their obligations to their children and implemented an innovative system of elementary or district schools.

In 1701, two years after Daniel Epes retired from teaching, the Salem Village parish voted Joseph Herrick, Joseph Putnam, and John Putnam, Jr., a committee to contact "some suitable person" to be a schoolmaster for them in "some convenient time." That it took seven years before they procured an instructor would seem to be stretching "convenient" to an unusual length of time.

These three men constituted the village's first school committee. School business was parish business until the incorporation of Danvers as a district separate from Salem in 1752. In 1756, town meeting chose the first Danvers school committee: David Gardner, David Purrington, Daniel Epes, Jr., Nathaniel Felton, Sr., and David Putnam. These men were instructed to "draw up something and lay it before ye District" concerning the schools. The charge seems as laissez faire as "convenient" had been interpreted more than a half century previous.

It was in 1708 that colonial education really started locally. Tired of this type of procrastination, the fifth Salem Village minister, Joseph Green, Samuel Parris's successor, paid most of the expenses for the building of a schoolhouse and the hiring of the first teacher.

In his diary during March of that year, Green has two brief entries about speaking to neighbors in regard to these matters. Having introduced the subject and received positive responses, he stood up at a meeting of the parish on March 22 and spoke confidently of his plans. "Neighbors," he began, "I am about building a schoolhouse for the good education of our children, and have spoken to several of the neighbors who are willing to help it forward, so that I hope we shall quickly finish it; and I speak of it here that so every one that can have any benefit, may have opportunity for so good a service. . . ."

The congregation's reaction to his proposal is also preserved. "Some replied that it was a new thing to them," he wrote, "and they desired to know where it should stand, and what the design of it was. To them I answered that Deacon (Nathaniel) Ingersoll would give land for it to stand on, at the upper end of the Training field, and that I designed to have a good schoolmaster to teach their children to read and write and cipher and everything that is good. Many commended the design and none objected to it." Recall that *good* here meant *moral.*

Further entries in the diary relate the progress on the schoolhouse. Most of those writing later on this incident believe the building was not used for its intended purpose, although church records show a receipt from that first teacher as having been paid five pounds for "Keeping School at Salem Village at ye School House near Mr. Green's."

In any case, what Green did before the work was completed was quite customary. He rented a room in a private home for a school. During the course of a year, the community would do this in various parts of the parish or town in order to allow equal schooling for children in all sections. Green rented that first room from James Houlton on what is now Prospect Street in Peabody, then part of the Village. The minister's two sons, seven-year-old John and five-year-old Joseph, were sent to this school, which combined the two types of seventeenth century schools—the lower, or reading school and the upper, or writing school. The second taught both writing and arithmetic.

For teacher, Green hired Katherine Daland, a widow for seventeen years who was of high moral character and might otherwise have become an expense on the community. A successful farmer as well as a parson, Green paid her salary for several years. It was not until 1712, according to Charles Rice in a First Church history, that Mrs. Daland was paid by Salem. In 1714, the first schoolmaster was hired. It was he whom "Capt. Putnam and Lieut. Putnam" hired cheap. He was Samuel Andrews, and he may have been retained for a Latin school. When he signed the receipt for his pay on November 3, 1714, he acknowledged having received seven pounds from the two Putnams and an additional forty shillings from "Several persons for teaching their children." Seventeenth century grammar-school masters, as noted in Chapter I, could retain the tuition paid them by out-of-town parents who sent their children to the master's school. Like the function of the schoolhouse, evidence is too slight to make a definite assessment here.

Nevertheless, we can almost be certain from what texts Mrs. Daland would have taught. There were invariably two printed works approved in Massachusetts Bay for very young scholars. The first was a hornbook consisting of a single sheet of paper attached to a paddle-shaped board and protected by a transparent layer of cow's horn. Printed on the paper were the great and small letters, the Roman and/or Arabic numerals, the Lord's Prayer and sometimes a benediction. The second text was the little *New England Primer*, written before 1660 and reprinted as late as the end of the eighteenth century. The book taught the alphabet in rhyming couplets (In Adam's fall/We sinned all); spelling, ending with polysyllabic words like *abomination, mortification, and purification*; and reading by the use of simple rhymes instructing in religion, conduct, and the consequences of bad behavior. At the conclusion of this part, there were eight quatrains,

"Praise to God for learning to Read." When the book had been memorized, young scholars might progress to reading the Bible and the Psalter.

When writing instruction began, students were given quill pens. Since paper was scarce, they practiced with a dry pen before using ink. Ruling on plain paper was accomplished by the use of lead plummets—at least in Danvers. However, penmanship lessons sometimes began at the grammar school level. Later, during the eighteenth century, a slate, a stylus or slate pencil, and a rag to be used as an eraser when wet, were given little scholars by their parents. Once the teacher checked an answer, the slate was wiped clean for the next problem The Danvers Historical Society has a slate with a red felt strip glued around the wooden frame. The function of the cloth was to muffle the clatter of the slate on a wooden desk top.

As far as the town supplying free textbooks and supplies, that service did not begin until 1884–1885, a good part of the reason being those damp rags that soon became quite filthy and so were thought to be unsanitary and the cause of childhood illnesses.

Cyphering texts like Crocker's 1677 *Arithmetick*, printed in London, were rare, but Crocker's went into many editions and was used in Danvers in the early 1800s. While books were available for grammar school scholars, they were not used on the elementary level where the instructors taught simple sums and the times tables.

As noted, Green's two sons went to a school combining primary and elementary levels. The former, when privately run by a local woman in her own home, was known as a Dame School. Samuel Page Fowler, born in 1800, was sent at six years of age to such a school in Danversport. His schoolmistress was Lydia Hayward, who conducted her lessons in the kitchen of the Joshua Kent house. Like all Calvinists, she drilled her scholars in the Bible, but her punishments were uniquely her own. For small offenses she would pin a little boy to her apron. A somewhat more conventional chastisement was administered when she caught her charges daydreaming. She would issue a smart rap to their bare toes with a long willow switch. Other 'Port teachers who maintained Dame schools in 1806 were Miss Rachel Putnam and Miss Hannah Carroll.

The most common complaint of those who attended early schools had to do with a lack of explanation. And this was true at all levels: the reading, writing, and cyphering schools; the nineteenth century ungraded district schools; and the grammar or Latin schools. In his autobiography, *Life of Samuel J. May,* this nineteenth century preacher and abolitionist, born in 1797, tells of an incident that took place in Mrs. Wallcut's Boston dame school. Following a reading from the New Testament, the children wondered what heavenly happiness consisted of.

"One little girl said she thought we should have plenty of burnt almonds there," wrote May. She was, of course, thinking of a favorite treat. "I told them I expected that we should sit up at table and drink coffee."

Major concern for the eighteenth century citizens of Salem Village, however, was less the quality of instruction than it was the lack of a tax-supported school for their children. As early as 1691, the villagers had petitioned the General Court for an allowance toward keeping a school within their boundaries. In the Danvers centennial celebration in 1852, Judge John Proctor gave an address on education in which he observed, "Previous to the separation but little attention had been given (by Salem) to supporting schools for the children on the borders." He meant Salem Village and Middle Precinct.

John Wells, author of *The Peabody Story,* mentions the fact that almost invariably Salem records referred to the citizens of these two villages or parishes as farmers. While the villagers themselves had designated their area as "The Farmes" in the seventeenth century, occupations were fairly diverse in the eighteenth century with the establishment of brick and pottery making and mills of various kinds. Such repetition of the term "farmers" as Salem employed indicates a superior attitude on its part, an attitude that led to keeping the Latin school and other tax-supported institutions close to Town House Square.

One exception came in 1733 as a result of the petitions from both outlying parishes to become separate communities. In that year Salem voted to have four schools, two within the town and one each in Salem Village and Middle Precinct. But this provision came too late to stop the popular movement for independence from Salem.

What finally made the efforts of these two villages successful was an unusual decision on their part to merge and become a single community. In 1752 they became a united district called Danvers. And in 1757 Danvers became a town.

Schoolmaster Epes's descendants were as worthy advocates of good education at this time as he had been in his day. His son and grandson, both named Daniel, signed the memorandum of agreement for separation from Salem in 1751. The son was on the committee to work with Salem and through the General Court for independent community status. At the first town meeting of the new district after the division was approved, the son served as moderator and the grandson as clerk. The son was on the board of selectmen for Danvers, and the grandson, on the second. They and the third Daniel's brother Samuel, a Revolutionary War hero, served as state representatives.

It is ironic that before the eighteenth century was ended, the grammar school Danversites felt so sorely the lack of was apparently no longer in existence. Middle Precinct had been on record as planning a Latin school as early as 1739. In 1756 the town of Danvers voted to select a committee "to regulate ye Grammar School." At the town meeting of March 3, 1757, it was voted to investigate the grammar school. The action seems to indicate a lack of school. On May 22, 1765, on the school committee's recommendation, it was voted to keep a grammar school half the year in the North Parish (Danvers) and the other half in the South Parish (Peabody).

The necessity for the last decision was partly due to the large area covered by Danvers at the time, making it difficult for a scholar in one end of town to get to the school at the other. As for the nomenclature, the term *Parish* was used for affairs within the town. In the same period, the terms *South Danvers* (Peabody) and *North Danvers* (present-day Danvers) were employed for business outside the town. The location for town meetings alternated annually between the two centers. These actions point up the very loose federation of the former villages. As time went on, sectional rivalry became more intense and led ultimately to their separation in 1855.

Why, we may ask, the sporadic existence and eventual loss of an institution like the grammar school? There were several reasons. The new township had now the full financial responsibility of funding its own institutions without any subsidy from Salem. Qualified teachers did not, in fact, come cheap. And military rather than educational matters occupied more and more of the town's attention. In this long period of transition, the decline of theocratic rule made the necessity of a school whose main purpose was the preparation of future ministers less imperative. Finally, the dominating themes in education were becoming God and country.

Under these circumstances, the small number of men applying for admission to the grammar school might not have seemed adequate to support the salary of a schoolmaster, especially in a community where control rested solidly in the hands of practical-minded farmers and businessmen.

During the eighteenth century there are records of only eleven native sons of the town who were college graduates. In 1852, Judge Proctor recited the names of ten, a list compiled by a centennial committee. Add to this roster Ebenezer Putnam, brother of Archelaus, identified by Harriet Tapley. There may well have been more. Most, if not all, of these men could have gone to the grammar school in Salem, or when they had one, in Danvers. That there are no seventeenth century graduates on record is not surprising since the Village was so late in being settled.

All eleven of these men were graduates of Harvard. It was not until the early nineteenth century that local young men went to Dartmouth, Amherst, or Tufts, or other New England colleges. Daniel Putnam, the earliest named of the eleven, was Harvard, 1717. He could have attended the Salem grammar school. The same can be said for Ebenezer Putnam, 1739, and James Putnam, 1746. Among those who might have attended a grammar school in Danvers were Daniel Epes, the old master's great grandson and himself later a teacher. He was Harvard, 1758. Moses Putnam and William Clark, the latter being the Anglican priest and Tory who spent time on a prison ship in Boston Harbor during the Revolution, were both Harvard, 1759. Tarrant Putnam, later a successful farmer, graduated in 1763 as did Archelaus Putnam, who became a physician, and so did his brother Ebenezer. Another James Putnam was Harvard, 1774. Samuel Putnam, who became a justice of the Supreme Court of the Commonwealth, graduated in 1787. And Israel Andrew, who, like Epes, became a teacher, was Harvard, 1789.

Danvers physicians like Samuel Holten, Amos Putnam, and Jonathan Prince, Jr., who might be expected to have been college graduates, apprenticed themselves instead to a practicing physician or surgeon. In the case of these three men, all learned their trade under Dr. Jonathan Prince, Sr.

In contrast to the extensive number of professions college graduates may choose to enter today, the young men of Danvers of this period had a much narrower scope. They all became either clergymen, farmers, lawyers, doctors, or teachers. For all that Danvers seems to have had few collegians, it should be observed, it probably had as many as any other agricultural community of its time and size.

The period between 1800 and 1850 saw the rise in popularity of alternative secondary schools to the Latin school. But these were still products of the eighteenth century. The first was the English grammar school or simply the English school. Originally started as private institutions, they often became incorporated into the public secondary school system. The second type was the private academy, the 1749 concept of Benjamin Franklin in Philadelphia. That the academies, with their secular courses of study, could come into existence when they did, particularly in Massachusetts, is more evidence of the waning control of the clergy in education. Courses for young men and women in these two institutions were more utilitarian and valuable for a developing country—mathematics, geography, navigation, surveying, sciences, and modern languages, especially English.

Most, if not all, of the eleven Danvers college graduates in the first half of the nineteenth century would have gone to nearby academies like those in Topsfield or Bradford. The most popular, nevertheless, was the more distant Pembroke Academy in New Hampshire. This school's 1842 catalog lists Israel Alden Putnam, Charles Henry Gould, William Needham, John Henry Porter, and Sarah Ann Kent, all of Danvers, in its student body. A common complaint in Danvers at that time was that many of the graduates from academies never returned to take up careers in their home town. School committeemen used that fact as one argument for having a high school in town.

But these eighteenth century English schools and academies had a profound effect on secondary education when it did come to Danvers in 1850. Even more affecting on American education was the work of two European philosophers, John Locke (1632–1704) and Jean Jacques Rousseau (1712–1788), who were setting forth ideas in the 1700s that, adapted by an educational theorist, Johan Pestalozzi (1746–1827), would revolutionize education in the succeeding century.

Meanwhile, the momentous change in local education came on December 1, 1777, in the North Parish meetinghouse when Moderator Archelaus Dale was handed a petition, headed by the signature of brickmaker Jeremiah Page, to set up ten schools throughout the town for the better instruction of Danvers children. Prodded by state mandate to the selectmen on a deficiency in its schools, the town voted for the petitioners' request. The intention was for these schools to be set up for three months during the winter. In 1780, the term "district schools" was first used. And in 1783, nine schools were finally funded to meet for two months each. On November 10, 1794, it was voted to have the selectmen "divide the town into as many districts as will best accommodate the town." The original number of nine eventually rose to thirteen.

When North Danvers and South Danvers separated in 1855, there were eight district schools established in Danvers itself: No. 1, Maple Street area; No. 2, Danversport; No. 3, Putnamville; No. 4, Hathorne; No. 5, Wadsworth (the Centre); No. 6, Collins Street; No. 7, Tapleyville; and No. 8, East Danvers. Because No. 6 was too close to Nos. 5 and 7, it was eventually absorbed into District No. 5. The No. 6 schoolhouse, later designated No. 8, was sold and moved to 53 Locust Street, where it was first converted into a shoe factory and then made into a handsome Greek-Revival residence, today the home of Marie and Eileen Lynch.

To run the district schools, the town created two committees: the committee-at-large and the prudential committee. The former, which came to be the school committee as we know it today, consisted of the town's three ministers (those from the First Church, the Second Congregational in Peabody Square; and the Third or Maple Street Church). Throughout the 1700s and even later, the first visit the teacher candidate made was to these men who would examine that person's credentials attesting to academic preparation and character. His religious beliefs would also be questioned in order to ascertain if they were orthodox. If, of course, he was a Harvard graduate, as most candidates were, the meeting could be pleasant since Harvard would not have passed a scholar unless he had all three qualifications.

The committee-at-large was further expanded in 1823 to include three laymen—Dr. Andrew Nichols, Judge John Proctor, and Nathan Felton. In 1827, a seventh member was added to these six, and this board became known simply as the school committee. It prevailed over the second board, the prudential committee, which consisted of one member elected by each district. A district built and owned its schoolhouse, hired and paid its teachers, and provided the school with fuel and supplies. Often it was the prudential man who hired a teacher for his district, but he was required to present the master's credentials to the school committee. Sometimes he did not do this, and this led to the charge of his being a czar. The harm to education was that unqualified teachers were allowed into the classroom.

It should also be mentioned that the town contributed some money to the districts. When the Massachusetts School Fund, started in 1844, returned money to the cities and towns, funds were generally meted out on a pro-rata basis to the districts by their population. The exception was that the least settled sections were given a little more so that children there would have a more equal opportunity.

The duties of the school committee, dictated by an 1816 revision of Dr. Benjamin Wadsworth's education code of 1806, included choosing the textbooks, visiting, and examining the schools "whenever they think proper," settling disputes between instructors and the people of the district, expelling any pupil on complaint of the teacher, and presenting the budget at town meeting.

This committee also wrote the annual school reports commencing in 1839. Even phrased diplomatically, their published reports were not always received kindly by the prudential men, especially when there were complaints about the lack of proficiency among the scholars, the absence of discipline, or a failure on the part of the parents to send their children to school. In the 1841 report, for example, the committee commented on absence: "In almost every school we have visited, we have received complaints from the teachers upon this subject. Scholars are allowed frequently to tarry at home on the most frivolous excuses, and often without any excuse whatever, other than the inclinations of the pupils themselves. Were parents fully aware of the vexation they give to instructors, and the injury they bring upon schools by their negligence in this respect, we are confident they would be more particular."

In the 1840s, the most difficult state requirement for the committee to observe was the two visitations annually to each school. Early in the decade the committee had formed for this task a three-man subcommittee, which soon also became overwhelmed, though they claimed truthfully that they went to the schools "as frequently as their own engagements would allow—although not so often, as they are sensible, as is enjoined by law."

In 1846, there were nine hundred students enrolled in these district elementary schools in Danvers. They had nine grades and children ranging in age from five to eighteen. Besides the regular subjects, older students in two schools could also study rhetoric, English composition, geometry, navigation, the rudiments of philosophy, and Latin and Greck. These were subjects that would be taught in a high school.

For years following the passage by the General Court of a bill making it mandatory for communities of five hundred families or more to have a high school, the town argued that the final years of some of its schools fulfilled the same purpose. What the committee could not argue away was the fact that not all qualified students could take these advanced courses.

Faced with such failures to observe state laws, especially the one on adequate supervision, the local school board members began to anticipate the day teaching would become a profession. They were also envisioning a new position for Danvers, a superintendent of schools who would primarily visit classrooms to give a professional evaluation of teacher performance. In 1853, they procured enough funding—$850.00—from the town to hire such a person for a half-time position. He was Charles Northend, who in 1839 had been the principal in District No. 1. He served for a number of years, and then the position was eliminated.

Aside from teaching in the summer school and later in the winter term as well, women had little to say, officially, in the choosing of teachers or the running of the schools. In 1874 women were permitted to serve on the school committee. Finally, in 1881 they got a limited form of enfranchisement, the right to vote for the members of the school committee. By then the district school, the great innovation of the 1700s, had been abandoned in favor of a centralized system.

In review, it can be said that the eighteenth century first makes us aware that any period of transition in education will be a long one. In this case, the change was from religious to civic control of the schools. As a result of this relaxing of the Puritan hold on New England, the Puritan revival movement of the 1730s attempted to scare people back to the fold with morbid sermons like the Reverend Jonathan Edwards' "Sinners in the Hands of an Angry God," which pictured the Earth's surface as a thin crust that could break at any moment and cast a transgressor down into Hell's fire. One unfortunate effect of such a tactic was to drive a number of young people to suicide.

By the end of the century even the *New England Primer* altered its emphasis when several printers in the 1790s introduced the characters of the good and the bad girl and boy. Naughty Miss Prat-a-pace, for instance, received none of the rewards meted out to good Miss Prudence. Paul Leicester Ford, an authority on the *Primer*, cites a poem, new to the text, that "should have made the true Puritan turn in his grave":

> He who ne'er learns his A,B,C,
> Forever will a blockhead be.
> But he who learns his letters fair
> Shall have a coach to take the air.

Turning again to Dr. Wadsworth's 1816 code revision, we find that the deficiencies an instructor had to correct assume a contemporary sound. Among them were "theft, cruelty to animals, impertinent talk and writing obscene words on buildings and fences."

After the dark years of the 1700s, the 1800s became a bright, dynamic century for education. However, with the goal of the Puritans gone and the subjects different from theirs, this was education very much the opposite of what they had intended for their descendants.

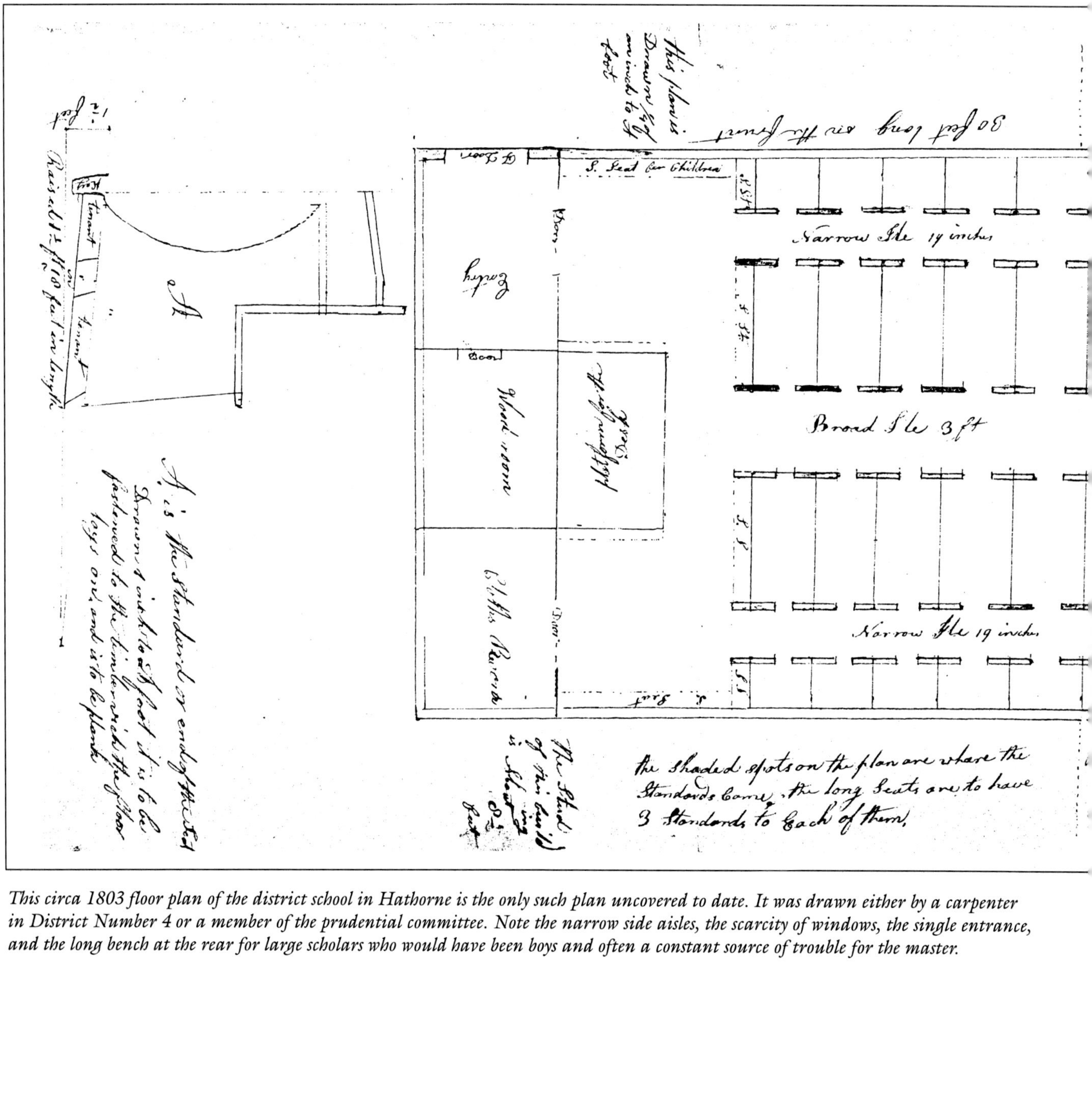

This circa 1803 floor plan of the district school in Hathorne is the only such plan uncovered to date. It was drawn either by a carpenter in District Number 4 or a member of the prudential committee. Note the narrow side aisles, the scarcity of windows, the single entrance, and the long bench at the rear for large scholars who would have been boys and often a constant source of trouble for the master.

CHAPTER III

Educating for Country—1800–1849

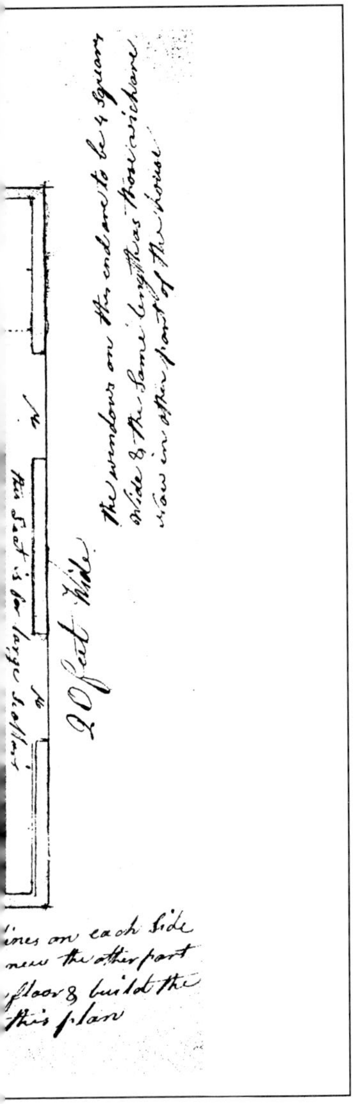

In 1793, Isaiah Thomas, the radical patriot and printer, and his partner C. T. Andrews published Samuel Freeman's *The Town Officers*, a volume enumerating the duties of all town officials from selectmen on down to fence viewers, inspectors of nails, and teachers. The placement of the last may appear ironic, but the number of college graduates going into teaching was insufficient for the growth of the population of New England. As a consequence, many who called themselves instructors were too often ill prepared and held in low esteem.

Summed up quickly, the duties of the schoolmasters, according to Freeman, were for God and the good of the nation:

It is the duty of all instructors of youth . . . (to teach) the principles of piety, justice, and a sacred regard for truth, love to their country, humanity and universal benevolence, sobriety, industry and frugality, chastity, moderation and temperance, and those other virtues which are the ornament of human society, and the basis upon which the republican constitution is structured.

With the exception of the new emphasis on patriotism, the century began much as the old ended. There were new schools, but teachers were using the same old harsh methods. Then an educational revolution commenced in the third and fourth decades of the nineteenth century during which profound changes occurred.

Once, a common expression has it, giants roamed the earth. Whether dinosaurs or creative forces, these titans leave a lasting impression. Massachusetts schools had at least three such giants: Horace Mann of Dedham, who transformed American public schools during his tenure as the first secretary of the state's board of education (1837-1848); John D. Philbrick, a former Danvers teacher, who as superintendent of schools raised Boston's system to be the nation's model public school system, the City on the Hill; and Elizabeth Peabody of Salem, the founder of the American kindergarten movement. A fourth innovator was a Danvers woman, Anne L. Page, a friend of both Philbrick and Miss Peabody. She attained a national reputation as a trainer of kindergarten teachers.

Revolutions develop slowly. First, a few adherents to a new cause. Then a host demanding change. That progression works in education as well as government. Great numbers of converts like these four were made in Europe and America through the works of two philosophers identified in Chapter II, John Locke and Jean Jacques Rousseau, and two educational reformers, Johan Pestalozzi, and his follower, Frederich Froebel, on the kindergarten level.

Rejecting the Calvinist doctrine, which held that children were born evil, i.e., in original sin, these men held that they are born good—or at least neither good nor bad. For Locke, the mind of a newborn was a clean slate upon which environment wrote, shaping the individual. Rousseau went further. He believed that children are born good, but are corrupted by our social institutions. His natural man, the noble savage, sent scores of world-weary European nobles to America's plains and forests in search of this creature so superior to the debauched figures of a king's court.

Pestalozzi took upon himself the task of translating these thoughts into educational methodology. Schools, for him, should provide good (pleasant), healthy surroundings. Children should be taught not by recitation and rote, but rather by means of familiar objects. For example, as a child in Lyndeborough, New Hampshire, Fidelia Pratt, whose family later farmed the property at 191 Centre Street, Danvers, was instructed by the Pestalozzi method of "the science of numbers." Her textbook, *Intellectual Arithmetic Based upon the Inductive Method of Instruction,* by Warren Colburn, contains in its introduction the story of "The Boy without Genius" to explain how students were instructed by the use of "sensible objects" in their first lessons.

Farmer Humphrey Acres has sent his son, as a last resort, to Solon Wiseman, the renowned schoolmaster, to see if any intelligence resides in this lad who has been a failure in conventional schools. In Wiseman's interview with the eleven year old Samuel, he ascertains that while there is nothing outstanding in the boy's intelligence, he can learn. The master begins the examination:

Have you learned any thing of accounts?
I went into addition, sir, but I did not go on with it.
Why so?
I could not do it, sir.
How many marbles can you buy for a penny?
Twelve new ones, sir.
And how many for a half-penny?
Six.
And how many for two-pence?
Twenty-four.
If you were to have a penny a day, what would that make a week?
Seven-pence.
But if you paid two-pence out of that, what would you have left?
Samuel studied awhile, and then said, Five-pence.
Right. Why, here you have been practicing the four great rules of arithmetic—addition, subtraction, multiplication, and division. Learning accounts is no more than this. Well, Samuel, I see what you are fit for. I shall set you about nothing but what you are able to do; but, observe, you must do it. We have no I can't here. Now go among your school-fellows.

Fidelia Pratt's first lesson in this text began with her fingers and concluded with a thorough study of fractions.

In the beginning years of the nineteenth century, an agricultural community like Danvers found one way to keep educational expenses down was to provide district schools that were no-frills institutions. For instance, Samuel Page Fowler related how the school kept in the kitchen of Aaron Putnam in Putnamville had for the scholars' desk a plank supported by barrels on either end. Another early nineteenth century school, this one in Danvers Centre, was recalled by a former student: "The old brown schoolhouse stood by a small barren, unfenced, unattractive triangle at the corner of Centre and Dayton Streets. There were rows of benches on each side of the house, one for girls and the other for boys. At one end there was a large open fireplace, and opposite it stood the master's lofty desk, to which he ascended by two or three steps. The windows were so high that scholars could not look out from the seats, and outsiders could not look in without climbing. No paint or ornament of any kind was indulged in."

Contemporary woodcuts of the country, ungraded, one-room schools often depict little scholars "toeing the line," i.e., placing their feet along a crack between two floorboards in front of the master's desk when they are reciting. Other children are seated on hard benches awaiting their turn to repeat their lessons. Generally, the master has a birch rod in his hand ready to punish unprepared or unruly pupils.

In his 1806 code, Dr. Benjamin Wadsworth of the Danvers school committee stated that pupils in a district school should be divided into at least two ability groups. In an 1887 biographical sketch of John D. Philbrick, who taught three winter terms in Danvers, Dr. W. T. Harris described the day's work in such a school: "Twenty-five pupils . . . admit of classifications into divisions of two or three pupils at the most, and the result is, forty recitations for the day's work, and five or ten minutes to each recitation. It is obvious that no thorough work can be done on this plan; no searching analysis of the recitation, no discussion of the thought, no experimentation to illustrate it—nothing, nothing, but mere committing to memory and repeating the words by rote—no explanation of the process of an arithmetical problem, but only a memorizing of the rule, and an inspection of figures in which the answer is stated. The ungraded school in which this method of procedure did not prevail was a rare phenomenon." Note here the words overlooked by teachers up to this period: analysis, process, discussion, and experimentation.

Through Horace Mann's writings school building and teachers were coming under scrutiny. Teaching was, as indicated, no longer the respected profession it had been in the seventeenth century. In fact, it wasn't a profession at all. Schools were kept for a period of eight, later twelve, weeks in winter. There were also short summer terms for the primary years usually taught by women. Many of these young female instructors had no education beyond that provided by a private academy. Others were only graduates of elementary schools. However, they had an advantage over their male counterparts, young men earning their way through college, since they had usually grown up in the districts where they taught and knew the scholars and their families.

Young male instructors regarded themselves as temporary workers and received, according to a Danvers school committee report in 1841, the "present meager rate of compensation." In that same report it was also noted, "Our teachers are usually composed of students from colleges, and other seminaries of learning, who resort to schoolkeeping as an expedient, by which to eke out a scanty income to aid them in the completion of their studies." By providing a long winter hiatus from their course work, colleges aided these young men to earn money.

Despite these male teachers' lack of experience, there was little or no supervision of their work by the local school committee. As early as 1817, a Danvers report noted, "In some instances the committee did not find the degree of silence and regular order which is necessary to enable scholars . . . to pursue their studies most advantageously." Apparently, school boys did not cow easily, for the customary punishment then was to apply the hickory stick liberally, despite an admonition in Wadsworth's code: "Every instructor shall establish and maintain order . . . not by inflicting cruel and unusual punishment . . . (but by) stimulating them in their duty by hope of reward."

According to Fowler again, one of his teachers was Caleb Clark, an elderly man who, over the years, taught in different sections of the town. In his younger days, this man continually whittled on a shingle while hearing his scholars' recitations. For punishment, he would have an unprepared or misbehaving boy gather all the shavings together into a pile in the middle of the floor, and then Clark would kick them around so the lad's punishment began all over again. On a hot day when the windows were open, this master hung a wire from the ceiling and compelled anyone he believed needed correction to stare at it until a fly landed there. At that moment, the child had to notify him by shouting out.

Several times Clark terrorized the youngest children by setting his shoulder under the classroom mantelpiece, threatening to topple the house down upon them all. But it wasn't only his severity that distinguished this man. He must, at least in old age, have suffered from some mental or physical infirmity. Fowler notes that he would sometimes place an arithmetic problem on the board for the older students and then puzzle over it for such a great length of time that the boys would sneak out to slide or skate.

Most teachers used their boxwood ferules to give a misbehaving child a stinging slap across his open palm. "Warming it sufficiently," Fowler noted. "Even on a cold day, [it] would not produce a blister, or wound the flesh like a heavy ruler." Two 'Port masters actually brought cowhide whips to use on the older boys. However, these students considered the treatment too servile. Determined not to allow themselves to be punished like slaves, they broke into the schoolhouse on a Saturday afternoon and cut up the offending instruments into small pieces and tossed them back into the masters' desk.

The expenses of the master's school were paid for by the town; those of the summer schools were paid by private subscription among the people of the district or by tuition. Because of the poor pay masters received, they were permitted to keep writing and singing schools in the evening and pocket the fees.

Women teachers tended to be less harsh than men. When double seats and desks were part of the nineteenth century classroom's furniture instead of rough benches, some teachers would compel a disruptive boy to sit beside a girl as punishment. However, there is a story that one female instructor in School District No. 1, the Plains, punished a boy or girl she caught talking by placing a sturdy but pliant busk or corset stay against the child's mouth. Pulling back on one end, she would suddenly release it, letting it snap painfully back against the offender's lips.

In a unique instance, kindness and dread existed in the same classroom. During the first half of the nineteenth century there were two sisters, Betsy and Hannah Putnam, who always taught together. They were the daughters of Dr. James Putnam, a physician who had been trained by his father, Dr. Amos Putnam. The children of the town made up a rhyme about the two men that does not seem to be a testimonial to the son's ability: Dr. Amos was very famous;/Dr. Jim was very slim.

According to one of the sisters' scholars, the Reverend Moses Kimball Cross, "Though like in temper, they were devotedly attached to each ether. . . .They had each of them, a chair and table and sat facing each other in the school room. They were both very pious; Betsy read the Bible and Hannah opened the school with prayer, and did the governing. Betsy was a very sweet and gentle spirit, and greatly beloved by the scholars; Hannah was fiery and quick in temper, and a terror to naughty boys and girls. I said they were both pious; they were also very polite. Some of my first lessons in politeness and sublimity were imbibed from them, though they were about as evanescent as the musk with which they were mingled. . . . I was something of a favorite, I believe, in those days in District No. 5; always with Betsy— sometimes with Hannah. Betsy's way of showing her regard, was by calling me out to read for her entertainment one of her favorite pieces in the *English Reader*. . . . Hannah's attentions were bestowed in a somewhat different manner. She took me once, across her lap before the whole school, and used—well, I can hardly say whether it was her hand or her ferule—but it was used with so much emphasis, that I remember thinking it must have been heard by all the girls in the house, —perhaps thirty or forty of them; for some of whom I cherished a very high regard; but who, I feared, would not think very highly of me after that."

Alden Perley White in his excellent history of Danvers in *The History of Essex County, Massachusetts* (1888), wrote that Hannah applied her emphatic correction "to that portion of a boy's body by nature designed to receive it."

Despite their inexperience, some of the temporary teachers employed in Danvers were outstanding. It was a practice of the school committee to recognize in its annual reports the system's best teachers. In 1817, they were Samuel Preston in the North Parish and Amory Felton in the South. The outstanding instructor in the North Parish in 1839 was John D. Philbrick, an ardent follower of Horace Mann. Philbrick became the only Danvers teacher to make an international contribution to education. Because of his work at expositions in Philadelphia and in Europe and through his writings and addresses, it was said that he was America's best known educator in Austria, Belgium, Great Britain, Japan, Spain, and Russia.

John D. Philbrick was the Hathorne schoolmaster and later innovative Boston superintendent of schools.

John Dudley Philbrick, a country boy with a drive to learn and a disposition to serve, was born on May 27, 1818, in Deerfield, New Hampshire. His father Peter, a farmer, gave him a sense of his own distinction when he told him that his birthday coincided with the day on which apple blossoms were at their fullest in springtime.

His uncle Elbridge Dudley in 1834 urged the boy's parents to allow their sixteen-year-old son to attend Pembroke Academy. There and at Dartmouth, which he entered in 1838, he had to pay his own expenses, so that his studies were interrupted by long absences when he had to either help his father with haying and other seasonal chores or teach winter sessions in rural, one-room schools. A few times he missed a whole semester. Fortunately, he was an excellent student who quickly made up his work. From the beginning, he proved to be a capable instructor with the result that he always found a teaching position.

At Pembroke he had made the acquaintance of several young Danvers men and women. During the Thanksgiving holiday when he was a Dartmouth freshman, Philbrick arrived in Danvers. Starting in Deerfield, he had walked from town to town seeking a teaching post. Two of his Pembroke classmates, Israel Putnam and Oliver Woodbury, had secured positions for the 1839 winter term in Danvers, their hometown.

Philbrick stayed with Woodbury, who took him the next morning to the Putnam shoe factory behind the General Israel Putnam birthplace. Moses Putnam, the father of another Pembroke classmate, introduced him to Ahira Putnam, the prudential man for District School No. 4.

When Philbrick had seen the pretty white Hathorne schoolhouse with its green shutters the previous day, he had thought it palatial compared to some of the rude schools he had been in. He promised himself that if he could get the teaching job there he would accept nineteen dollars a month pay and board instead of the twenty and board he was looking for. As the two men were talking, they were closely watched by Julia Putnam from the homestead where she was doing her Monday morning chores. She was particularly interested in this prospective teacher as she taught No. 4's summer term. Four years later, after he had taught three winters in Danvers and one year at Roxbury Latin School, they were married on August 24, 1843.

For one who had influential friends in District No. 4, Philbrick's first evaluation did not start out well. The visiting committee wrote in the annual report that at mid-term they had found some concern with his work, but at the end of the term he received a strong endorsement: "We have seldom found in school so general and thorough acquaintance with the various marks of punctuation as was possessed here and as a necessary consequence we have found some of the best readers here that we have listened to in town."

Fortunately for Philbrick, two of the subjects stressed at Pembroke had been composition and declamation; in those days the North Parish of Danvers prided itself on the quality of its hometown orators. Dr. Wadsworth's code stated, Item 8, "Each instructor shall endeavor to give those who read. . .a correct knowledge of punctuation, notes of interrogation, and admonition of accent, emphasis and cadence and correct whatever is improper in their tone of voice or manner of reading." Lacking any kind of recording devices, the voice was that generation's most powerful communications medium.

Another reason for Philbrick's improvement may have been that the teachers in Danvers that year held a convention during which they discussed individual problems and received suggestions for improvement.

It had been Philbrick's intention to become a lawyer after Dartmouth, but following his experience in Danvers and after that, as master at Roxbury Latin, he decided to make education his profession. For forty years, this man whose personal philosophy was, "The chief end of a man [is] self-culture, with a view to use his talents and acquirements for the benefit of others," would become the school administrator who brought an end to the upgraded, recitation-filled method of instruction.

In 1847 Philbrick was hired to take over as head of the Quincy School in Boston with the responsibility of establishing the nation's first graded institution. The general design was in place; the details and the job of making this innovative program workable were his. Now instead of large study halls in city schools for the preparation of lessons with little regard to grouping students by ability, children who had attained approximately the same level of development were assigned their own room and their teacher. Here, as in Roxbury, he insisted that each pupil have his own desk and chair.

Furthermore, Philbrick had the best instructor freed from some classroom duties in order to give model lessons and to point out to the rest of the faculty what techniques were being well performed by different instructors within the school. First called the principal teacher, this position grew into that of principal as we know it today. In 1875 in Quincy, another educator, Francis Parker, first brought many of the elements of progressive education into that system.

One of the immediate benefits of the new program was the very precipitous drop in disciplinary cases. No longer would a Boston master boast, as one had in 1845 without being considered ineffectual, that he had whipped up forty rattans in one morning suppressing a rebellion among the boys. Positive reports about the Quincy experiment spread, with the result that graded schools were adopted throughout the country.

Everywhere he went, Philbrick impressed those educators he met with his vast knowledge of the history and major philosophies in education. No one in his period was better read than he. He boasted that he possessed the country's largest private library on the subject in America. "Study education as a whole," was his advice to those in leadership roles in the field. His own papers were the best examples of what he meant. One of these on granting teacher tenure in Massachusetts was ably argued and filled with references to what other countries and experts had to say on the subject. (See Larkin Duntin's *A Memorial of the Life and Services of John D. Philbrick* from which this material on Philbrick has been taken.) In contrast to the days of indifferent teaching by untrained and often undereducated temporary instructors working their way through college, what was needed, according to Philbrick, was for school systems to secure "persons of ability and culture . . . devoted to teaching, as a life work (since) the best criterion of merit in a school system is to be found in the characters and qualities of the teachers in the service." He often said, "Schools good enough for the rich are poor enough for the poor." By this he meant that public schools from the primary grades through the high school that dealt with children of few advantages needed to be better taught and better equipped than private schools.

Any one of the innovations Philbrick made to education would have been sufficient to make another person's reputation in the field, but in addition to what has been written so far, he introduced into the Boston public schools courses in physical education, music, and art that were adopted nationwide. When he got the first two approved by the school committee, he advertised for a teacher of physical education and music!

When Philbrick died in 1886, the best educators in the region gathered at his home at 428 Maple Street to pay tribute to one who had performed so effectively for the well-being of America's school children. By then both he and Boston's schools were referred to as "The City on the Hill."

It detracts in no way from Philbrick's contributions to say that he was inspired by the work of another great American educator, Horace Mann.

For years after the passage of a bill in the Massachusetts legislature making it mandatory for communities of 500 families or more to keep high schools, the law had been widely ignored. Its success was due principally to the ability and determination of Mann. His future wife, Mary Peabody of Salem, hailed him at the time of his 1837 appointment as secretary of the Massachusetts Board of Education as the "High Priest of Education in our Land." It was an apt title. His annual reports to the General Court detail, among other subjects, the growth of the number of public secondary schools during his tenure, which ran until 1848. His lyceum lectures and particularly his 1841 Fourth of July address in Boston on public education were reprinted throughout the land.

As far as high schools were concerned, Danvers was one of the hold-outs. One question Judge Proctor once asked him in 1839 had to do with the size of the fine the state might levy on the town for its noncompliance. "I see no reason to doubt," Mann replied cooly, "that a town with the requisite number of inhabitants (will receive) the full penalty prescribed. . . ."

Mann's annual reports and his articles in the *Common School Journal*, for which he was editor and almost sole writer, gave instructions on such diverse topics as school construction, classroom management (he advocated the abolishment of flogging), and the education of teachers. It was he who in 1838 was responsible for the establishment of the nation's first normal or teacher-training school in what was then Lexington. Whatever he wrote on the subject of education had a wide readership among the new corps of professional teachers like Philbrick.

The Danvers school reports of this period frequently echo Mann's sentiments. His thoughts on the necessity of public education to the nation's preservation appear in the 1841 report as:

Education may well be considered the cornerstone of our national fabric. It was through the intelligence of the people that our Republic was originally organized and established—and it is only through the intelligence of the people, that its blessings can be perpetuated from generation to generation.

Mann's thoughts on teacher training appear in these words:

To raise our public schools to the high standards of which they are susceptible—to enable them to put forth all their elevating and salutary influences in the community—it is necessary to secure a class of men devoted entirely to the business of instruct-

ing. School teaching should become an established profession, as much as the ministry, or the law, and as honorable.

One of Mann's strongest statements in his July 4 address was "Select (private) schools for select students should be discarded." It was prompted by several experiences. One occurred in Salem at a convention on November 10, 1837, when one speaker, as quoted by Louis Tharp in *Until Victory: Horace Mann and Mary Peabody,* "questioned the expedience of endeavoring to get the educated classes to patronize public schools." Mary Peabody wrote her future husband, "He spoke, he said, in the interests of mothers who preferred. . .to have their children grow up with those of their own class. No one spoke on the American side of the question."

The frequent appeal to patriotism was a calculated one by those advocating the free education of all the nation's children. Informed townspeople in communities like Danvers were attempting to convince their fellow citizens to underwrite an expensive encumbrance. "The education of the mass of the people should be the great object aimed at," wrote the chairman of the local school board in the 1841 report. "In such a government as ours, it is with the mass, that our liberties rest, rather than with individuals."

"Mass of people" did not just mean poor, native-born children. Around Boston in the 1840s it included Irish Catholic immigrants and their families who had fled from the effects of the potato famines. Poor, illiterate, living in unhealthy, substandard tenements, they were not welcomed by many in Boston, the cradle of liberty. At the onset, education was not uppermost in the minds of these parents when every cent earned even by the youngest children was needed.

For their benefit and certainly out of principle, Horace Mann became engaged in the most intense struggle he waged as secretary of the board of education. An added impediment to getting immigrant children into the public schools came when a few clergymen tried to have not only Bible reading but also Bible interpretation included in the day's program. While Mann upheld the former, he rejected the latter. At the time, Danvers school children were taught from the Holy Bible and texts with titles like *Sacred Extracts, Assembly and Shorter Catechism, Evangelical Primer, Biblical Catechism,* and *Sabbath Lessons.*

Mann had no objection to the reading of the Bible and the recitation of the Lord's Prayer, but Bible interpretation was something else. Reverence, he expected; sectarianism, he rejected. And his will prevailed. "If we do not prepare our children to become good citizens," he wrote in his 1844 report, "if we do not develop their capacities, if we do not enrich their minds with knowledge, imbue their hearts with love of truth and duty, and a reverence for all things, sacred and holy, then our republic must go down to destruction, as others have gone before it."

These are appropriate words for one whose personal motto was, "Be ashamed to die until you have won some victory for humanity."

Speaking of this era to the members of the Danvers Historical Society on March 25, 1912, Attorney William B. Sullivan in his address, "Celtic Danvers" said, "God bless the town of Danvers. The common (public) schools of New England have regenerated the Irish race; the common schools of Massachusetts have put us on our feet; our people came here poor, unlettered, friendless, homeless and they came out here [to Danvers] realizing that the first thing to do was to educate their children, to give back to their children the means of education that Cromwell took away, and our fathers went to work for $1.50 a day or less, raised their families, built little homes, lived within their means and never sold their vote. They are now sleeping in their graves on our hillsides here in Danvers; a finer race of men and women never lived."

During this period, all levels of education had their pioneering geniuses. This was, after all, the commencement of modern education. There was another contribution that Philbrick made, which was overlooked in the many eulogies delivered at his home on February 2. He was also responsible for making possible the first public kindergarten in America. A good part of the credit also lies with his wife, Julia, whom one of the speakers characterized as the perfect "helpmeet."

Julia Philbrick had been an early patron of Elizabeth Palmer Peabody, Mann's sister-in-law, who had set up the first kindergarten in the country in 1861. Miss Peabody was a follower of Friedrich Froebel. As publisher of *The Kindergarten Messenger,* she popularized his work in this country.

Through the efforts of Julia Philbrick and some wealthy Boston families, she was allowed to set up free kindergartens within the city schools in 1870–1877. She included them in the North End and other depressed sections of Boston, as well as in the more affluent districts. When private financial support was withdrawn, the Boston school committee declined to fund the program. Disappointed but not discouraged, Miss Peabody helped set up privately run kindergartens around the city.

Anne L. Page, a Danvers woman who had taught kindergarten in a room in her family's barn on Elm Street, was inspired by this woman's example. Born on October 5, 1828, she was the ninth and youngest child of John Page, like his father Jeremiah, a leading brick manufacturer. She grew up in a bright, congenial family. Everyone loved her mother Mary, the subject of a Lucy Larcom poem, "Her Garden." Anne's brother Charles, who played in local theatricals, organized many parties for cousins and friends. When their kitchen was filled with the rich aroma of baking gingerbread cookies, she knew their grandfather's former slave Dill had come to visit. Every year the family piled into carriages to drive down to River Street to see the annual Indian encampment and to buy baskets made from the sweet grasses growing there.

Anne loved learning, although she had to wait until the North Parish had its own secondary school in 1850 in order to receive her high school diploma. She was then twenty-two years old.

The happy voices of her little scholars were a clear contrast to the type of traditional instruction we have so far observed. Mary Mann had described most of the early childhood teachers then as "hard, knotty women, young or old." In the beginning, however, Anne Page was more probably influenced by Bronson Alcott, Louisa May's father who ran the Temple School, a private institution in Boston. Alcott believed in developing the threefold nature of childhood: the spiritual, imaginative, and rational faculties. Miss Page agreed. She was convinced, "The young and tender plants require more care and attention. . . . When the twigs are all bent wrong, it is too late to incline the tree."

Dressed in a white muslin or blue print dress, this tiny woman opened the school day by reading a Bible passage. After discussing the day's reading, she and her pupils knelt by their chairs to repeat the Lord's Prayer.

There were two levels in her kindergarten, the upper and lower. Much learning was conducted through games and music. Alice Hanson Witherbee, a student in the 1860s, recalled in the Danvers Historical Collections (vol. 39) that their favorite song taught them their phonics. Besides the three R's, they learned elementary French and botany. They walked with Miss Page and an assistant or two to the stream running through Walnut Grove Cemetery to gather plants for their fish tank and to Burley Woods for leaves to feed their silk worms. They learned all the parts of the plants as they studied them. "Analysis is a mental microscope," she told her training assistants, "synthesis, a mental telescope." While the children worked, Miss Page would talk about the unity of all things. Like Miss Peabody, she was a follower of Froebel, and he had taught that man and nature were governed by the same rules and came from the original Unity (God).

During study periods the young scholars were left on their own. They ob-

Anne Lemist Page 1828–1913

served an honor code. When they wished to communicate with a friend, they wrote a message and left it in a letter box in the front of the room. They could whisper if they felt it necessary, and they could leave the room without permission. Discipline was a quiet talk with Miss Page after classes let out and everyone had shaken hands with her as she stood smiling beside the melodeon. After school, her pupils often played in the Pages' backyard. On occasion they visited the little Page house conservatory at night to see the flowers close up their petals.

In 1879, Anne Page went back to school. She was fifty-one at the time. She attended a Boston training school conducted by the Misses Weston and Garland. In connection with her course work, she taught in a North End Kindergarten. She learned there, "We help others not by changing their environment, but by revealing new ideals to them so that they may choose." She saw the occasional need for prodding, nevertheless, and she spoke out locally to allow Catholic women into the Danvers Home for the Aged.

She became national secretary of the Froebel Union and served on the Danvers School Committee. She translated and adapted for students a French botany manual *Flower Object Lessons* and wrote articles for periodicals and chapters in textbooks. Some of her observations are well worth reviewing today: "Creative work is the ancestor of knowledge. . . . Creation is a self-builder and a world-builder." To her training students she advised, "Do not shun alien thought. Talk respectfully with people who do not agree with you." And "Train a child to be deliberate. His power to choose should enable him to select and refuse materials offered for the structure of his life."

Her most famous training student was Annie Moseley Perry, founder of Perry Kindergarten Normal School. Mrs. Perry once wrote to her alumnae, "You owe to her (Anne Page) so much of what has come through me to you." The training school at Wellesley College was named for Miss Page.

Interested in the cultural and social life of Danvers, she opened her home for the organizational meetings of the Danvers Women's Association (1882), the Danvers Historical Society (1889), and the General Israel Putnam Chapter of D. A. R. (1895).

She came out of retirement in 1897 and for several years conducted the free kindergarten supported by the DWA, first at Danversport and then in Tapleyville. Charles S. Tapley, one of her pupils at the Tapley School, recalled going up Pine Street with the class to collect wild flowers and at another time churning butter in the classroom. True education for Miss Page was "drawing forth the child's power of observing, comparing, and doing." When the DWA no longer funded the program, the town, like Boston, refused to continue it.

Today what she regarded as world-improving may be seen as traditional, since the less structured Montessori method is favored by many parents. Anne Page would have been unhappy. "[Marie Montessori] mistakes the channel for the stream," she once wrote. "She was a laboratory woman, and Psyche never worked in a laboratory." This woman who really did gladly learn and teach passed away quietly on May 27, 1913.

The country's motto *E Pluribus Unum* is now rejected by minorities too long prevented from enjoying the full benefits of United States citizenship; however, these four educators—Mann, Philbrick, Peabody, and Page—recognized that in order to attain the ideals propounded by the founding fathers of the Republic, public education would be the greatest unifying institution and therefore the great strength of our democracy They believed with Benjamin Franklin, "We must all hang together, or assuredly, we shall all hang separate." Their work had a dynamism, articulateness, and ability to inspire others that carried American education on the momentum they provided for a hundred years.

The Quail Trap, the second North Danvers high school, now located at 15 and 15A Essex Street and vinyl-sided. In this photograph of the original siding, note the similarity between this exterior and that of the third high school. Both entrances in these two buildings had flushboards while the sides were clapboarded. Both had circular windows to ventilate the attics.

CHAPTER IV

Holten High School—1850–1899

After years of delay, Holten High School was hailed as an overnight success. George Peabody was honored for, among other philanthropies, encouraging scholarship. Social reformers turned their attention toward truer universal free education by having truancy laws enacted as part of a campaign to eliminate the exploitation of very young children in the labor force. The followers of Pestalozzi strove to achieve child-centered programs. And toward the end of the century, educators began to concern themselves with having students learn by being more involved in the "real world." Danvers hired a new superintendent of schools who attempted to have the local teachers employ the new methods—then fired him—and then tried to rehire him. Finally, there began to be inserted into the country's schools an attempt to eradicate some of society's most unsolvable problems.

Within three years of setting up high schools in the North and South Parishes, the Danvers school committee reported in 1853 that there had been a measurable improvement in the education of elementary school pupils. It was as Horace Mann had predicted on April 24, 1839, in answer to Judge John Proctor's query about the town's failure to keep a secondary school. Mann had written then, "[A high school] holds out a very strong inducement to the scholars who will be admitted to it on examination, to study." Furthermore, he added, such a school, "improves the character of the other schools, by giving better specimens of scholarship."

Danvers school reports make clear during the latter half of the nineteenth century that its secondary school was "the queen in our free school system." In addition to the benefits cited by Mann, another local one was the realignment of the lower grades into three divisions: primary (1, 2, 3), intermediate (4, 5, 6), and grammar school (7, 8, 9). In Danvers, as noted, the primary schools had always been taught by women; any school for those seven and older, by men. It wasn't until 1863 that the school committee expressed the thought of no longer accepting young college men without pedagogical training for the winter term, but instead, hiring its own local women teachers, some of whom now had normal school educations.

For most of the remainder of the nineteenth century, the grammar school was regarded as the alternate terminal level for those not going on to high school and as such continued, for a short time, to offer courses like bookkeeping that were not then available at the secondary level. Since the grammar school had also become a feeder institution for the upper division, great pressure was applied to its teachers to better prepare those students aspiring to a high school education for the rigorous entrance examination. As a result, grammar school instructors, in their turn, demanded better results from those teaching in the elementary grades.

When the first qualifying test was held in North Danvers in 1850, the crowd of townspeople who arrived to witness the event was so large that the site had to be moved from the cramped, rented quarters of the North Parish high school, ironically named Belvidere Hall, on Conant Street opposite present-day Alden, to the new, spacious brick grammar school in New Mills, which educated pupils from the 'Port and the Plains. Questions, particularly in arithmetic, generally had to do with agriculture and commerce:

A. purchases a farm of 400 acres at $60 per acre; and sells B. 40 acres at $75 per acre; to C. 50 acres at $59 per acre; and to D. 33 acres at $40 per acre. For how much must he sell the remainder to realize a profit of 19 per cent on the speculation? (This problem was taken from the 1848 final examinations for Grade 9, but the same question with figures changed could have been reused for an entrance test.)

A ship is worth $16,000, and a person who owns 5/16 of it sells 3/8 of his share; what share has been remaining and what is it worth?

Much of the examination was oral. The erudite Samuel Page Fowler gives us a picture of such tests in "Old-Time Schools in Danvers" in the Danvers Historical Collections (DHC, vol. XII), where he tells us that the chairman of the committee would present a question to a student who would then recite the answer. Other committeemen might also interrogate the scholars in their areas of expertise. Businessmen, for example, could ask questions relating to mathematics. For the rest of the committee, "Wise men as they were, kept their lips closed," wrote Fowler, "and sat twirling their thumbs."

Mrs. Cornelia E. Whipple in her reminiscences (DHC, vol. 6) relates how one primary school teacher in the 'Port, Sarah Ann Osgood, developed an almost foolproof method of seeing her pupils successfully through their tests. Miss Osgood, who remained at her post until she was teaching the grandchildren of her original pupils, "would answer her own questions by motions of her lips on which the eyes of the children seemed to be fixed."

For the popular spelling bees, a final part of this program, one boy and one girl were chosen by the master to pick their sides. Then the teams faced each other in the middle of the classroom, and the elimination began. "None of those who have stood up on the floor in those old school houses," recalled Fowler with affection, "in a spelling match have experienced the excitement and heart-flutter caused by one of these contests in orthography."

Some answers to questions, especially in letter writing, were included each year to reveal a command of composition and good penmanship. In 1893 the school report actually included and compared letters written by Danvers grammar school youngsters with letters of application received from graduates of Harvard and Wellesley. The committee felt that in those cases cited the public school pupils had done a better job.

Having passed their qualifying examinations, Danvers high school students felt privileged, and attendance records in the North Parish reflected their pride. For the first term in 1850, there were 38 initial students enrolled, a few as young as twelve years of age. Their average daily attendance was 37; the second term, 41 were enrolled and the average daily attendance was 39 3/5; and for the third term, the numbers were 43 and 39 13/34.

Such an impressive rate contrasts with the attendance figures for the lower grades the previous year when the two parishes together ranked 168 out of the 300 towns of the Commonwealth. "We know of nothing peculiar to the size of the Districts . . ." wrote a disappointed Rev. Milton Braman, committee chairman, "that serves as an apology for our standard below so many other towns." For the rest of the century, the secondary school figures remained high and much better than those of the elementary grades; in fact, much better than most of the other communities in Massachusetts.

And so from the outset, the high school succeeded. The first North Parish principal/teacher was John P. Marshall. The committee was pleased with its choice. Like John Philbrick, Marshall was another representative of that new breed of professional teacher, well educated and skilled, in Marshall's case, "in communicating instruction and awakening interest and activity of thought in the minds of the scholars." In demeanor, he was described as quiet and well mannered, just the opposite of old classroom tyrants like Caleb Clark.

References to Marshall's school identify it as an English high school because of its practical course of study. There were three terms to the school year. Marshall's classes met for six hours each weekday and three hours on Saturday in a cramped, low room with the master's desk at one end and the recitation platform at the other. In between there were only three rows of double seats. There was little space outside for recreation. Graduation came in three years.

According to John Proctor in his Centennial Address in 1852, two-fifths of the town's revenue was being spent on education—$10,000 out of the total $25,000 in taxes. Since school reports at the same time made pleas for higher teachers' salaries, and the introduction of the high school into the system was delayed for so many years, it indicates that taxes were being kept low. But this happened not just in Danvers. James Truslow Adams observed in *The March of Democracy,* "The notable contribution of these decades (1830–1850), however, was to the theory of free education for the masses of the people. This was largely brought about by pressure from the working-class groups and against much opposition by the taxpayers." As Proctor concluded in his speech, "If the schools of Danvers are not advanced in proportion to their appropriation, the defect is not chargeable to the mass of inhabitants—their *will* is to have *first rate free schools.*"

Unfortunately for the town, teachers like Marshall had their choice of positions. He remained here just one year before being lured away by another community for higher pay. But even before his departure, the committee had been concerned about the drain of instructors. Two school reports in mid-century contain admonitions about the low rate of pay: "In selecting instructors, the object should not be those who will work the *cheapest,* but rather those who will work the *best.* The *cheapest* teachers are generally the *dearest.* Those who are willing to engage for the least compensation are often the least competent. . . . The habit of beating down the wages of teachers, to the lowest possible mark, is one of the deepest and most serious evils with which our common schools have to contend."

As to the lack of permanence of the headmaster/teacher in the high school, the Reverend Charles Rice, a long-time committeeman, kept records showing that the next four men to hold Marshall's position also moved fairly quickly to more prestigious posts, even though they, like Marshall, united "in a most happy degree the accomplishments necessary," for effective teaching. (See list of principals, p. 68).

The first public exhibition, meaning entertainment, given by the students of Holten High School was held on March 11, 1831, in Granite Hall, the basement of the Maple Street Church. On May 1, 1886, the *Danvers Herald* printed the schedule from John S. Learoyd's program of the event. More importantly, on the fourth page was a handwritten list of the students attending the school.

Who the families of these young people were, as far as social or economic status was concerned, is revealed in their names: Bates, Black, Endicott, Eveleth, Fowler, Hunt, Learoyd, Ober, Perley, Perry, Porter, Preston, Putnam, Sawyer, and Silvester. Here were the children of the town's first families—of tanners, merchants, store owners, mill operators, successful farmers, etc. They were just the ones who at first opposed public secondary schools for Danvers on the grounds that they were an added tax burden for those parents who were already paying to have their children educated in private academies. Now they could send them to a local public high school where they could still be with their "own class." By the end of the century, the schools were considerably more democratic.

Bright and with a sufficient amount of leisure, these first high school scholars had the time to prepare such an entertainment as they presented, on March 11. Their skits and recitation pieces were both humorous and serious and reflective of their educations. William Franklin Endicott welcomed the assembled guests with a Latin salutatory. Recitations included selections like "School Girl's Offering," "Gratitude Due to Our Ancestors," and Samuel Fowler Eveleth's original "Wrongs of the Red Man." There was the obligatory homage to Erato, "Beauty of Poetry," a piece that oozed couth with characters like Terrestria, Oceana, Chrysomline, Celestia, and Psyche. There were also a humorous skit with characters' names out of Restoration comedy—Ned Madcap and Miss Snivel; a short portion of *The Merchant of Venice*; and John S. Learoyd's valedictory.

Apparently the rent for Marshall's school was considered too high, although the official reason stated for the removal from this building was that it was not centrally located. In 1831, the Free Evangelical Society's chapel, a few hundred yards down the way at the convergence of Holten and Sylvan Streets, was leased. This structure stood where the war memorials are today in front of the town hall. Owned by the Wesley Society, a Methodist denomination, it was familiarly known as the Quail Trap as it was here on Sunday evening services, according to Frank Damon in *The Salem Evening News*, that young men came to "catch" young women.

The original teacher at this second school was Ambrose Stuart, or Stewart, who was paid $750 per year; his successor, Nathaniel Hills, was the first in that position to have an assistant. She was Clara Flint. The town was following custom here, the man having the higher grades and the higher wages.

The rapid series of changes in the principalship in no way deterred the growth in the number of scholars seeking entrance into the high school. The 1895 school report gives enrollment figures for a forty-year period, 1855–1895. On February 1, 1855, the whole number registered was 50. On the same date in 1863, it was 94. Then the Civil War and the economic depression following temporarily reduced the number. In 1885, the number was 105; and in 1895, it rose to 204.

Two events in 1853 mark it as an exceptionally memorable year. First, the high schools were named for two of the town's illustrious natives. George Peabody, the international banker, gave his name to the South Parish school, and Samuel Holten, the North Parish's distinguished physician, patriot, and judge, had his name selected for the other. In choosing these names, the citizens of Danvers were singling out men who, they hoped, would be the best role models their children could pattern themselves after.

Then, from London on November 30, Peabody announced an annual gift of two hundred dollars during his lifetime to be spent on "prizes for distribution as rewards of merit to the pupils (of both schools) at their annual examination." This recognition was to be given to all members of the graduating classes for scholarship and deportment. Precedent for such an award was the little, hand-colored paper rewards of merit that Victorian teachers gave deserving elementary school pupils. Even later, in the twentieth century, kindergarten and elementary school teachers placed gold stars or colorful stickers on an excellent paper or the collar of their good students.

Either Peabody medals or books by famous English authors were presented over the years. The latter were awarded for outstanding achievement. In 1856, the first Peabody medals were received by the three Holten High School graduates that year and eight others who had previously completed the three-year course. This medal had Peabody's profile in the pose of a Roman emperor and his motto, "Education—A Debt from Present to Future Generations," on one side, and on the other, the pupil's name and year.

There were actually several different types of medals struck. The original, a large silver medal, was given out from 1856 to 1868. From 1869 to 1893, smaller silver medals were distributed. From 1894 to 1905, a gold-plated medal was designed and given out. And from 1906 to 1913, silver medals similar to the first were awarded. By 1913, when the final medals were distributed, 1,415 had been cast.

In 1868, the year of George Peabody's death, the trustees of the Peabody Institute Library received a bequest from his estate for $2,000 to continue procuring medals for future generations. This they did until 1913 when the funds ran out. In 1868 also, the old South Parish, which had changed its name to South Danvers in 1855 when it separated from North Danvers, changed its name once again—this time to Peabody. It was then that North Danvers became simply Danvers.

The pride and pleasure of receiving the Peabody medals was described by Judge Alden Perley White to a Tennessee audience gathered at George Peabody College for Teachers in 1895 on the centennial observance of Peabody's birth. White was handed his "signet of George Peabody," as he called the medal, on the stage of the old 1869 Gothic-style Peabody Institute Library. He said, at that time, all graduates received one in the lyceum hall beneath the great oil portrait of its founder. It was, for the generations of graduates there, the culmination of the exercises on that "day of days."

When this library burned in 1890, the portrait, all the books, and some of the furniture were saved. The new Colonial-Revival style library still in use today was designed by another Holten High School alumnus, Lester Couch, of the architectural firm of Little, Brown and Moore. Completed in 1892, its lyceum hall with the sloping floor served for graduations into the early 1960s.

The third North Danvers high school and the first to bear the name Holten High School was mainly Greek-Revival in style. In addition to features pointed out in the Quail Trap, this building has indented corner boards, and an octagonal cupola. The Civil War monument is approximately on the site of the Quail Trap.

On April 10, 1854, the Quail Trap being considered inadequate for the increasing size of the student body, town meeting voted to erect a new municipal building capable of incorporating into it the town offices and a new high school. On May 30, shoe manufacturer Joshua Silvester sold Danvers almost an acre of land. This lot included both the site of the Quail Trap and the land behind it. Silvester then had the obsolete school removed to 15–15A Essex Street, where it was converted into a duplex dwelling.

For $9,298 a two-and-a-half-story Greek-revival style structure was built on the new property. In addition to a meeting hall, classrooms, and the town offices, the building contained the town's 1,500-volume library with the high school principal Nathaniel Hills also serving as the librarian for an extra one hundred dollars added to his salary. The basement even had a "holding tank" to temporarily house tramps.

In the fall of 1856, the student body of Holten High School, and indeed all the other young people in North and South Danvers, were agog with the knowledge that their patron, the sixty-one-year-old Peabody, was returning to the United States and would visit them. The leading citizens of the two communities formulated plans for one of the longest parades ever assembled in the region—one that would include all 1,700 of the school children and their teachers and administrators. Yards and yards of thin, glossy silk ribbon were being imprinted with Peabody's portrait and his famous motto to be cut into badges and worn by the students and all the other participants of the occasion.

These girls and their teacher from School District Number 2 are passing under one of the many triumphal arches erected for the October 9, 1856, parade in honor of George Peabody. Note the use of American and British flags and bunting and the second banner, "Onward and Upward," a sentiment for an optimistic age.

Mothers were busy preparing new clothes for their children—straw bonnets with blue velvet edgings for the girls and red sashes for the boys of Holten High School. Banners were prepared with legends like "In God We Trust," "We Rejoice to Welcome You," and "Onward and Upward." The students were being trained to march in unison. The young men and women of Holten High were drilled over and over again in precision for their special part in the festivities. Danvers wouldn't see such a display by its high school students until the 1890s when the school's cadet corps led by Captain Elliott Perkins with his lieutenants Lewis Abbott and Charles Webber, dressed in immaculate white uniforms, took their places for Fourth of July and Decoration Day parades.

According to the writer of "The Procession" in the special book printed after the celebration with a title almost as long as the parade itself—*Reception and Dinner in Honor of Geo. Peabody at the Old Town of Danvers, Oct. 9, 1856*—"The sun rose on the 9th of October bright and beautiful. It was one of those bland Indian Summer days peculiar to New England in the Autumn months, the serene atmosphere and clear skies contributing in no slight degree to the pleasure of the occasion." In all, 20,000–30,000 spectators lined the streets of the parade route. The various contingents of the marchers in South Danvers following the preliminary reception in North Danvers would stretch for a mile.

Festivities started near the Maple Street Church. Seated in the lead barouche were Peabody and the Honorable Robert S. Daniels, Peabody's friend and host. The chief marshall was Major General William Sutton. One of the first banners the guest of honor saw was the one stretched across the new Maple Street Elementary School, which read "Free Schools, the Nation's Strength." In fact, flags and banners and bunting decorated every public and commercial building and most private homes Peabody passed that day. Welcoming arches of greenery spanned the main streets of both towns.

The parade began around ten o'clock with the firing of one hundred guns. Military units, the long cavalcade of private carriages bearing Peabody, the Governor of the Commonwealth, dignitaries including New York bankers and British officials, and then two smartly dressed equestrian contingents, one of men and one of women, proceeded down Maple, High, Water, and South Liberty streets. Bystanders cheered and threw bouquets and nosegays into Peabody's open carriage. Gilmore's Brass Band provided the cadence.

At Wilson's Corner, they were joined by almost four hundred firemen with their brightly painted handtubs and hose reels, the names of each emblazoned in gilt or gold—*General Scott, Torrent, Eagle, Ocean*, and *Volunteer*. Following them were the students of the two high schools, led appropriately by those in Peabody High, and then behind them the fourteen district schools.

As the Peabody carriage appeared, the Holten High students—the young women dressed "in black waists and white skirts, with scarlet trimmings; the young men wearing Peabody badges on their red sashes—presented a brilliant appearance:

> *Each unfurled a flag not till then displayed; and, being so arranged that the American and English colors alternated, the effect was very fine when, in honor of their trans-Atlantic guest, the two were crossed, and, throughout their ranks, the stars and stripes mingled with the British cross. Their banner presented on one side, "Holten High School, Danvers. We Welcome Our Benefactor"; and on the reverse, "One Generation Shall Praise Thy Works to Another."*

George Peabody

The long parade eventually arrived at the Peabody Institute Library in South Danvers and the reviewing stand. As they approached their destination, the fire companies lined up on either side of the entrance to the grounds. Peabody and the other dignitaries and guests passed between them into the stands and the school pupils filed onto the grounds of the library.

Peabody's brief and homely address noted the changes in his native town since he had left it. What the "humble boy" saw denoted progress. The fields on which he had once played "now resound with the hum of busy labor." But the greatest part of his speech was directed toward the young people.

To the boys, he enumerated the qualities they should strive for: "steadfast and undeviating truth, fearless and straightforward integrity, and an honor ever unsullied by an unworthy word or action." To his young female friends went the reminder that they too could be great, "great in their domestic graces, as daughters, wives and as mothers." All in all, it was a soul-satisfying day, except perhaps for those young women planning to attend state normal schools or women's colleges and aspiring to a life that might not include domestic duties.

The year after this public display of gratitude to Peabody, Holten High students were thrilled to have the great man himself visit them. Apparently it was not to be the only time he came to see them. The school's visitors' book had in it his signature once, and his name twice more in someone else's handwriting. During this era, those logs, one in every school, recorded that as many as 3,000 guests toured Danvers schools, observing classroom teaching and attending the periodic examinations. In 1893, the number of guests was still high. Between school committeemen and women, parents, and others, 871 visitors made their appearance.

The examinations and other competitions were exciting to parents and townspeople who received annual invitations in the school reports to make visitations and see how well their money was being spent. On the other hand, these reports also censured parents for what was seen as deficiencies—failure to send their children to school regularly, drinking and smoking in front of their children, etc. In one issue, parents were exhorted to drill their sons in spelling at least one half hour a day, it being a known fact that boys were naturally deficient in this area of learning.

Should parents forget why they were sitting in on classes, Superintendent Northend reminded them in 1855: "Have you done what you could for the improvement and prosperity of these schools?. . . Have you manifested a deep and true interest in the school duties of your children? Have you cheered them on? Have you rendered to the teacher—who, for a time being, stands in your place—that prompt, cheerful, and judicious cooperation to which they are entitled? . . . Have you thought kindly of the teacher—spoken charitably of him, and acted the part of an elder brother and fellow-laborer, or have you been ready to indulge unkind thoughts, harbor ungenerous and groundless suspicions?"

The compulsory attendance law, passed in 1852, helped to decrease the truancy rate in the lower grades. In that year the Danvers board discovered that there were 167 pupils between the ages of five and fifteen who had never attended the winter term. Townspeople thought that the situation could be better, for they, like most Americans of their day, believed in education for the masses in order to attain and preserve a more perfect Union.

From 1850 until the end of the nineteenth century, reformers worked to stiffen truancy laws by establishing enforcing officers and raising the compulsory school attendance age until it reached sixteen. The expert in these laws, according to President Grant's commissioner of education, General John Eaton, in 1891–1892 was John D. Philbrick. Aware of the situation in Boston, as elsewhere in the nation, where poor immigrants needed the money their children could bring into the family, he was also aware of what was a perpetuating cycle that kept these families in poverty from generation to generation—the lack of education.

Children as young as five years old were set to work picking rags in city slums, sorting coal in mining operations, or tying broken cotton threads on clattering, mechanized looms; in short, in every menial, unskilled work that others would not or could not do because of size constraints. Factories then brought prosperity to the few and misery to the many. They also spelled finis for the old apprenticeship system that, while not always kind, provided a plentiful supply of skilled workers in the trades.

There was another negative side to the compulsory attendance laws, since they allowed for more children entering the schools than ever before. For the twentieth century public school systems, especially urban ones, it meant that students were forced to remain in school until they were sixteen, whether they wanted to be there or not. The result, wrote Lawrence Cremin in *The Transformation of the Schools,* was "The dream of democratic idealists may have resided in compulsory attendance laws, but so did the makings of the blackboard jungle."

In the 1860s, a grammar school diploma was considered adequate for all except those not entering the professions. Then toward the end of the century, when more young people sought entrance into college, high school training was regarded as essential. An additional reason in Danvers and elsewhere was the introduction of commercial subjects making it possible for those who completed the course to find better paying white-collar jobs.

Not surprisingly, pressure was applied to the school committee to eliminate the entrance examination. The members of the board were opposed to this: "High schools are established, not to supersede the grammar school, or to take its place, but to secure a higher and more advanced education to those, and those only who are fairly qualified to avail themselves of the advantages they afford." In 1892, the board was still arguing against making admissions easier. Eventually, of course, public opinion prevailed. A resolution came in 1895 whereby a compromise was made. Promotion into the high school would be determined by taking the average of a ninth grader's daily work and the results of three examinations spaced approximately three months apart. The grading system instituted then was E(xcellent), 90–100 percent; G(ood), 80–90 percent; F(air), 70–80 percent; P(oor), 50–70 percent; and VP (very poor), any grade below 50 percent.

The committee stated that this new system would create "no yawning chasm" between the different school levels. "After all," the board chairman pontificated, "The school department's motto should be 'The School for the Child,' not 'The Child for the School.'" It was a rather pompous but high-sounding attempt at saving face. Since the followers of Pestalozzi had been striving since the 1860s for a child-centered (their term) system of instruction, it indicates that Danvers citizens were not in the forefront of educational thought.

Educators knew differently and as a result most American students then and well into the twentieth century were exposed to Ralph Waldo Emerson's essay, "The American Scholar," in which he wrote:

"I learned," said the melancholy Pestalozzi, "that no man in God's wide earth is either willing or able to help any other man." Help must come from the bosom alone. The scholar is that man who must take up into himself all the ability of the time, all the contributions of the past, all the hopes of the future. He must be an university of knowledges. If there be one lesson more than another which should pierce his ear, it is, The world is nothing, the man is all; in yourself slumbers the whole of Reason; it is for you to know all.

Recall now how Horace Mann had fought hard, risked all, and prevailed in his determination to eliminate religious instruction from Massachusetts school programs. He had waged the good fight partly in order that Irish Catholic immigrants would send their children to public schools.

Town records show a dramatic growth in Irish families settling in Danvers in the 1850s. Beginning then and progressively more so toward the end of the century, local industries like the iron works, the gristmills, the tanneries, and the shoe factories had need of blue-collar workers, both native- and foreign-born.

In 1865 two of the latter, Daniel and Bridget Doherty, watched proudly as their son Edward graduated from Holten High School. He was followed in 1866 by Annie Waldron. John E. Maguire and N. Daniel Crowley received their Peabody medals in 1870. John E. Crowley graduated at the head of his class in 1874. In 1883, Elizabeth Ahern and William B. Sullivan were graduates. By 1895, a third of those entering Holten High School were first generation Americans of Irish ancestry. Among those matriculating that year many had Irish family names: Callahan, Farley, Fennessey, Finnerty, Flynn, Guiddry, Harrigan, Kirby, Lyons, Mullaly, Murphy, Neil, O'Connell, Quinlan, Tufts, Wrest, and five Sullivans. In addition, three of the Danvers teachers were also Irish-Americans—Elizabeth Ahern, Alice Clancy, and Annie Sullivan. Helen Gallivan, who entered in 1896, later succeeded Miss Ahern as principal of the Danversport school.

Several of these sons and daughters of Irish immigrants gave back to their hometowns the benefits of their educations. Daniel Crowley and William B. Sullivan resided in Danvers following their college training and became outstanding attorneys. Elizabeth Ahern and her sister Margaret, both of whom graduated at the heads of their classes, left an endowment for one of the earliest Holten High School scholarships. But children of other nationalities also became beneficiaries of American public schools at this time. In 1895, another of the graduates, Alice Steutermann, was of German descent. In 1895 also, Fred Geroux of French-Canadian parentage and in 1896, Leo Brissette and Emile Deschene entered the high school. Jerome Fossa was the first son of Italian parents to call Holten High School his alma mater from 1898 to 1900.

With this growth in the number of children, Danvers was engaged in the building of new schools and the expansion of existing ones. In 1883, the combined high school and town hall building was expanded at a cost of $14,000 by cutting it in half and moving the front end forward twenty-five feet. But by 1895, this Holten High School was already overcrowded. There were 205 students crammed in—sixty to a classroom. "When classes from the large room (study hall) are to recite, those thus seated in the recitation rooms interchange, marching and meeting each other and getting by each other in the best way they can, in the congested aisles. Much time is thus wasted and much confusion is unavoidable," wrote W. A. Baldwin, the superintendent. "Public schools," he reminded Danvers citizens, "are established for public good, for the advance of civilization, the security of good health, good morals, and *good order.*"

The expensive business machines—the "Atwood machine, the Electrical machine, four typewriters, and the Dynamo and Telegraph Instruments"—were definitely vulnerable to the adverse conditions in the high school. Without properly vented laboratories for chemistry and other sciences, the fumes created by experiments were ruining this equipment. In hot weather, the temperature in the classrooms sometimes rose to over one hundred degrees Fahrenheit and "the complete lack of ventilation produced frequent cases of illness among the students."

In 1896, at a cost of $32,000, a further expansion was begun by Mead, Mason and Company of Boston. The result of their effort was an impressive Colonial-revival style structure with deep quoining at the corners. Its outstanding feature was twin, blue-domed towers rising ninety-three feet, both contained in new side wings. In the left tower was a large clock given to Danvers by wealthy George Augustus Peabody of Burley Farm and president of the library trustees. In the right hand tower was the school bell. Holten High was then in session from 8:15 to 1:15 with a fifteen-minute recess. With these hours there was no need for a cafeteria. The length of the school year was now officially forty weeks.

Unfortunately for Danvers, Mead, Mason and Company was not a good construction company, at least so far as this remodeled building was concerned. Almost immediately leaks developed around the towers, causing water to seep into classrooms during rain storms. While the morale of the students remained strong, by 1910 they were too well aware of the school's physical deficiencies. And they were not silent about them. In the April issue of the school magazine, *The Holten*, appeared this poem:

Holten High
Not of its glories I'll relate
Though it has some that I could state,
But of its needs, I'll tell you all,
For it has many, great and small.

First: when we have to stay quite late,
Preparing lessons for Miss Cate,
And when our eyes ache as we read,
We know electric lights we need.

Second: no mirrors for the girls
To fix their "psyches" and their curls.
No drying room. In case of storm
We sit in wet clothes all the morn.
Third: a playground, too, we surely need.
'Twould keep the boys from all misdeed,
And make recess a perfect treat,
With no more mischief on the street.

Fourth: there's not a place to drink or eat
Except on stairways or the street.
A lunchroom then you must confess
To cure our hunger at recess.

Fifth: another need of Holten High
Which must be realized bye and bye,

Is a splendid, new and longed-for gym
To give our pupils strength and vim.

If I should stop to sum them all
'Twould take from summer time till fall,
And we might talk for aye and aye,
Just telling "needs" of Holten High.

Dear School Committee, just and fair,
Listen, we beg you, to our prayer,
That in the near, sweet bye and bye,
We'll have a reconstructed High.

If the "sweet bye and bye" is measured in decades, it took two of them to change matters, for this school, built to house 300 students, served as Holten High School until 1931.

As modern as this remodeled school appeared to local citizens in the 1890s, one colonial custom that survived then and right into the 1950s on the elementary level was the separation of boys and girls in filing in and out of school and at recess time. At the town hall, boys entered Holten High from the Sylvan Street entrance; and girls, from the Holten Street side.

In the elementary schools, boys played in one section of the schoolyards; girls, in another. Marie Lynch, a principal of the Tapley School, told me that boys did not trespass onto the girls' side whenever a schoolyard had an imaginary boundary line between the two adjacent areas. If the boys' ball landed beyond their half of the play area, they waited until a girl tossed it back to them. At the Tapley School, boys played in the backyard on Washington Street; the girls, in the front on Holten Street.

The Class of 1881 had its picture taken at a side entrance of the school in 1879. The lady on the left of the back row is Miss Sarah Frances Richmond. The gentleman at the opposite end of the row is Headmaster Frank M. Hawes.

The end of recess was signaled by a teacher or the principal blowing a whistle. One teacher was assigned to supervise the line of girls waiting to reenter the school, and another, the boys. When everyone was quiet, the pupils filed silently back to classes through separate entrances. Cadence in some schools was provided by a teacher or line guard tapping on a metal triangle. Another teacher, Ann McNamara, has described how at the Maple Street School pupils marched out of school at the end of the day to Sousa marches played on the Victor machine or phonograph. When they reached a landing, pupils would take three steps in place and then proceed on the fourth step. While it all sounds very San Quentin- or Sing Sing-like, if a boy winked at a favorite teacher, he was generally met with a smile and not a reprimand.

Although no young man would take the liberty of winking at her, Miss Sarah Frances Richmond, a mathematics and science teacher who was also the principal's assistant beginning in 1872, was the most endearing instructor in Holten High School during this period. A short, neatly dressed woman, hair parted loosely in the middle, she appears in photographs like a pleasant, approachable Queen Victoria. She was beloved by her students, who affectionately called her Sally behind her back, for her fairness and her ability to remember them and their names long after they had graduated.

Another statement about her uncovered by archivist Richard B. Trask also reflects the affection she inspired. "I believe," said one of her former students, "that no Danvers person has had more influence than Miss Richmond in instilling into the minds of our boys and girls the old-fashioned principles of New England life and good conduct."

Parents and school committee boards admired her "for exactness of scholarship and for skill and thoroughness in imparting instruction." Despite all this adulation, in 1892–1893, she announced her intention of resigning, and the school report for that year stated she had determined to "enter upon some different work."

What disturbed Miss Richmond was another pay cut. For several decades following the Civil War, the United States economy was in a period of recession. In 1878–1879, teachers' salaries were cut back. The committee resorted to rhetoric to justify the action. Noting that teachers received "much more than the ordinary profits of business," a board member reminded them that "they are a part of common humanity with like interests and like destiny and in life's stormy voyage subject to like exigencies. The sun cannot shine for their especial benefit more than for any, or all the rest."

Happily, in the instance of faithful servant Sarah Richmond, in spite of life's stormy voyage, she prevailed. The din of protest over her impending departure was such that the committee undoubtedly raised her salary, for "she was induced to remain." And stay she did until her retirement in 1914.

Nowhere is there in Danvers' educational history a better example of the clash between old-line views and educational leadership than occurred here in 1897. The incident involved Israel W. Andrews, a long-time member of the school board, and W. A. Baldwin, the new, part-time superintendent. Baldwin had been hired on April 17, 1894, with the instructions, "Go ahead, and do as you have been in the habit of doing (in Andover), until fault is found." Baldwin interpreted that statement as meaning he was being encouraged to do what he felt had to be done. But he should have read more closely the committee's report for the year ending February 1, 1895. If he had, he would have found in the following statement an implicit warning not to move too swiftly—at least on programs that required tax money: "The cost of our schools have increased at an alarming rate of late, and the shadows of the future are dark and ominous. Failure and ruin are to be dreaded, but they often follow extravagance." School report prose in the 1880s and 1890s was often phrased in such melodramatic tones. In this case, the writer must have been Andrews, who was characterized by the committee in 1894 as one having no faith in the new or different.

For most of its history, Danvers has been a conservative town. Its innovative teachers have done their work after leaving Danvers. John Philbrick is the best example of that. For years it had postponed the inevitable about setting up its high schools. In the second half of the nineteenth century, music, art, and manual training programs were put off as long as possible. The school committee's recommendation in all these subjects was to defer action or to have the classroom teachers perform these functions. In the matter of physical education, the committee believed children could exercise beside their desks. The result was that physical education was performed as an afterthought or not at all. There was no systematic development from one grade to the next in most subjects.

Often what has caused change here has been the threat of penalties exacted by the General Court. Well intentioned though legislatures may be or have been in demanding new programs, they have not always provided necessary funds. This was true in the 1880s with the law requiring communities to supply students with paper, pencils, erasers, and other supplies.

Under this kind of pressure from outside, what begins to disappear with the success of the schools, the high school in particular, is the idealism and willingness to sacrifice seen in mid-century. In 1855, for instance, the school report had quoted Dr. William Ellery Channing about sacrifice for good schools:

There is no office higher than that of a teacher of youth, for there is nothing on earth so precious as the mind, soul, and character of a child. No office should be regarded with greater respect. The first minds in the community should be encouraged to assume it. Parents should do all but impoverish themselves to induce such to become the guardian of their children.

Unfortunately for himself, Baldwin, an exceptionally capable administrator, was very much aware of current thought in education. To translate thought into action would be expensive. While his views were enthusiastically accepted by his faculty and the women of Danvers, they were definitely not by Israel Andrews.

During 1895, the superintendent had worked to produce a sequential program of studies, grades 1–9, in geography, language, reading and spelling. Baldwin expressed his belief that teachers would integrate the work in the various subjects: "Nature studies and geography should furnish splendid opportunities for language work." The new teaching method was investigation.

Baldwin's 1896 report indicates he was even more ambitious for the welfare of local children. He recommended the establishment of a public kindergarten. Philosophically he was out of step with any conservative member of the board like Andrews, for he wrote that he would adapt school work to the needs of the child. Teachers should become the children's friends. It was this theory that helped bring an end to the harsh discipline of previous eras. Their work together would find teacher and pupils enjoying a new pedagogical tool, "out of door expeditions." Clearly in these matters, Baldwin was influenced by Anne Page.

To Judge Andrews, not the man of foresight that John Proctor had been, all this obviously sounded like pie-in-the-sky thinking. When the superintendent went on to recommend not only the hiring of kindergarten teachers but also the raising of teachers' salaries, Andrews exploded. Not always an astute observer of what went on in a classroom, Andrews believed, according to his fellow-committeemen, "with a good teacher no amount of supervision is needed and with a poor teacher, no amount of supervision can do much good."

Andrews was convinced that any boy or girl whose handwriting was neat and clear was "in all ways a good scholar." Cornelia Whipple, who recalled his visits to her classroom back when he was the prudential man for District No. 6, wrote in "Some Wise Words of Old People" (DHC, vol. VI), "On one occasion while making the customary remarks to the children . . . he glanced at the blackboard on which some one of the naughty children had drawn a caricature that evidently set his emotions a'whirring. Can't you see his angry face," she remembered, "as he abruptly turned his subject for praising children to, 'Who did that work? I would like to see the father of the one who did it.' I'd tell him what I thought of such actions. The rising generation is going to destruction."

"That boy," concluded Mrs. Whipple, "was said to be his own son."

In order to understand what Andrews did to rid Danvers of Baldwin, it is necessary to know that in the 1890s, town meetings could last for ten or eleven sessions over a period of several months. On March 3, 1897, Andrews moved for reconsideration of the article requesting $28,000 for schools, etc. What he specifically wanted was a reduction of $500, the salary paid Baldwin. A motion to table this motion failed. Then F. H. Caskin amended Andrew's motion to change the amount deleted to $1,000. The motion, as amended, carried.

Danvers mothers were furious the next morning when they learned of this. Andrews and his cohorts had waited to the end of the meeting when many had left in order to bring up the matter. Those ladies in the DWA who had worked closely with the superintendent were especially angered. Under the leadership of Evelyn Masury, one who had proved herself a preeminent parliamentarian in several national women's organizations, the mothers decided to do something about it. They sent a set of resolves to the selectmen along with a request for a conference. They felt the former administration of the schools by the committee and the prudential men "had been a constant source of uncertainty, irritation, and disappointment." Furthermore, they knew that Danvers wasn't even close to being the leader in the state when it came to the amount of money appropriated for schools. In 1894, for example, the town ranked 162 out of the 352 communities in the Commonwealth in its funding for each child, there being 545 pupils in the local schools at the time.

At the tenth session on May 12, the town clerk read the resolutions prepared by the DWA. James A. Farmer, not appreciating the power of women scorned, moved to table the matter. The motion failed. Then the Reverend Charles Rice moved that the school committee report to the town what added appropriation would be necessary to engage the services of a superintendent, Baldwin having left in the meantime. The Rice motion carried 52–5. In the end the Superintendency was restored, and it cost the town $400 more than originally budgeted. Baldwin was rehired, and the women were impressively victorious.

But only for a few months. Baldwin resigned because of ill health. For its part, the Danvers school committee was delighted to be free to return to its old ways. Later the finance committee and then the school board recommended that the office of superintendent and that of the principal of the high school be combined. It wasn't until 1903 that a new superintendent, Louis A. Pratt, was hired because state law forced the action.

A final area of concern to teachers and school committee during the late 1890s was the subject of a child's physical development and school design to promote a more healthful environment. In 1850–1851, teacher A. J. Demeritt wrote the committee that she was sorry to see "some little children, whose pale cheeks and drooping eyes show they had been sent from home before their strength had returned sufficient for them to bear without injury the confinement and atmosphere of a school room." When the new, larger elementary schools for a centralized school system were built in the late nineteenth century—the Danversport in 1893, the Highland's Wadsworth in 1897, the Tapley in 1895, and the Maple Street in 1898—the concern for a child's physical development and health was evident in the large-sized windows in each classroom. At the time tuberculosis was endemic. To keep their children healthy, some parents had them sleep in unheated, open porches. The need for fresh air and exercise led to the elimination of homework for elementary school pupils in order to give them more time outdoors.

Of all the baleful influences on the health of secondary school students during the final three decades of the nineteenth century and into the next one, two of the most common worries were about "demon rum" and the "noxious weed." This was the era when temperance societies for men and for women were formed. At the time, the local Women's Christian Temperance Union and other WCTUs around the country were admonishing men, "Lips that touch liquor never shall touch mine." Two questions used on Holten High School examinations in physiology (later called health or hygiene) were:

Mention three diseases of the brain which are often the effects of alcoholic drinks.

How many cubic feet of air does a man breathe in daily? If all the vapor which he exhales in a day were condensed to water, how much would it be?

In 1893, Dr. W. S. Frost, school board member, wrote in his portion of the annual report, "If the teaching in the public schools is to be depended upon to stop the smoking of tobacco by boys, that teaching will need to be in some way made more vigorous than it is." In 1908, a student writing for *The Holten* used smoking and drinking as an argument for the benefits to be derived from athletics: "Football tends to overcome the cigarette evil, for every player knows that to be strong, he must abstain from these muscle-weakening things. The liquor habit is removed in the same way. Football occupies the boy's mind and keeps him off the streets where he might fall in with bad companions."

In 1909, Fred C. Mitchell, principal of Holten High School, prepared a message for the school report that is unusually blunt, to the point of seeming to be foolhardy, concerning attendance, smoking, and general deportment. However, he had submitted his resignation. He placed the blame on the parents, who, he felt, were spoiling their children and being lax about sending them to school. To support his point, he quoted an old story, undoubtedly apocryphal, about one parent who grew tired of writing excuses for the frequent absences of his child. Therefore, he "wrote out a few dozen, stuck them together in a long roll and sent the package to the teacher with the instruction, 'When in need of an excuse, tear one off.'" Mitchell reminded townspeople that without parental support, teachers were powerless.

As to the subject of general manners, despite his assurance that most students were "normal, industrious, well-minded, and well-behaved," a reader of his comments wonders just what mean street life or fantasy had taken the man:

Little boys hardly out of knee pants smoke in public and on the sly; little girls in short frocks indulge in coarse familiarities and flirtations; these children meet and loaf in the streets and hang around resorts, and once in a while, some of them fall into mental states and into practices that are depraved and vicious. Some parents live in blissful blindness to it all. The children run things, their doting parents included.

In the same report, a more conciliatory committee member explained, "It is a hard thing to teach in school that the things done in the home are immoral or in anyway injurious or unsuitable. . . . Now, the laws being as they are, we are not at liberty to change the teaching in the schools. . . . Would it not be well then in such cases if the teaching in the home could be changed?"

The main point of all this is that a new responsibility had been placed on the school since it is the only institution through which practically all children can be reached. Because of the very success of the nation's public schools, Americans were confident that they could change what society and the churches hadn't been able to. Where the identification of physical problems was concerned, success could pretty well be assured. However, where problems like smoking and drinking were thrust on them, the schools were now being asked to eradicate society's unsolved or unsolvable problems without, necessarily, society's cooperation.

"An Ounce of Prevention" is the apt title for these ninth-grade students exercising at the Maple Street School in 1910.

Mabelle Spofford went to A. O. Elwell on Danvers Square to have her graduation picture taken in 1901. Albert O. Elwell had himself once studied at Holten High School.

CHAPTER V

Holten High School—1900–1929

The twentieth century was to be America's. European, especially German pedagogical theories, were supplanted by a New World one—progressive education. At the end of the nineteenth century in the era of rapacious Robber Barons, progressive reformers worked to restore the promise of the land of opportunity to the downtrodden. Settlement houses like Jane Addams' Hull House in Chicago were set up in large cities to aid the destitute, instruct immigrants from southern and eastern Europe, and provide healthy recreation for inner-city children.

Progressive education had its beginning at the famous Quincy School twenty-three years after John Philbrick had left. In 1875, Francis W. Parker, the newly arrived principal, introduced more group learning activities in a less structured setting. Textbooks were abandoned in favor of teacher-made materials; and newspapers and magazines were often utilized.

Elsewhere, as time passed, student-teacher contracts for academic work were made out, and new forms of texts called workbooks took students step-by-step through a project or unit of work. The result was an expanded, individualized curriculum more fully realized in private than public schools where the buildings favored by architects and school committees had discreet classroom units enclosed by immovable walls inhibiting expandable learning spaces for varied work.

John Dewey, progressive education's chief spokesman, held that schools should be communities. Besides job-oriented courses like typewriting and shorthand, manual training, farming, printing, and domestic science were included in the programs of studies. Student councils, clubs for foreign languages and other subjects, and publications like *The Holten* in Danvers were organized.

Locally the turn of the century saw the commencement of arguments over who should receive high school diplomas. In 1879, the school committee analyzed the needs of secondary school students as (1) those (the majority) who would complete their formal learning at this level, (2) those who wished to enter the business world, (3) those who wanted to enroll in three-year teachers' colleges, and (4) those who planned to matriculate at four-year colleges and universities. The solution, according to the board, would be to have a course of study sufficiently flexible to meet the requirements of all students. Danvers was in the spirit of progressivism and the new educators who were asking, "What shall be taught?"

As an aid to American commercial interests, business subjects had been accepted before the end of the nineteenth century. Other vocational courses took longer and came partly as the result of pressure exerted by the country's manufacturers apprehensive about the decline of their traditional apprenticeship system. Before the end of the century, at the urging of progressives and industrialists, practical courses like manual training, agriculture, printing, and home economics, the last originally called practical arts and then domestic science, were included in the course of study. The words "arts"and "science"gave these subjects the cachet of established academic courses.

When one learns that the teaching of this kind of education was then over one hundred years old, the question becomes, "Why did it take such a long time to become acceptable in the United States?" In 1774, Johan Pestalozzi had taken twenty orphans into his home in Zurich. In addition to their regular subjects, he had the boys instructed in farming and the girls in domestic work and sewing. The reason was twofold: they could help pay for their educations by working while acquiring skills for future occupations.

The real innovators in vocational education were the Scandinavian followers of Pestalozzi, proud of their traditional folk crafts, who had instituted courses in the 1860s. Familiar with their work, Anne L. Page, while a member of the Danvers school committee from 1873 to 1875, wrote, "All artesans [*sic*] and laborers, every woman who makes a garment, every man who makes a shoe or ploughs a field, or even digs a trench, will do it better if the eye has been trained, and the hand made skillful by early use."

The point Miss Page may have overlooked was that Americans were aspiring to rise above the laboring class. In 1911, a year after manual training was first taught in Danvers, Martha Chandler, editor-in-chief of *The Holten*, saw the benefits of vocational education as affecting all: "The practical side of education is becoming very important. Exhaustive knowledge of dead languages is no longer considered adequate to educate a person well without the aid of a training in something which he can apply to real life. . . . Some people object to manual training because the students do not wish to be carpenters. In the words of our new instructor [Clinton Low], its object is 'to make boys use their eyes and think for themselves.' It involves disciplined accuracy, practice in the use of the hands, and the exercise of muscles seldom used." Miss Chandler was voicing the strategy by which vocational education became acceptable to an upwardly mobile society, and that was that this form of education was a help in whatever occupation—professional or blue collar—a student might enter.

The Maple Street School was the flagship of the Danvers grammar schools (grades 7, 8, and 9). It was the first to establish departments, with the students going from room to room. In an illustrated booklet to parents, written around 1910, Frank Poor told of manual training with its hand tools and benches in the basement of the school. For the first half year, the boys worked on projects required by the teachers; but in the second, they worked on their own. Sometimes they went with their instructors to make products for other schools.

In 1909, equipment was set up in the boys' basement of the new Maple Street School for all ninth-grade boys to learn whittling, sawing, planing, and chiseling. To underscore the dignity of such a subject, the superintendent himself chose to be one of the two instructors. Townspeople concerned over the direction the high school had taken with the inclusion of this vocational course were assured by Superintendent H. C. Sanborn in 1910 that subjects emphasizing manual as opposed to intellectual skills would only be scheduled if they had "inherent practical value or [are] already correlated to subjects having such value."

In 1911, Clinton Low, a graduate of Brown University, was hired for manual training. He had prepared himself by taking special work at the Sloyd Training School in Boston and student teaching in Methuen. Low's first major assignment in Danvers was overseeing the installation of benches and machines for advanced manual training for tenth-grade boys in the basement of the town hall/high school. To demonstrate to the citizens of the community how they were deriving an immediate return from the expense of purchasing the equipment for this shop program, he had his students make a large bookcase for the study hall, laboratory equipment for chemistry, tables for the new biology laboratory, and even a stand for a large plaster bust of Benjamin Franklin.

By 1914 so popular was Low's course that he began an extension class two evenings a week. "We were besieged," he reported to the board, "by a small army of boys from all parts of town who wished to come into this night course." But out of all those applying, only twenty could be accepted.

Despite the passage of the Smith-Hughes Act in 1917 providing federal funds to subsidize the salaries of vocational teachers and equipment for shops, Danvers did not opt to set up a trade school because of the limited number who would be enrolled. Instead, the town has paid the tuition of those few who are able to enter trade schools in surrounding cities. While many Danvers adolescents would have preferred going to either a technical or agricultural school, their parents kept them in Holten High on the assertion that the education from the vocational schools was inferior. The problem had more to do with their social standing than education.

For several years after manual training became a part of the school's offerings, domestic science had progressed little beyond the old classroom projects involving sewing and basketry. Then a cooking area was installed in the girls' basement of the Maple Street School. There were other practical courses suggested for the high school curriculum. Although printing was one of them, it was never introduced. However, a two-year course in agriculture was. Many adolescent Danvers boys were interested in farming. Large cultivated fields were commonplace throughout the Onion Town. In 1910, *The Holten* printed a well-researched essay, "The American Poultry Industry," by Wallace Cook. Although Cook was not destined to become a chicken farmer, a great many boys of his generation enjoyed keeping gardens and raising animals. Wheeling flights of homing pigeons could be seen circling above their lofts in almost every neighborhood. Added to the early morning factory whistles, roosters crowing in backyard coops were that era's alarm clock.

Of domestic science introduced in 1917, for grammar and high school girls, Grace Ingalls wrote, "The equipment consists of twelve small gas stoves arranged on benches with drawers for cooking utensils underneath. A cooking stove, refrigerator, sink, supply table complete the outfit." Girls also sewed useful items like aprons, dresses, and underclothing by hand.

The agricultural courses at the high school became redundant after 1913 when the Independent Agricultural School in the County of Essex, called for brevity's sake Essex Aggie, opened in Hathorne. Following their graduation from Holten High, Paul Killam and Ralph Hussey of the Class of 1913 took postgraduate work there. After that year, many young Danvers men and women completed their full secondary schooling at the Aggie.

As with manual training, art, including mechanical drawing, was finally accepted into the public schools mainly at the behest of manufacturers seeking a plentiful supply of expert draftsmen. In 1871–1872, United States Commissioner of Education John Eaton had quoted from a report on the importance of drawing to arts and manufactures by Professor C. O. Thompson of the Free Institute of Worcester: "Drawing is indeed the language of form. A master workman is almost as helpless without it as a scholar would be without the ability to read and write. . . . It is clear that the proper time to learn the elements of drawing is in childhood."

Two of the art teachers Danvers had at this time were Jennie Aiken and then Mabelle (later Mabel) Spofford. The period during which they taught is known as the arts and crafts movement in architecture and decorative arts, an era when artisans were in revolt against cheap, mass-produced goods. The reflection of that locally was the time spent learning the use of hand tools in manual training and needlework in domestic science. As a result of their normal art school educations, both ladies had studied jewelry design and mechanical drawing.

Misses Aiken and Spofford had their classes design a piece of silver jewelry. Both ladies taught drawing in all the elementary schools. At least transportation was easier for Miss Spofford in Danvers than in her previous assignments in Vermont and Boxford. There were trolleys here to take her to her various schools rather than horse-drawn sleighs in winter.

This slight woman was the kind of person who, when she thinned out her garden each summer at 8 Cherry Street, would place the excess clumps of iris rhizomes along the sidewalk together with a neatly lettered sign reading, "If you can use these, please take them." In the Victorian novels that she read, Miss Spofford was known as "a lady of tender sensibilities."

At an advanced age when most people would have avoided active civic involvement, Miss Spofford was organizing and heading fundraising drives for Cerebral Palsy. In appreciation of that service she became the recipient of the North Shore Cerebral Palsy Association's Humanitarian Award. Some years into retirement, Mabel Spofford was named Danvers Woman of the Year.

Of more immediate concern for most high school students than practical courses was the lack of a town-funded athletic program. One wonders what compensations kept student morale so high at this time. The absence of a gymnasium, for example, meant they had to walk to other buildings and fields around the Square for their sports. The girls took their gym classes in the old Company K armory at 128 Maple Street. At one time a girls' intramural bowling league competed on the lanes in the basement of this building.

At a field on Lindall Hill and later at the Danvers Park, the girls played field hockey. "A Faithful Alumna" writing in *The Holten* told how tuition students from Middleton in the 1870s had to walk to the Square for their trolley; those from Topsfield and Boxford were excused fifteen minutes early in order to catch their train home.

Faithful Alumna, who, I believe, was Mary Nichols, also noted that before the cafeteria program began, students had just fifteen minutes at recess time to go to the Union Store on the corner of Essex and Elm Streets to spend five cents for cookies. At an adjacent bakery, for the same price, they could buy a slice of warm cake coated with a thin frosting. As an alternative to these sweets, a lady in a nearby house sold sandwiches from her porch. A few students even ventured as far as the Square for snacks. The school day ended at 1:30, which meant that make-up work was performed between three and four o'clock after they returned from taking their lunch at home.

Helen Richards and Helen Vaughn costumed for Margaret Wood's assembly play Le Voyage de M. Perrichon *in the 1920s.*

The few sports mentioned previously for girls were better than nothing. And nothing is what they had had earlier. In her 1909 graduation honors address, "Physical Culture and the Public School Girl," Naomi Kerans told the adults in the audience, "The gymnasiums of the larger towns and cities, our colleges, the social settlements, and the Young Women's Associations place opportunities within the reach of all except the public-school girl. Shall nothing be done for her? Large cities and towns have already answered in the affirmative. How about Danvers?" It was a bold question Naomi asked when you recall that her generation grew up with the repeated injunction, "Children should be seen and not heard." In somewhat pseudo-scientific terms, she saved her most convincing point for last: "Muscular exercise, rightly directed, conduces to the strength of the body, which in turn is necessary to the storing force of the brain. Therefore, this physical train-

In 1912, the girls' basketball team took themselves in their middy blouses and bloomers to William Taylor's photographic studio on the Square. Their teacher, Minnie Packard, is the center young lady in the back row.

ing besides strengthening the body will produce saner thinking and better mental work."

The young men of the high school sympathized with their female counterparts. George Newbegin supported their desire for physical education in the June 1910 issue of *The Holten*, even though the quotation that follows seems to be ironic: "The girls in our school can get no athletic exercise at all in connection with their school, and they certainly show the need of proper exercise under supervision."

In 1911, the young, attractive Latin and history teacher, Minnie Packard, started girls' basketball on a field on Lindall Hill, after she was named coach of "out of door sports" for girls. In the same locale, she had them playing Hare and Hounds, rules for which were printed in the school magazine in November: "Each Wednesday, [the girls] start for a run through the woods. Half of the number are hares and the other half, hounds. The hares go ahead and when they have gone some little time, the hounds follow. Arrows are marked in chalk to show the way. As soon as the hares are seen, the hounds try to overtake them. When all the hares are caught, the game comes to a close. It is very exciting!"

To collect money for tennis, basketball, and Hare and Hounds, Miss Packard also helped the girls form an athletic association that same year. The roster of the girls' basketball team in 1912 is one of the earliest lists for their sports that we have. In that year, the girls and Miss Packard went to Taylor's photography studio on the Square to have their picture taken. I found a copy of the postcard they had made up from that session at Pownalborough Courthouse in Maine. Eleven of the girls were Katherine Blanchard, Beatrice Brown, Lurana Butler, Eleanor Caskin, Martha Chandler, Gertrude Collins, Anna Cooke (Captain), Helen Doyle, Catherine Glover, Helen Learoyd, and Audrey Lynch. The twelfth girl was the sender of the card, who had coyly written to her Maine friend, "See if you can tell who I am, and I will write in a day or two to tell you." Of course, the card was unsigned.

It was only by accident that her identity was uncovered. I had that picture beside me one day at the Archival Center when Henrietta Newbegin Sears came in with some pictures taken by her aunt Gladys Damon. She picked up the picture and began naming the individuals. When she said, "And that's my aunt Audessa Newbegin,"I let out a triumphant hoot.

The boys also formed athletic associations to support their programs. These associations, both girls' and boys', collected a fee from each student, generally a dime to a quarter. In addition, they held entertainments in the assembly hall or the Peabody Institute Library to which they sold tickets. In the spring of 1910, the boys' baseball team, according to the writer of the "Sporting Column" in *The Holten*, conducted a program at the library during which they recited poems, sang, and showed motion pictures and thereby realized "a neat sum."

There were other forms of entertainment to raise funds. Dances were the most frequent. But on St. Patrick's Day in 1919 a minstrel show, a now discredited type of show in which the end men performed in black face, was held. The director was Cornelius F. Dunn, then a new teacher of history and music. The interlocutor was Frank Cooke, who had discovered "some intimate facts of general interest concerning certain of the faculty." Among the numbers most appreciated was Raymond Welch's "Wild Women" skit, rated "the *howling* success of the evening." In their enthusiasm, the students had decorated the front of the town hall in black and white bunting, setting the colors for the entertainment. The end men wore black and white striped suits and the costumes of the chorus had the same color scheme. The evening grossed the association $115.43. More importantly, this was the genesis of the popular sweater benefits held at the Richmond auditorium for years and directed by either Mr. Dunn or commercial teacher Gladys Damon.

On November 11, 1922, the football team played two games beyond its regular season to raise money for equipment. The players got into their uniforms at 8:00 A.M. and didn't get out of them until 6:00 P.M. Three athletes—Ronald Wilks, my father Paul Zollo, and Tubby Spencer—played every minute of both games. The average weight of the team was 135 pounds. The lightest man was Richard Shinnick, who weighed 102 1/2 pounds; Lester Coffin, the heaviest, weighed 180. It is an indication of the team's size that Coffin was nicknamed Bull. As light as these athletes were, they held Gloucester to a 13-13 tie in the morning and Manchester to a 6-6 tie in the afternoon. In the scheduled games that season, my father, who played left halfback, made ten of the twelve touchdowns.

Football had a reputation for being a game played by hooligans. In 1917, disappointed at not having had a football team for several years, another student writing for *The Holten* observed, "The members of the school living in the 'Port issued a challenge to the rest of the school for a football game. The challenge was immediately accepted; here was a chance to revive the grand old sport in Holten High. Alas, our hopes were dashed to pieces when, because of lack of knowledge of the rules, the game started in a free-for-all fight between members of the two teams."

What finally rescued the game from its reputation for rowdiness was the 1923 hiring of Lewis S. Crosby, one of the finest gentlemen ever employed in the Danvers athletic program. Mr. Crosby, who had been an outstanding backfield player at Colby College, did not allow any display of bad sportsmanship from his players.

The 1926 souvenir football program supports that last statement: "He has not only produced good athletes and very creditable football teams but has accomplished his work in a manner that is fully appreciated by every fair-minded citizen, without a single harsh word, not one act of violence, or a threat to an athlete aspirant."

On March 14, 1951, Mr. Crosby was talking to hockey coach Raymond Funchion in the cafeteria when he suddenly collapsed and died. He had been both coach and athletic director; he was also appointed assistant principal in 1934. Eliot Duncan, head of the commercial department, succeeded him as assistant principal.

Baseball had a very different reputation from football. For years Danvers was known as a baseball town. The game was played here at least as early as 1868. Some of the nineteenth century athletes for this sport were Thorndike Hawkes, George Bradley, Ed Caskin, and Sam King. They all went on to the big leagues. Dennis Cashman was offered the opportunity, wrote Tom Shehan in "The Old Twilight League" (DHC, vol. XLII), but preferred to stay home because factory or mill players got paid better than national leaguers.

The 1909 high school game against Swampscott was a memorable one. Mark Cronan, who wrote the sports column for the school magazine, noted, "With a tie score, two outs, and a man on third, Swampscott's best batter drove a high liner into left field; (Cyrille) Kerans ran back and stuck his bare hand up and caught the ball and saved the day for Danvers. We scored the winning run in the tenth inning."

In order to get basketball started, boys argued that all that was needed was a ball and two hoops. When they were finally successful in entering a North Shore basketball league, they practiced and played on the third floor of the Pillsbury Block, a large, old shoe factory at 17 High Street. It was not so far from the school as the Danvers Park, where the boys played football; and the girls, field hockey.

One amusing aspect of this student struggle to achieve town-funded athletic programs was the cheers shouted at games. An enthusiastic supporter of sports was Paul Moore. He wrote a poem, "Base Ball," in which he created the following cheer:

> Hobbo! Gobbo! Rickety R!
> Are we in it? I guess we are.
> Hobbo! Gobbo! Rickety I!
> Who are we for? Danvers High.

Cheers in print lose their vitality, but not their inaneness. Around 1919, this cheer was adopted:

> Boom-a-lac-a,
> Boom-a-lac-a,
> Bow-Wow-Wow.
>
> Chic-a-lac-a,
> Chic-a-lac-a,
> Chow-Chow-Chow.
>
> Boom-a-lac-a,
> Chic-a-lac-a,
> Cis-Boom-Bah.
> Danvers High School,
> Rah, Rah, Rah.

In matters of athletic competition where outside teams were involved, the name Danvers High was used, not Holten High.

Two other high school inconveniences at this time were overcrowding (actually throughout the system) and the rapid turnover of teachers and principals. Consider overcrowding first. In 1910, the superintendent reported that four out of every forty-six children in Danvers failed. There were 112 pupils kept back that year, enough to fill three good-sized schools. In that same year in the high school, several students were not allowed to take science because there were not enough stations for them in the laboratory. The superintendent's recommendation was for a promotion based on something besides academic performance in order to keep educational expenses down. Here is the local origin of what became known as social promotions.

It wasn't until 1918 that the school committee finally acknowledged in print the need for a new high school. To make another building more attractive to taxpayers, the board envisioned one that would be a civic center in which evening classes could be held. These courses would constitute "a people's college,"and, according to the committee, such a center would enrich Danvers spiritually, culturally, and socially. Thirteen more years were to pass before the Conant Street facility was opened.

Whenever teachers' pay has been discussed in this history, it has been about the effect of low pay in Danvers. In fact, around World War I, other school systems throughout the state were undergoing a similar problem. However, low salaries in Danvers meant that local high school students were continuing to experience first-hand the frequent loss of well-loved faculty members. The roster of principals of Holten High School printed below shows the repeated replacement of men in that position. In 1875, four different principals were appointed and left!

High School Principals in Danvers

The North Parish High School
John Marshall, 1850–1851

Holten High School
Ambrose P. S. Stewart, 1852–1853
Nathaniel Hills, 1853–1865
John C. Proctor, 1865–1866
James Fletcher, 1866–1871
Orville B. Grant, 1871–1872
Myron O. Harrington, 1872–1873
Albert W. Bachelor, 1873–1874
Edward D. Mason, 1875
Joseph W. Keene, 1875
Henry H. Hart, 1875
Frank M. Hawes, 1875–1879
Howard P. Burrington, 1879–1890
Ernest J. Powers, 1890–1900
Herbert J. Chase, 1900–1904
William J. Rushmore, 1904–1907
Fred C. Mitchell, 1907–1909
Charles F. Abbott, 1909–1912
William A. Spooner, 1912–1919
Edward L. Montgomery, 1919–1920
Roy M. Strout, 1920–1921
Ivan G. Smith, 1922–1928
Cornelius F. Dunn, 1928–1958
Ernest April, 1958–1962*

* Mr. April continued as principal of Danvers High School.

Frederick Mitchell had assumed the position in 1907. When this well-liked principal resigned in 1909, the senior class willed a box containing all their class funds to be given to the school board with the wish that it dole out to Mr. Mitchell "a sum sufficient to enable him to retire from his professional duties, *but* throughout the fifty years (before then), they shall freely draw upon these funds so that his service in Holten High School shall be secured and he shall not find it worth while [*sic*] financially at least, to go elsewhere." To his scholastic degrees, the class added one more, " F. C. Mitchell, A.B., M.S., O.K."

In 1913, popular Minnie Packard, who had given so freely of her time each afternoon for girls' sports, left to go to Lexington High. And Mrs. Margarethe Allmanritter, a teacher of English, Latin, and German, left although the town would seem to have found a great bargain in this linguistic marvel, since she resigned in order to teach French and German in New Britain, Connecticut. Principal Charles T. Abbott, as popular in his few years here as Mr. Mitchell had been, left in 1912 to study at Harvard and then became a professor of history and political science at Middlebury College in Vermont. Abbott had been interested in developing the social life of the students along collegiate lines. He and his wife held well chaperoned parties at their house at 141 Holten Street for the seniors and for the language clubs.

The loss of Miss Carrie Q. Cate in 1912 after seven years of teaching French and German was also keenly felt. Her surprise farewell party on November 25 illustrated just how much her students appreciated her. When she arrived at the assembly hall at eight that evening, she was placed in a receiving line with the presidents of all the classes to greet her friends and students. Then she was given the seat of honor on the stage for a program that included Marian A. Niles' opening song, "Then You'll Remember Me," followed a little later by Mabel A. Blanchard's "How Can I Leave Thee?"

Before the affair grew too lachrymose, the classes of 1913 and 1914 presented her with a bar-pin set with a large amethyst. After the formal program, the senior class president escorted Miss Cate to the punch bowl. There they "touched glasses" and drank to everyone's good health. Dancing and games followed. In another of those ambiguous notes editors wrote for their magazine, we read, "Although this was a sad occasion, it still was a merry one, and the merriest of all was the one who was about to leave us."

School physician Charles Deering at ground-breaking exercises for the "new" Hunt Memorial Hospital, August 23, 1955.

Fortunately for the student body of Holten High School, there were compensations which, although they could not ameliorate deficiencies in the building or the course of study or the loss of faculty, helped to offset some of the disappointments. Among these counter-balances was the size of the school. "She is small enough so that we can all feel a personal interest in whatever she does," wrote *The Holten* editor in 1911. "We can all know each other well enough and so work together like one great family to further her interests. Everything we do counts toward her reputation. Indeed, in becoming a member of the school, each one has become a part of her; . . . therefore, it's 'up to every one of us' not only to help maintain her present high standards, but to do our very best to make them even higher."

Though the legislature might force communities to hire a school physician and later a nurse, their eventual presence in school systems like Danvers was regarded as a special beneficence of the school committee. In 1907, Danvers hired its first school physician, Dr. Harry C. Boutelle, a year after the state made such a position mandatory. In 1915, Dr. Charles Deering became the physician, a position he held, with the gap of a few years in the beginning, all through the remaining existence of Holten High. An alumnus of the last class to graduate from the medical school at Bowdoin College, he was an innovative team doctor for baseball and football.

Some call him a pioneer in sports medicine. His son Bob remembers that on Saturday mornings before a football game, he would bring two to three dozen fresh oranges into the kitchen and ask his wife Bertha to cut them into quarters. These the players consumed at half time. They were Dr. Deering's equivalent of today's quick-energy beverages.

This doctor for all his virtues was a little absent-minded. Previous to departing for a game, he would hastily pack his medical bag and drive off for the field. A few minutes later, he would often return and search through the silverware drawer in the dining room at 38 Elm Street until he found what he had forgotten—the spoon he used to set broken noses. As one who had specialized in orthopedics, he became adept at setting broken bones right on the field. By doing so, he believed the pain ended sooner, the swelling was reduced, and the bone set quicker. From the field, the injured athlete was sent to the hospital.

Dr. Deering never wore cleats even if the field was sopping. He would return home wet up to his knees. At Saturday night dinner, Bob or his sister Jean would ask him what the score had been that day, if they hadn't been able to attend. He seldom knew. In fact, he never learned the rules of the game for either baseball or football. What he did know was that his duty was to take care of the athletes, and he exercised his authority when it came to making the decision as to whether or not an injured player could reenter a game. Despite the protestations of a coach anxious to have a good athlete back in the game, Dr. Deering would mildly say, "No. I don't think he'll play today."

When he was eighty-three, Bob asked him one day, "Dad, what was the most important thing that ever happened to you?" The doctor thought for a few minutes before replying, "I guess for an old country physician, it was having that stadium named for me." In 1962, the town officially called its large, new football facility in Woodvale after him as "a tribute well deserved for his many years of loyal service to the Town and the school system," according to the annual town report.

Around 1916, the first school nurse was engaged. Sometimes, during the initial years, the Danvers Visiting Nurse Association provided that person. The nurse's duties included assisting the school physician in his examinations, helping to administer and then read the results of the Schick Test, which checked for immunity to diphtheria, identifying potential medical problems of individual students and notifying parents to check with doctors. The responsibility of follow-up work was also hers, as well as checking every child for head lice and nits. Because of some of these duties, it became the custom for the nurse to be a member of the Board of Health, thus giving her a source of funds to aid families in need of medical assistance. Those other sources, also included the DVNA and the Danvers Women's Association.

School nurse Theresa Creeden is at work here in her suite in the Richmond Junior High School in 1954, the year of her retirement after thirty-two years of service to Danvers school children.

In 1932, Theresa Creeden, an alumna of the school, became the school nurse and remained at that position until her retirement in 1954. By that time no one knew more about local children than Tess, and gossiped less. She had earned, Editor Leonard F. Nolan, Jr. wrote in *The Holten*, the title of "school mother." For twenty-five years she was a member of the Board of Health and for some years its chairman. She also worked regularly with the American Red Cross on its blood drives.

Although she had town funds available to her and used them, Tess was careful about spending town money. If, for example, a girl lacked a white dress for graduation, she would call her sister Etta Callahan to see if she could borrow the dress her niece Elinor had worn at her graduation. Sometimes she spent her own money, since during the Depression there was a great need among children for adequate dental care, eye glasses, and clothing, especially shoes.

Miss Creeden had been an army nurse in World War I, probably the only Danvers nurse to be sent overseas. From France in the summer of 1918, she wrote home:

Dearest Mother:

This is the first opportunity I have had to write as I have certainly kept very busy, as of course, you have read of the big drive the Allies made. Can you picture me living in a tent? It certainly does rain over here. I am in a receiving station and at present on all night duty. I remove clothing of the soldiers and dress wounds. I have had the excitement of an air raid. This is no place for people with nerves. If you don't hear from me often, keep writing, as my letters are my only consolation and as the unit I am with keeps moving with each drive, it makes it hard for me to get much opportunity to write.

The Americans are making a great drive. They certainly can hold their own. They are a wonderful crowd of boys. Tell people that you know, to write often to their boys, as only God and themselves know what they are going through.

I will have to close now as my time is limited, so, mother dear, don't worry about me as I am fine and will come back all right to you.

For all her brave talk, Tess didn't return all right. Like a lot of soldiers home from the Western front, she suffered what would be called today, post-traumatic stress disorder. For the men in those days it was called being shell shocked. The worst of what Tess experienced came on a day when she went out on a battlefield with the stretcher bearers. Surrounded by bomb craters, twisted barbed wire, and the dead and the dying, she was attending to the wounds of a badly injured soldier when she heard a feeble voice behind her say, "Miss. Miss. Please get him off my chest."

She turned to see a black soldier, a gaping wound in his chest, and working away at it, a huge rat. All the blood and carnage had attracted great numbers of rats that had also gone "Over the top" to dine. Terrified, Tess looked around and, seeing a wooden handle long enough to fend off the rats from the dying doughboy, she stayed with him until he died.

Holten High School students remember Tess Creeden best at assemblies honoring the nation's veterans. She sat on the stage, her navy blue overseas cap perched jauntily on her head, and her Red Cross cape thrown back over one shoulder. Whenever we sang "Over There," "My Buddy," or any of the other tunes popular during the War to End All Wars, her voice could be heard above the others, for Miss Creeden was a belter, and like all her family, she loved music.

As a member of the Overseas Veterans of World War I and a charter member of the Drapeau-McPhetres Post 180, American Legion in Danvers, she was a familiar sight in Memorial and Armistice Day parades marching proudly along shoulder to shoulder beside her "boys." It would be difficult to think of anyone who deserved the honor more.

Among the young Danvers men who were cited for bravery in World War I was David Stambler, whose artillery regiment, the 104th, repelled the Germans in the Americans' first engagement. A French general was so impressed with their courage that they all received the Croix de Guerre. Stambler was later sent home to recover from a serious shoulder wound he received in another battle. Another local man who received the Croix de Guerre was Esmond (Ekka) Farmer. Wounded in the left hip by machine gun bullets that had not penetrated very deep, he was crawling back across no-man's land to his lines when he came upon a man wounded so badly that he could not move although he was in danger of being hit by enemy fire. Farmer got the man across his shoulders and carried him to safety.

Paul Moore, who as an undergraduate in high school had composed his "Hobbo!

Gobbo!" cheer, was cited for bravery for coolness and bravery under heavy fire and poison gas at Verdun when he was with the 102nd Field Artillery. These were the fortunate ones. Raymond Knowlton and Hadley McPhetres were killed when a German shell landed in an ammunition storage area beside them.

Paul Moore in his World War I uniform stands beside his grandfather, Charles Newell Moore, a Civil War veteran, who once was the stage coach driver on the two-day trip from Boston to Providence.

For the students, a new basement cafeteria was another advance, in addition to a school nurse that their high school was making, even if after rain storms portions of the cellar flooded and they had to walk over planks to get there. A school lunchroom was first suggested by principal William Rushmore in 1906. Knowing the conservative ways of the town, he said students should be provided with "light fare, suitably selected, cooked and served as human nourishment and not as rations for an army."

However, no cafeteria materialized through the subsequent two-year principalship of Fred C. Mitchell or Charles F. Abbott's three-year term. Then in 1912, when William Spooner was acting principal, the General Israel Putnam Chapter of the Daughters of the American Revolution began serving students with a choice of four or five sandwiches, simple desserts, cookies or cupcakes, and milk or cocoa. Later Mrs. Marcia Ricker was made the cafeteria manager. Her success at this work got her appointed as a domestic science teacher.

While it was an unlikely place to inspire romance, one did blossom there in 1923. He first spoke to her as she passed him on the stairs. He turned and admiring her trim ankles said, "*Quelles jambes*," in his best high school French. Since he was a star athlete, she turned, smiled, and asked him what he had said. After that, they met in the cafeteria every recess period because his sports left them little time to see each other after school. He gladly ate the hearty, homemade rye bread sandwiches her Norwegian mother prepared, but she was ashamed of. She nibbled on the white bakery bread sandwich he bought her at the lunch counter. They married in October of 1925, and that was how my father met and wooed my mother.

Another exciting and valuable asset for the students was the school magazine that has been quoted so often in this chapter. *The Holten* gave the students a voice, one that, as the progressives had foreseen, would develop their sense of community and connect them to other secondary schools and colleges across the country. It was a stimulating challenge for excellence in writing in a print-oriented age.

"Exchanges" was the publication's department that reported helpful criticism of their magazine from other schools just as their editors commended and criticized other periodicals. In the June 1910 issue, the editor thanked thirty-six different institutions that had sent their publications to Danvers. These included the *Harvard University Gazette* and the *Tufts Weekly*.

This department also provided readers with more humor in addition to that provided by "The Knocker":

> Teacher (grasping frisky freshman by the collar)—
> "I believe Satan has got hold of you, young man."
> Freshman—"I believe he has."

For intramural topics, there were "Editorials," "School Notes," and "Athletics," all of which discussed school spirit, dances, assemblies, games, etc. A department begun in 1923 by Ruth Ellery was a creative addition on the order of Addison and Steele's Spectator—"The Corridor Crow." Charlie Crow, later joined by his wife Carrie, lived in the rafters of the school, and as the two gazed down on students and faculty passing by, they made comments about some of them. The big secret to the column had to do with who wrote it. Almost throughout its existence, no one knew each year's editor. Some students were convinced it was Mr. Dunn. As time went on, the purpose of the column drifted. Part of the prob lem had to do with credibility—there were no exposed wooden beams in the Conant Street facility—and part was that it began to duplicate many of the types of items in the humor column.

The most repeated cover design was a silhouette of Judge Samuel Holten. Long before popular periodicals like *Esquire*, personified by its popeyed Esky character, and *The New Yorker* by its monocled fop about town, Eustace Tilley, the students in Danvers had conceived of the idea on their own.

For the senior class will, history, prophecy, and grinds, students in the June issue wrote parodies from their readings in English literature like *The Lays of Ancient Rome* ("By the nine gods they swore"). Probably the very best of these was Ernest Clayton Pitman's class history in 1910. He selected "Hiawatha" to imitate. Its sing-songy meter sometimes served him better than it had Longfellow since Pitman was being deliberately amusing. His introductory lines follow:

Should you ask me whence this story,
Whence this legend of Holtenah,
I should answer, I should tell you—
In the records old and secret,
Chronicles of Nin-ten-tenah,
Found I many simple legends
Of the school-rooms of Holtenah
And the class that came to dwell there,
Noble class of Nin-ten-tenah.

Toward the end of his history, Pitman paid tribute to the teachers. The best of these, according to this senior, was Sarah Frances Richmond:

But the grandest of our teachers
Is our dear Miss Sarah Richmond,
'Neath whose loving hand and guidance
We have learned to face our battles.
So the class of Nin-ten-tenah
Gives its love, respect, and honor,
To this noblest of all teachers.

In 1929, Ernest Pitman became the first principal of the Richmond Junior High School.

Pitman's use of his full name was a sure indication in his day that he had aspirations of becoming a poet on the order of Percy Bysshe Shelley, Henry Wadsworth Longfellow, Samuel Taylor Coleridge, John Greenleaf Whittier, etc., all of whom he would have read during his three years of high school.

He was not alone in employing this device. Another Holten High School poet who used his full name was Thurl Dryden Brown (sometimes T. Dryden Brown). His verses have been printed in the *Danvers Herald*, where he worked for a decade as a reporter, and in World War II service publications like *Blizzard* and *The Rucksack*. Brownie, as he is often called, or Gremlin by his fellow ski-troopers of the 10th Mountain Division, is now the poet laureate of the latter.

Henry Moscow, editor of *The Rucksack*, tells in the preface to Thurl's *Rucksack*

Recollections how their Gremlin won the hearts of his buddies. In the summer of 1943, Thurl was on board the USS *Zeilen*, which was carrying troops through the North Pacific to Kiska in the Aleutians. The journey was often fogbound, and the soldiers' fear of being sunk by a Japanese submarine was realistic:

One morning, a group of them (ski-troopers), sprawled or squatting on deck, were joined by a small, lean, taut, crewcut man who resembled a slightly grizzled elf. Within a minute or two, their somber talk had given way first to chuckles and then to bursts of laughter evoked by the wry comments of the newcomer, delivered in the accents of his native New England.

As a man who loves skiing, Thurl is a keen observer of weather, and so, understandably, the seasons and the elements make up a large part of his poetry and its imagery. In the Spring, 1938 issue of *The Holten*, he submitted to the "Alumni" editor this poem:

A Poem
Be the storm! not of it.
Swing with snowflakes, wild.
Chase the wind and be chased;
Be the dark cloud's child.

Rage and shriek! Be Terror!
Gnaw stone walls and trees.
Spit your frozen vapor.
Ice the stream and freeze.

Feel the frozen vigor
Solidify your veins;
Clothe yourself in Winter!
Hate the balmy rains.

Hush all men with whiteness.
Choke them with your smoke.
Be New England Winter.
Wear a brittle cloak.

In the next decade, there was a poet, one among a surprising number of Danvers professional writers, called "one of the most rewarding of New England poets." He was Samuel French Morse, Class of 1932. His earliest poem was probably published in *The Holten*. His first published poems for national periodicals appeared in *College Verse*, *Poetry*, *Smoke*, and *New Republic*. His work was also accepted over the years by *The New Yorker* and *The Atlantic Monthly*.

When he had a sufficient number of poems, they were collected into a volume, *Time of Year: A First Book of Poems* (1944) with an introduction by Wallace Stevens. " That Wallace Stevens should have volunteered to write an introduction for a book of mine," he wrote in *World Authors*, 1950–1970, " was as flattering as it was unexpected."

In addition to Sam's first book of verse, he published several other volumes, *The Scattered Causes* (1957) and *The Changes* (1964). He wrote two books for children—*All in a Suitcase* (1966), a rhymed alphabet book, and *Sea Sums* (1970). Of these two volumes, he noted, "The pleasure of reading poetry aloud to children has led to some trial flights with writing poems for children. The experience has been a good one; it has, I think, added a dimension to my work."

For the same issue of *The Holten* in which Thurl's poem was printed, Sam Morse submitted two sonnets, parts of a longer work. Here is the first:

From Two Sonnets
Frost decorates the grasses with its thread,
The silver bends across the steaming brook;
She wonders how the vivid summer fled
Remembering August and the tawny look
Of immensities of cloud, the hullaballoo
The thunder made; of June, and circus tents
White in the fields of Dover and Caribou . . .
The twisted woodbine shivers on the fence . . .
But this is past: and she will not forget.
Because the sunlight wanes, that river course
Choked with the swirling leaves, the timeless threat
That spends eternity with sullen force.
The frost dissolves along the withered stem,
A paradigm of suns, Sun's stratagem.

Finally in this category was an alumna and a member of the faculty who began writing poetry as a young girl and continued until she was in her late eighties. She was Margaret Proctor Wood. Except for the publication of a few of her poems in Boston newspapers, they were not generally known to her students even after she published a small volume of them in 1959 under the title *Rhymes of a Lifetime*, followed in 1964 by *More Rhymes of a Lifetime*. Miss Wood's choice of the word "rhymes" is reflective of her modesty or, as the students of the Class of 1921 recognized, her honesty.

In terms of service, Miss Wood was the oldest of the instructors on the faculty in the last two Holten High School buildings. She taught French for thirty-seven years. After her graduation from Wheaton Seminary and Brown University, she traveled in France for two summer vacations perfecting her French accent. She studied also at Middlebury College and McGill University.

The writer of her biographical sketch in *A Margaret Proctor Wood Sampler*, printed posthumously, stated, "She was strict with herself." For example, to be near the high school during the winter months, she boarded at 19 Cherry Street away from her beloved family home, the eighteenth century Proctor Farm on Conant Street. To generations of her students, she was remembered as a strict, not severe, teacher. There was no small talk in her classes. In those days the emphasis in language study was on reading, not speaking, although we all spent time in front of our bedroom mirrors practicing the proper pucker or moue for some of the French vowels.

It wasn't until I began teaching at Holten High that I began to know her as a person. After my first bicycle trip through France in 1947, I brought her back an old map of a favorite Normandy landmark of hers, Mont Saint Michel. She hung it on her living room wall. When I visited her on an early autumn afternoon, she would have a fire burning in her Franklin stove. Mr. Marmalade, or another of her favorite cats, would be curled up fast asleep.

Miss Wood's lyrics reflect an excellent sense of humor, a love of small children and her pets, a close observation of the world around her farmhouse during the different seasons, and most of all her home itself:

Courage
Sorrow had best be buried.
 Hide your own;
Earth's skies are dark enough
 Without your moan.
Each has his own grief.
 Why add yours?
God knows, and for the asking,
 Courage stores.

Fire
Where fire burned the hill
Runs a clear path of living green.
Where love seared life
Runs a new path of comforting belief
In things before unseen.

Some Curricula
Some curricula activities are silly,
And some are pedagogically sound.
A thorough course in gym
Makes corrections in the slim,
Not to mention alterations in the round!

If Ogden Nash
If Ogden Nash
Makes words to suit him,
Who am I
To undispute him!

Little Boys
No wonder that the small word noise
Rhymes so well with little boys!
Faces beaming, voices high,
"We've come to visit you," they cry.
Raincoats dripping, boots all mud,
My spotless floor is soon a flood.
What to do but let them in?
Worth it, such goodwill to win!

A story that Margaret Wood enjoyed telling about herself concerned a tour she gave a group of school children through her home. She was discussing witchcraft and her relationship to John Proctor, one of the victims who had shown great courage in challenging the Puritan authorities in 1692. She concluded her account with the statement, "He was hanged right there in Salem, on Gallows Hill." One child, fascinated by the drama of the whole incident, responded, "Gee, I'll bet that made you mad."

Newspaper writing was another field in which Holten High School graduates excelled. William Crouse was editor of the *Woonsocket* (Rhode Island) *Call*; Francis (Tip) O'Neill wrote for the Hearst newspapers in Boston; Marilyn Twiss was news editor of the *Summerville* (South Carolina) *Journal Scene*; Alfred Hutchinson wrote feature articles for the *Danvers Herald*; but the newspaper that employed the greatest number of Danvers people was *The Salem Evening News*. Cyrus J. Newbegin,

James O'Neill, Jr., Lawrence Blake, and Peggy Shehan. Tom Shehan, Peggy's father, wrote for the old *Boston Transcript*. Of most interest here are Jim O'Neill and Tom Shehan, both of whom graduated from Holten High in the 1920s.

"What happens to a dream deferred?" Langston Hughes asked in "Harlem," ending ominously, "Does it explode?" James J. O'Neill, Jr.,never let disappointment turn into bitterness or rage. Born to write, he was forty-three before he found employment in journalism, and forty-seven when his big story broke. By then no one was better prepared for his job, and no one worked harder at it. "Hours meant nothing to 'Jim' O'Neill," his editor at the News once wrote, "when he had his teeth in a story."

Everything Jim had learned came to a climax on March 25, 1952. What began as a Mack Sennett comedy ended in death. About 10:15 that morning three guards for the U.S. Trucking Corp. left their green armored truck, "Big Baby," parked and unlocked outside Ropes Drug Store on the east side of Danvers Square while they went in for a cup of coffee. Moments later three other men in a stolen black Buick drove up and began withdrawing bags of money from the "traveling bank" to their car. By the time Officer Edmund Noonan went over to investigate why they were double-parked, they had $681,700 safely stowed away.

Spotting Noonan's approach, the men jumped into their car leaving $88,250 behind, and sped directly at the Danvers policeman, who leaped aside but managed to get their license number. Road blocks were quickly set up, but the thieves made good their escape.

As the first daily reporter at the scene, Jim worked fast, taking notes on what proved to be the nation's greatest larceny. Since no one had been placed in fear during the actual theft, this put the Danvers crime technically in a different category from the earlier Brink's $1,200,000 robbery. Jim earned himself a national by-line. Of necessity, his articles were hastily composed, but they were also well-written and factually accurate.

He was on hand two years later when Big Baby returned briefly to the Square so that the jury in the trial of George O'Brien of Wollaston could inspect the site of the crime. O'Brien, a small-time gambler with a prison record, had been found with $438 of the stolen money after he went on a spending spree, purchasing a new home and three cars mainly in cash. He was found not guilty, however, for lack of credible evidence placing him in Danvers on March 25. Two months later he shot himself through the head in his parked car.

Jim's most appreciative audience became his grandchildren for whom he wrote a series of eagerly awaited letters from MacGregor, his terrier, telling of canine adventures and complaining of Jim's unfair treatment. On Sunday, January 16, 1972, having completed his Middleton and Boxford columns at home, he was getting ready to deliver them to the Danvers office when he suffered a fatal heart attack.

A writer, who appeared in *The Holten* as an adult was Tom Shehan. His essay "The Life of Riley" was printed in April, 1938. Tom provided his high school audience with a description of what it was like being a sportswriter and also, in the process, revealing much about himself: "On the sports pages you will find a humanness that is missing from the editorial pages, humor that no cartoonist can express in the comics, and a personality that papers neglect expressing in their regular news columns." However, the phrase that is most telling comes when he refers to himself as "one who likes life spiced with variety."

As a writer, Tom Shehan has had that. He has been a sports reporter for the *Boston Evening Transcript* and the *Maine Sunday Telegram*, along with many other newspapers; publicist for the defunct Boston Shamrocks and the St. Louis Gunners; correspondent for *Yank*, the World War II Army magazine; ghostwriter of Sam

Snead's *Natural Golf* and Ben Hogan's *Power Golf*; author of local history articles for the *Danvers Historical Collections*; and an editor and publisher of the Derry (New Hampshire) *News and Enterprise*, *The Horseman's Journal*, and *The International Trotter*.

If you're wondering why Tom never became a professional athlete himself, ask yourself how many five-foot, four-inch baseball or hockey players you've ever heard of. Like Thoreau, Tom Shehan listened to the beat of a different drummer, and as a high school student, it often distracted him from completing his homework. But back in the 1920s, English teacher Sally E. Dow led him to the path of self-education, and that is the best legacy an instructor can bestow.

Miss Dow was a graduate of Smith College, who came to Danvers to teach because of its proximity to Boston. Proud of their Searsport, Maine, origin, she and her younger sister Kate were thoroughly cosmopolitan. They regularly attended the Boston Symphony and the theater in Boston and New York City. They traveled to Europe together. Each sister wore a handsome Limoges enamel ring with the profile of a Renaissance noble, which they had had made from a pair of cufflinks brought back to America by a sea-going ancestor.

Sally Dow was always neatly and expensively dressed. She often wore silk blouses and English tweed suits. Girls envied her smart leather shoes. Her hair was neatly dressed. However, her appearance was not enhanced by heavily tinted eyeglasses. Tom wrote for the *Salem Evening News* on October 21, 1988, that she came alive in the classroom. Paul Cotoia, another of her students, claims that she was a teacher's teacher, and he knows what he's talking about. For years Paul coached Twilight League and boys' athletic teams.

Miss Dow was particularly valued for her deep concern for her students. No one who tried failed her subject. But work was involved. She was one of the few instructors who strictly enforced a school regulation that for each day of absence, a student had to have an afternoon help session with each teacher of a major subject. One Highlands girl, absent for several weeks, resented the fact that she had to remain behind hours with Miss Dow. Even though she was receiving individual attention, she was also missing her afternoon bus home.

In her undergraduate days, Miss Dow, like so many of her college contemporaries, studied the works of professors of education like William DeWitt Hyde of Bowdoin, who in *The Five Great Philosophies of Life*, asked his readers to ask themselves, "Do I get at the individuality of my students, so that each one is different to me from every other, and I am something no other person is to each of them? Then I have the high school teacher's special gift, and shall be a power of good all through my students' lives." When it came to her pupil, Tom Shehan, Sally Dow almost fumbled the ball.

One day she left her study hall for a few minutes. A class bully in her absence seized the cap of another student from atop his books and threw it out the window. The outraged boy shouted an awesome oath that froze everyone in place. That, of course, was the moment Miss Dow re-entered the room. Without hesitation, she said, "Mr. Shehan, will you please leave the room."

Despite all his protestations of innocence, she remained adamant. So Tom went off to Principal Ivan G. Smith's office, where it was suggested that he apologize to her. "I don't think that I owe Miss Dow an apology," he said. "I think she owes me one." In the meantime someone had told Miss Dow of her error.

The following day, she had Tom stand in class and publicly admitted that she had been wrong. "So I was sold on Miss Sally E. Dow's rectitude, both as a woman and as a teacher," Tom later wrote. Not long after this, when she was his English instructor, she also became one of his earliest fans despite his errors in syntax, spelling, and punctuation. She appreciated his compositions' interest and special style. And she urged him never to let anyone change it. Since she recognized, according to Tom, that sports lore "was oozing from my pores," she recommended he start reading something else—quality periodicals like *Harper's.*

Those magazines proved very different from Tom's favorite reading, the two hundred or so Frank Merriwell stories written by Gilbert Patten, and he thought that Miss Dow had given him some poor advice. When he told her that he had tried reading them from cover to cover and didn't enjoy it, she suggested that he pick out the one poem, article, or short story that appealed to him and just read that. Tom is still reading them while pitcher Merriwell and his double breaking curve ball are just pleasant memories.

Some years after her retirement from Holten High School in 1949, she spent "a night at the races" with Tom and his first wife Harriet (Bishop) when he was general manager of Scarborough Downs in Maine. That evening one of Tom's employees asked her if Tom had been a good student. "No," she replied, "Tom was not a good student, but he was an interesting one."

Sally Eaton Dow got her integrity from her family, especially her father Captain Leroy Dow, master of the three-masted Down-Easter *Clarissa B. Carver.* A modest woman, Sally did not tell many of her pupils his story. But on the night of June 7, 1885, a clear, serene night, Captain Dow's ship was struck by the heavy, steel-hulled British steamship *Glamorganshire* as it was entering Hiogo Bay in Japan and sank within forty minutes. Despite the fact that a sailing ship had the right of way over a steam vessel and that the *Carver's* running lights were in order, he lost the first trial held in a marine court of inquiry. Dow remained in the Orient for almost a year and a half fighting to recover the damages for his ship's shareholders and to restore his own reputation. Clerking for different shipping companies to support himself, he continued the litigation until he was vindicated and $84,244.38 in Mexican dollars for damages and interest were paid the owners of the *Clarissa B. Carver* on October 18, 1886. The conclusion of the last court, wrote John R. Richardson in *The American Neptune* in 1980, was that the steamer's look-out was "not a sharp hand, (but) dull in the extreme."

Today, the Penobscot Marine Museum has on display many of the beautiful objects Captain Dow brought back to Maine for his family because Sally and Kate willed their property to the museum, even their childhood home, which is now the residence of that institution's curator. In the gift shop of the museum you can find a copy of a booklet Sally Dow wrote, "Profiles of Some Searsport Master Builders."

As you read her biographical sketches, notice the writer's singling out in her subjects the quality of integrity. She quotes Captain William McGilvery as saying, "I value my business reputation more than all else I possess." And she describes Marlboro Packard as "a man of sterling worth, of sturdy independence, of unswerving honesty, and one whose word was quite as good as his bond." She might well have been characterizing herself.

One of the few jobs high school boys could find in the 1930s was that of weeding on local farms. Here is such a work crew at Pat Shea's farm in Tapleyville. Work was hard, and the pay was low on all the farms.

CHAPTER VI

Holten High School—Depression Years
1930–1939

Holten High School instructors like Margaret Wood, Sally Dow, Frances Wadleigh, and Gladys Damon, educated before World War I, were taught by professors to take both a moral-and a character-building approach in their classes. Harvard professor George Herbert Palmer of Boxford told his classes that teachers and students existed together in a "dependent fellowship"; and because both were human beings, he advised, "We (teachers) must be ready with spiritual aid."

In 1931, Superintendent Ivan G. Smith in Danvers wrote in his annual report, "The first charge of the school is for the health and happiness of the boys and girls." They must, he felt, be prepared to be "mentally alert, physically strong, and morally right." "Happiness" was a new word in the lexicon of pedagogy. It was an added responsibility of the schools to career and college preparation, citizenship, health, morality, etc.

As a result of their training, school teachers of the period were convinced that they needed more than methodology to be effective. They held with English poet Alexander Pope: "Just as the twig is bent, the tree's inclined." Thus, they were not reticent about dispensing advice along with learning, and during the Depression, they were very often successful at both without causing a great deal of resentment from students and their parents.

Their pay may have been small, but the respect given them was great. This was also an era when young people looked to adults for direction. Male students heeded the advice of coaches like Lewis Crosby or Charles Vye. As for their principal, Cornelius F. Dunn, they welcomed assistance from one they regarded, in the words of Ray LeColst, as "a square shooter." In those deprived years, *The Holten* editor, Francis Caskin, wrote, "The teachers may be surprised to know that, in the minds of the students, the warmth-giving adjective *understanding* means more than the cold adjective *brilliant.*"

No students ever had a better champion than Cornelius Dunn. Nothing was too good for them. One of his disappointments was that his faculty did not always provide what he considered to be sufficient extra-curricular activities. He certainly had as a teacher, and when he became the school's chief administrator in 1928, he almost immediately resurrected the Peabody Honor Society and formed Holten High's first marching band. Despite his complex tasks, he never forgot that his first responsibility was his students' well-being. He was always a visible presence who knew the names of every student, even forty years after they had left him.

That explains why, when Danvers Town Clerk Daniel Toomey was asked, "What was the best thing about Holten High School?" he answered without hesitation, "Connie Dunn!" He gave as his reason this man's remarkable skill at communicating with young people.

In 1958, the year Mr. Dunn retired, Norman Brown of the Class of 1922 wrote a tribute to the one who had been his American history teacher and later his boss when he himself taught English in Danvers. The first stanza of Brown's poem reads, "Long after we've forgotten what he taught, We still remember him. He had The power from God alone, As natural as a summer's day, To make us dream, to see, to understand." *Dreams*, of course, is a common word in the writings of adolescents only that which is desired alters. Half a century ago, dreams stood for careers, success, marriage, and family. Young people idealized these commitments regarded as essential to a full and satisfying life.

Richard Crosby, valedictorian of the Class of 1932, expressed in his graduation address a sentiment that puts one in mind of Dr. Martin Luther King's dream for the advancement of race relations. "May we never, any of us, stop dreaming and hopefully expecting. Let us keep alive within ourselves the spirit of inspiration. Even though we never enjoy the complete fulfillment of our dream, when we die may the world say of us, 'He left a dream.'"

However, for Norman Brown to have written "To make us dream" reflects Mr. Dunn's ability to awaken within his students greater ambitions than they had aspired to.

A good deal of this youthful idealization came through classroom reading. In those days, students of American history were taught that a brave Christopher Columbus, not a cruel exploiter of indigenous people, discovered a New World of opportunity. The nineteenth-century doctrine of Manifest Destiny prompted the westward expansion of the United States, opening the country to wide-scale wheat farms and cattle ranches despite the onslaughts of ruthless savages, not dispossessed native Americans. Heavy industry became the basis of the nation's greatness and wealth, and little mention was made of the resultant pollution. Smoke, in fact, was often the symbol of strength, as it is in the poetry of Carl Sanburg.

The course of study then was a conservative one with the reading of the same classics one's parents and grandparents had studied, i.e., works in English class by Tennyson, Macaulay, Scott, Shakespeare, Dickens, Emerson, and Addison and Steele. Despite the unevenness in quality represented here, the writings of these authors promoted a sense of community between the generations and a recognition of accepted values, both stabilizing influences in a period of bewildering change.

By the 1920s, as we have seen, in addition to overcrowding, there were serious physical defects within the combined town hall/high school. These and a burgeoning elementary school population made new buildings imperative for the upper 7–9, which would be taken into the Richmond Junior High School, and years 10–12 into Holten High School when they were constructed.

In 1926, the building of the junior high school began. When it was completed the following year, it included seventeen classrooms to house 600 students. In addition, Archivist Richard B. Trask reported to the Massachusetts Historical Commission, there were "a library, lunch room, sewing room, manual training department, drawing (art) room, auditorium with a seating capacity of 700 which included a gallery, stage, anterooms, and motion picture booth; locker rooms with showers for girls and boys; a suite including a waiting room, private office and private toilet for the superintendent of schools and another for the school's principal; clinic with toilet; a rest room for women teachers and one for the men; toilets for boys and girls on every floor; storerooms; a boiler room designed for future expansion; outside coal pocket; and janitor's room." Approximately $300,000 was appropriated for the school with its furnishings, plus classroom clocks, an intercommunication system, fire alarm, flag pole, etc. Everything was completed within budget.

In 1928, three years before the new high school opened, Superintendent John Anthony resigned. To fill his post, the school board promoted high school principal Ivan Smith to that post, and Cornelius Dunn, whom they had passed over previously, became the new principal. A reporter for the *Danvers Herald* concluded from a poll he conducted that the appointments of these two men "who have done so well in their respective positions, who are well-known to the teachers and citizens, and who understand the system is well merited."

List of Danvers Superintendents of Schools

W. A. Baldwin	1895–1897
Louis A. Pratt	1903–1904
Arthur J. Collins	1905-1908
H. C. Sanborn	1909–1918
John Anthony	1922–1927
Ivan G. Smith	1928–1954
Clifford J. Good	1955–*

*Mr. Good's term extended into Danvers High School years.

Mr. Dunn, whose hometown was Baldwinville, had first come to Danvers in 1918 to substitute for just two weeks, but he stayed here as an educator for forty years. He had taught previously for one year in Dracut, where, Tom Shehan told an audience in 1958, the superintendent said Mr. Dunn lacked discipline. And then he taught for one year in Penacook, New Hampshire. He resigned that post when the school committee assigned him to the high school. He preferred working as an elementary school teacher. His own education included study at Fitchburg Normal, Bridgewater Normal, and Boston University.

When he first came here, he was twenty-eight years old. His good sense of humor quickly gained his students' affection. As a handsome, blue-eyed bachelor, he had a special appeal to the girls.

In 1921, after three successful years of teaching here, he submitted his resignation to accept a job in Fall River. Alarmed at the loss of this instructor, more than 300 students and their parents, again according to Tom Shehan, "not only signed a petition requesting the school committee to ask him to reconsider, but delivered it themselves to the town hall when the board was in session." The committee did make the request, and toward the end of the summer, Mr. Dunn announced his intention of staying.

Two incidents will help to explain why he was so popular. In 1922 he was teaching United States history in a small tower classroom. Aware that cheating was going on during a test, he could have made an unpleasant scene. Instead he said, "Miss (Olive) Durkee, why don't you pass in your paper. If I grade yours, I'll have the marks for the entire class."

Before proceeding to the second example, it can be added parenthetically that this class was a particular favorite of his. In 1929, one of the prettiest Danvers girls, dark-haired, blue-eyed Helena Cashman became the superintendent's secretary. Mr. Dunn began to court her, and in 1933 they were married. He was forty-three at the time. They had a son, Neil. A devoted husband, he telephoned his wife from school each afternoon to tell her all that had gone on that day.

Now for the second example. On a miserably cold, rainy spring morning in the 1920s, underclassman Thurl Brown, who had been assigned a study period in the back of Miss Jessie Petrie's commercial class, was idly examining the wall beside him. If there was a saying in those days about twig bending, there was another that said, "Idle hands do the Devil's work."

For the first time, Thurl saw a button above him that he had never seen before. It resembled the buttons that a teacher could press to call the principal's office. There was no sign indicating its function. So Thurl pressed it. Immediately, the rapid clang of the fire alarm bell sounded, doors flew open, and the whole school began to rush out into the chilly deluge.

Horrified at the confusing scene he was immersed in, the rapid swirl and eddy of loudly complaining students, Thurl ran from line to line explaining that it was all a mistake: "You don't have to go out! It's a false alarm!" No one paid the least attention. Helpless, he watched the last figures being sucked out through the heavy exit doors.

Never one to duck the blame if he were at fault, Thurl went to the principal's office to confess. "It was an accident," he told Ivan Smith and Mr. Dunn. "I'm sorry. I didn't realize what that button did." Mr. Smith heard Thurl out and then said he had no choice but to suspend him. Mr. Dunn interceded for the boy. Such an action, he felt, was not necessary. Thurl had voluntarily owned up to his action. He was sure that the other students would not follow Thurl's example. Mr. Smith remained firm.

Exhausted from the morning's events, indignant at what he believed was an unjust punishment, the boy ran up to his father's clothing store on the Square. Although Charles Brown was sympathetic, he now explained a fact of life, "Thurl, you're going to encounter a lot of injustice in this life. It's up to you to learn to rise above it. Now you'd better go home and tell your mother what happened."

When his mother Eleanor and his sister Bessie heard the story, Bessie was incensed and wanted to take the matter before the school committee, but this was an age that, wisely or not, almost always obeyed authority. While the Browns made no complaint, Thurl recalled almost seventy years after that there had been one that day who stood up for him.

As previously noted, one of the first major projects new Principal Dunn undertook was the formation of a marching band. Two aspects of high school life that he particularly enjoyed were football and music. In fact, he had taught music when he first came here as a substitute teacher. For years he never missed a football game. What he did now was the traditional practice of raising funds for instruments and uniforms. In 1930, he went to publisher Victor Elmere, who agreed to a plan whereby students would sell subscriptions to the *Danvers Herald* in return for a percentage of the money collected. The Danvers Rotary Club, as it almost always does, made a generous donation. And on May 10, 1929, the student musicians gave a fund-raising concert.

Among its numbers, the orchestra played selections from Wagner's *Tannhauser*. Singing teacher Rachel Kerans had her Glee Club follow with songs by a full chorus and solos like "The House by the Side of the Road," sung by Osborne Linnekin and "Do You Know My Garden?" by Edith Damon. Verna Andrews gave a dramatic reading, "The Country Postmistress," and in similar elocutionary style, Imogene Skillings read Alfred Noyes's "The Highwayman." Finally, the curtains parted revealing the new band, which opened with "March Down Main Street." Its concluding number was "Heads Up," and, *The Holten's* "Class Notes" editor commented, "No one in the audience had any inclination to put his head down."

On Memorial Day that year the editor-in-chief predicted, "They will be marching down main street and band music will issue forth to awaken the echoes of a Past not so ancient. The streets of Danvers will again feel the tramp of young feet. The roar of the rattling drum and the rhythm of the other instruments will all tend to quicken the pulse of every Danvers citizen."

In addition to the band, there was a baton squad. Reminiscing about her days in this precision group, Marie Lynch recently wrote me:

About twelve of us formed a line behind the head twirler, Sally Snow, and later her sister Mary Lou. We were followed by the drum major of the band, Henry Luscomb, in about 1933–34. We wore dark blue skirts and sweaters of our own with white blouses. We had no commercial uniforms at that time. . . . We in the line never all caught the batons when we tossed them in the air. Sally and Mary Lou never missed! I was probably one of the worst for letting the baton drop. I worked hard at it all my waking hours at home, hoping some day to look like the pretty blonde Snow girls.

The Holten High School band and baton squad in the late 1930s. Where athletics was involved, the cheers and letters on sweaters always denoted the school as Danvers High School. During that championship season, one cheer combined both— "D. H. H. S./D. H. H. S. Rah. Rah. Rah."

The instructor who gave these girls their lessons was Ollie Ahearn, who charged them a quarter a lesson.

A new instrument was added to the band in 1938, a glockenspiel, the instrument of choice of Prussian military bands. It was an apt addition to a game often referred to as a gridiron battle where a bevy of frenzied followers urged their bloodied warriors to "Give 'em the axe, the axe, the axe," and followed that with "Rack'em, stack'em, put'em in a basket." While this is said in jest, isn't it interesting that the imagery is so consistent?

(A story of doubtful veracity was attached to the gentle, dignified Ivan G. Smith at this time. Several claimed he used to shout, "Pierce the line fiercely, boys!")

In 1929, town meeting appropriated $325,000 to build a new high school. Plans called for a building with twenty-seven recitation rooms; a science lecture hall and laboratories for physics and chemistry and a combined classroom laboratory for biology; a large study hall with a small adjoining library; a gymnasium divided by a long, roll-up canvas curtain creating a boys' and a girls' side, plus shower and dressing rooms with lockers, and offices for the two physical education instructors; a cafeteria with a modest kitchen; two tiny teachers' rooms; a suite for the principal and another for the dean of women. A very small classroom next to the principal's office became the band room.

Except for a tall, white cupola and the small marble foyer, the building was spare and functional. By way of contrast, Edward N. Robinson Jr., Class of 1930, who became writer of stories and articles for magazines like *The Saturday Evening Post,* described his old twin towered cathedral of learning in these terms: "[It] was not your characterless, present-day schoolhouse, but a unique place with lots of individuality."

The individual, of course, did stand out in the new building, but the school's rigid interior walls encouraged traditional teacher dominated instruction. Only where there were principals, like Mr. Dunn, who permitted highly motivated students the opportunity to circumvent lock-step programming, or only when academic teachers encouraged and provided extra opportunities for talented students, were there attempts to fulfill one of the chief tenets of progressive education, unleashing the genius of the individual.

The day of departure from the old building was January 14, 1931. Mr. Dunn demonstrated his sensitivity to his students' feelings. They looked back at their town hall days with fondness for the close friendships they had formed there and the traditions they had followed. Their sentiments were more personal than those of the superintendent, who described the old school as "a tool once sharp and bright, well fitted for the work to be done, but now grown rusty, worn, and dulled by time and use," but then Mr. Smith was addressing taxpayers. Elizabeth Merrill of the Class of 1931 voiced what the students felt:

Before leaving this school, let us remember that it has smiled upon another generation besides ours, that it had its day of glory. Not because we are superior to (old) Holten High School, but because we have out-grown it, do we move away.

The first activity on that departure date was a last assembly in the old auditorium. At the conclusion, the students sang "Auld Lang Syne," and the band's trumpeters played "Taps." Then the students formed outside by classes. It was also Mr. Dunn's idea for them all to march right through the center of town and down Conant Street to their new headquarters. As a money-saving measure, he had faculty and students alike carry their books rather than hire a trucking company to haul them.

Further embellishments to the parade were reported as spontaneous ones. There was the decision of five of the oldest alumnae to march along: Helen Putnam Learoyd, Class of 1858, who had been a student in the town hall in 1855, its first year of operation; Anna Bradstreet Southwick, Class of 1861; Ellen Allen Gunn and Emily Pope Abbott, both Class of 1866; and Annie Allen Newhall, Class of 1867. More recent graduates like Everett Elliott, a student at Northeastern, also elected to join the parade. And Sergeant Richard Kirwin (later Chief Kirwin) and a squad of Danvers police officers arrived to head up the procession.

At nine o'clock the trek began. When the units passed through Danvers Square, they attracted the attention of more and more townspeople. The small contingent of officers in their heavy navy blue uniforms and white gloves stepped briskly along to the strains of "On, Wisconsin" and "The Washington Post March" played by the band following directly behind them. Next in line came the alumni and then Mr. Dunn and Mr. Lewis Crosby, the assistant principal, at the head of the faculty and student body.

As they progressed down Conant Street, the junior high school pupils waited excitedly, according to a *Herald* report, to salute "their new neighbors." As soon as the parade came into view, they broke into cheers. The police held back the crowd lining the front walk of the new building. Mrs. Learoyd unlocked the front door, and under the lintel inscribed "Dedicated to Character," strutted drum major Newell Griffin, the first student to officially enter Mr. Dunn's Holten High School. The boys in the Junior class, who had been good long enough, broke into a raucous chorus of "Hail, Hail, the Gang's All Here!" After depositing coats and hats in their brand new lockers, students entered their assigned homerooms to await the start of the third period of the day.

A motion picture taken by Frank Cooke captures the parade on the grainy film of the day. Whenever it is shown at class reunions, eager old alumni drop their dignity and point excitedly to any classmates they can recognize. One of the easiest to identify is tall, thin Sidney Martin, a good-natured Gulliver among his scurrying Lilliputian fellow students.

In the fall of 1932, the student body had even more to celebrate. "There isn't much talk of depression in Danvers," wrote sportswriter Tom McCabe of the *Boston Herald*. "There is not time to think about it."

The reason was the undefeated football team that year. I once wrote a number of articles for the *Danvers Herald* on the subject of local history for a series entitled “Danvers Yesterday.” One of those columns was “Vye’s Undefeated Teams Brought Life to Football.” The teams were those of 1932 and 1941. The coach was Charles Vye. *Gruff* was the adjective most often associated with him, but to his athletes he was always addressed with respect as “Coach.” To the press and the general public he was Charlie. In 1932, reporter McCabe noted, “Today, if the Danvers folks could bring it about he could have the presidency of these United States.”

Charles Vye came to Danvers in 1931 following five years as assistant football coach at his alma mater, New York University, where he had been center on the football team. He had also played varsity hockey. At Holten High, he was also boys’ physical education instructor until he became athletic director in 1957.

At the start of his career in Danvers he was the man who changed the game from the mindless hurtling of bodies against bodies and forward passes into one described as a scientific game where “it’s all wing-backs, spinners, and laterals.” His players always described him as tough but fair. He drilled both his teams and his classes hard to get them into condition. LeRoy Atkinson, another Boston sportswriter, noted that Vye’s emphasis on training was reflected in the fact that his ’32 team requested only two time-outs . . . and had only three injuries that season.

Besides conditioning, this coach paid attention to details that could otherwise have been left to an assistant. The fit of a uniform and protective gear were among his first priorities. John MacGrath, who coached football and baseball when Vye was the athletic director, said in 1991, “Football had the best helmets and pads then conceived. . . . There was never any expense too great when it came to student-athletes.” A former player, Barry Robertson, related, “He got us our first face masks in 1957, newer, modern pads, shoes. . . . He made Danvers the showcase facility.”

The original uniforms Coach Vye bought in 1931, by which time the town was supporting athletics, had blue jerseys to replace the old black ones. They gave the team a new name that replaced Oniontowners—the Royal Blues. The Coach insisted that the men touch up any chipped paint on the broad white stripe in front of their helmets, that their shoes were polished, and that even their white laces were clean before they ran out onto the field on Saturday afternoons.

No matter how well the men looked, Charlie Vye saw to it that they didn’t develop swelled heads. When Dick Spencer was playing baseball, he fanned out in one game. Of his third strike, he shouted angrily at the umpire, “The ball wasn’t over the plate.”

“Yeah?” the coach commented dryly. “Neither were the other two you swung at.”

An advantage of working with more than one sport, as Charlie did, was that he could encourage a young man in one sport to try another. The ’31 and ’32 teams had athletes who were trackmen as well, so that the team was good at defense and fast on offense. Tony Morose, right halfback, could run the 100-yard dash in 10.1 seconds. It wasn’t until 1955 that track and football standout Mickey Ouimette ran the hundred under ten seconds. He did it in 9.8.

A second advantage was that most of the players on the ’31 team were juniors. When the fall of ’32 came around, they were seasoned veterans who enjoyed playing together. John Peterson summed up the reason for the team’s success in one word, *camaraderie*. Steve Hawkes concurred, “We always got along well together. There never was any fighting. We even practiced the plays on a field on Lindall Hill every morning before school.”

A third advantage was the versatility of several of the players, even with their impressive size, for this was one of the heaviest teams Danvers had fielded up to that time. John Fleming, “a jack-of-all trades and master of a bunch,” according to one newspaper story, could play end, tackle, or backfield. Captain Gardner Trask, “the juvenile mastermind of the gridiron,” generally played center, but he could and did play in other positions. He was so dependable that his coach told reporter Tom McCabe, “I almost feel he could handle the team if I was not around to direct it.”

The undefeated 1932 football team. Seated: Albert Collins, Leo Mercier, James Gaffney, Robert Stuart, Stephen Hawkes, Captain Gardner Trask, Oscar Perkins, John Peterson, John Fleming, and Richard Churchill. Standing: Tony Morose, James Finnegan, William Eisenhauer, Roger Pennell, Leonard Powers, Marshall Young, James Conway, and Harvey Dempsey.

First team players were James Finnegan, Robert Stuart, John Peterson, Leo Mercier, Dick Churchill, Courtney Johnson, Tony Morose, John Fleming, Stephen Hawkes, Roger Pennell, Oscar Perkins, Harry Barnes, James Gaffney, William Eisenhauer, Joseph Litwin (captain-elect of the '33 team), and Gardner Trask.

Because families remained in a single community for generations in pre-World War II years, several players were members of athletic dynasties. Steve Hawkes, for example, was the younger brother of Wellman and Walter Hawkes, both high school star athletes. Wellman, who participated in five sports, received thirteen varsity letters; he was also the batting champion in 1925. Walter Hawkes was only fourteen when he was elected captain of the football squad in 1927. A football program that year described Walter this way: "He pulled the unexpected play and more important than anything else, he always held his head above water, never becoming alarmed, no matter how discouraging things appeared." He also never wore a helmet.

An equally capable athlete at Springfield College, Walter was a magnet for nicknames. In college he was the "Driver" and elevated himself there to the All-American ranks. At the same time, he was the "Blond Driller" in wrestling. Back in Danvers, he had inherited his brother Wellman's cognomen, "Pickles." Finally, because he was a tow head, he became "Whitey." "Coach" was the name people in Reading called him. They had such affection for him there as coach and then athletic director that they named a sports facility the Walter E. Hawkes Field House. As an elderly man undergoing dialysis treatment, his nurses hailed him as "Wally."

Walter, however, was not the only coach in the Hawkes family. Following his graduation from Bowdoin, Steve's son, Robert, who coached at Worcester Academy in Massachusetts, has for some years been coach at Berwick Academy in Maine. Like his father and uncle, Bob was an all-round athlete at Holten High playing football, baseball, and basketball. He was the Northeastern Conference batting champion. He was voted the school's Most Valuable Player in 1955, and he also received the Lewis S. Crosby Award.

That Steve, Bob, and Walter were all baseball players is fitting since their uncle, Thorndike Hawkes, was a big league ballplayer. And not to be left out, Steve's father, Timothy Hawkes, was once a sprinter wearing the colors of the Salem YMCA.

Jim Gaffney and Oscar Perkins were the sons of men who had also been athletes at Holten High. Oscar "Iron Man" Perkins, Sr., was president of the D Club in 1932. It raised funds for school athletic programs because the field the teams played on at the Danvers Park was an open one making it difficult to collect admission money except by passing the hat at half time. James Gaffney Sr. was an attorney and the chairman of the building committees for the junior and senior high schools.

This team gave the greatest credit for its winning season in '32 to Charlie Vye. "He was great to work for," said Steve Hawkes to me. "He was good to us." Jim Gaffney cited three vital contributions of Vye's to that famous team: change, inspiration, and encouragement. Most important of all, said Gaffney, "He instituted a system of conditioning every bit as good as what we had in college." Precision timing emerged from all that extra practice. The result was that after the Thanksgiving game, not only was Danvers undefeated, it also led all other teams in the state in scoring, amassing 249 points to 19 for its opponents. Several players were named to all-star teams. Oscar Perkins made the *Boston Herald's*; and Gardner Trask, the '32 All-Scholastic teams by all Boston newspapers.

So much attention is given to the 1932 football team that other young men's and women's sports tend to be forgotten. Called the Royal Blue Nine, the baseball team placed second in the Northeastern Conference in 1933 and were the champions in 1936. Danvers baseball players were regularly named to All-Conference teams. Outstanding athletes in this sport were men like Mel Dempsey, Joseph LePage, Frank Bennett, George Gongas, and Ernest DiPaolo. In the early thirties, an alumnus of Holten High School, Granville "Duke" Wallace, was playing professional ball with the Boston Braves.

Coach Charles Vye about 1942 surrounded by admirers, from left to right, Nadja Melta, unkown, Karen Hurd, Nancy Moulton, Constance Duncan, and Lucille Dupray.

The famous summer Twi-Light League was almost entirely made up of former local high school players. For a number of years these teams competed in exhibition games against clubs like the Cuban Giants, an all-Black nine. There were also the Pittsburgh Hoboes and the New York Convicts, who played in uniforms appropriate for their names. One outstanding Danvers athlete, Ray Funchion, organized some college players who called themselves the Collegiate Clowns, modeling themselves after the famous Broadway Clowns. Ray, who was nicknamed Chatterbox because he was seldom, if ever, silent, had his athletes choose aliases like Zilch and Doolittle. He himself was Al Capone. In 1952, the high school baseball team played the Georgia Chain Gang, losing 8-1.

The boys' basketball team won the Northeastern Conference in 1937 under the coaching of Gardner Williams. Track, coached by George Mannell at one point, had, as previously mentioned, many of the football players competing in it. In a meet against Beverly, Robert Stuart was hauled out of the stands to run a few dashes because Tony Morose had been ruled out of further events by the meet doctor who felt he had competed enough that day. Trento Picillo and Gordon Allen were other valuable trackmen. The Fleming brothers, John and Joseph, played on the golf team. John, who was the captain, was recognized as one of the outstanding young golfers in the state. Arthur Harrigan and Herb Martin were two other team members.

For the girls, the 1930s marked the beginning of their coming-of-age in sports. More and more, they were regarded as athletes, not frail vessels. In 1932 there was a Twilight League for girls set up by the Park Department. That summer the Tapleyville Lasses, Captain Dorothy Smith, beat the Plains Girls, Captain Frances Flynn, 16 to 15 for the championship. A number of the Plains girls—Flynn, Muriel Estey, Phyllis Mosher, and Bernice Bragdon—hit homeruns. Outstanding for the Lasses were Smith, Jean Powers, and Olga Kossowan.

Miss Lee Page, women's physical education director, organized annual athletic demonstrations in June. The different events were held on Saturday afternoons in the Park for the general public. While the field hockey team played against other schools like Manchester and North Shore Country Day School, most sports were intramural, the girls being divided into the Blue and the White teams. In 1933, the captains were Agnes Tutko and her twin sister Mary. These girls were so evenly matched that they amassed the same number of points that year and were each awarded championship cups.

Mr. Dunn was well aware that there were other projects that developed character besides athletics. He wanted his students to learn to be aware of the needs of those less fortunate than they. Years later he gave voice to these sentiments in the 1955 yearbook; "Give careful thought to others. Cultivate and practice kindness towards your fellow men. I can think of no greater quality to promote peace and harmony. Kindness in thought and deed will endear you in your relationships, for it is a Divine virtue."

An example of what he meant was the collection of food by students before Thanksgiving and either food or toys for Christmas. Before their distribution to local families, the whole student body filed past the wide central stairway to view what they had accomplished—the lavish display of donated food, great overflowing cornucopias of good will. At Christmas time a student dressed like Santa Claus would distribute the toys.

An incident when students were less charitable occurred in 1931 or 1932 at an Armistice Day observance in the auditorium. One of the invited guests was Mr. Eli London, the local junk dealer. At that time, no one knew what a distinguished service record this man had had in World War I. At least we didn't until Hollywood made a film, *The Fighting Sixty-ninth*, starring James Cagney and Pat O'Brien. Then we were told London was portrayed in one of the film's important roles.

When Mr. London was called upon to speak that day, all he could say was, "I didn't know I was going to be called on. I don't know what to say. It was terrible over there." And struck by stage fright, he kept repeating himself until the whole audience burst into laughter. The assembly ended shortly after he sat down.

Everyone filed back to homeroom to wait for the passing bell to the first recitation period. The wait seemed interminable. The reason was that Mr. Dunn was going to every single room delivering one short message: "Of course, you people are so superior that you can afford to laugh at someone else." As short as the message was, it was unforgettable. His approval was important; his disapproval stung.

As its class gift back in 1931, this group had given the initial contribution for the Holy Grail pictures that were hung above the dark green lockers lining the second floor corridor on Conant Street, reproductions of the Edwin Abbey murals that can be found in the Boston Public Library. "The Quest and Achievement of the Holy Grail" is their title.

According to Medieval legend, you recall, the Grail was the cup from which Christ drank at the Last Supper. A vessel of incomparable properties, it had been brought to England by St. Joseph of Aramethea. However, having disappeared, it would appear again only to the perfect knight. Tennyson's version of the story was perhaps read longer at Holten High than at other secondary schools in Essex County because it was linked so closely with the school's motto.

Back in 1904, Superintendent Louis A. Pratt had stated as the goal of his school: "We would teach good manners and good morals as the foundation of good character and the basis of true citizenship, and would endeavor to inspire in the hearts and minds of all girls and boys a high ideal and genuine desire for a noble life."

Building on the theme of character, Cornelius Dunn took the ideal of the noble life and coined a brief but memorable school motto—Ladies and Gentlemen Always.

About the Holy Grail story, the question becomes, Did Mr. Dunn expect his students to be perfect as, at various times, Sir Gawain and Sir Galahad came close to being? As one of his teachers, I know that he liked to think that the forces of good will win out over evil in this imperfect world. His favorite radio and later television program was *The Lone Ranger*, and he habitually left school dances early enough to enjoy another episode in the adventures of that white knight of the Old West.

Times change, moral and ethical codes appear to alter, all that we regard as immutable seems to shift over the years, but that ideal or goal toward which Mr. Dunn asked each of his students to strive could give meaning to their lives. For his students, he knew that it was the quest that was important, not necessarily the achievement.

Early spring of 1936 was wet and dismal. Great flooded areas covered much of the country from the Mississippi River east to the Atlantic seaboard. The only thing that brightened the lives of the flood victims was the generosity of people who, in the Great Depression, had little to give. Nowhere was that more evident than in Danvers.

Heavy rains in March had melted February's snowbanks and sent tons of water pouring into major rivers. Newspaper rhetoric waxed more and more graphic as the water levels rose: *New England Rivers on a Rampage; Ice-Choked, Swollen Streams Carry Death and Destruction; 18 People Perish, 8,000 Homeless, 50 Communities Isolated.*

As Thurl Brown so aptly wrote, "It was spring at a price!" The meadows in North Beverly were under water and a flooded section of Route 1A between Beverly and Ipswich had to be closed. Towns along the Merrimac River were hit hardest. On March 19, the water was 43.57 feet above the dam in Lawrence. And the river was rising seven feet an hour. All industrial activity halted.

Two Danvers organizations, the Red Cross and the Citizens Committee for Flood Relief, aided those driven from their homes. On Sunday, March 22, Edward Mulry, local Red Cross chairman, called an emergency meeting at the town hall. Three committees were formed. The headquarters committee was led by Mrs. Arthur Perkins; a donation committee, by Joseph Murphy; and a transportation committee, by Leo Nimblett. School nurse Tess Creeden asked that only clean bedding be given since in previous drives things had been donated that were "of absolutely no value."

The Relief Committee coordinated the drives for funds and supplies. The Knights of Columbus held a novelty party that week; there was a beano party at the town hall; and the Tapleyville Improvement Society sponsored a gala dance with entertainment.

The Danvers fund quota was set at $250. Businesses and organizations had already offered contributions before the quota was announced. Employees of local institutions and companies took up their own collections. The largest amount given came from the workers at the Danvers State Hospital. Another $120 they had raised went directly to the stricken area. By March 26, the Relief Committee had received $900. At the end of the drive on April 2 donations reached $2,221.19.

There were other forms of assistance. Men from the Danvers V.F.W. Post, under Commander Percy Melden, went to Lawrence and then to Haverhill to direct traffic and prevent looting. Roger Estey from the Water Department went to North Andover to help officials there in solving problems relating to the contamination of drinking water.

Chief Joseph Kelley, with the men of Engine Two from Tapleyville, went to help cover Andover but they were quickly dispatched to North Andover to extinguish a blaze in the large Bolton summer mansion. Marguerite Reagan Morris remembers that her father, Francis "Deacon" Reagan, was sent a little later with Engine Three, the Ahren-Fox Pumper, to Lowell to pump out cellars.

But the real Danvers heroes were the students of Holten High School. Mr. Dunn had quietly suggested at Mulry's meeting that his six hundred students could render valuable service in the work at hand. Fortunately his offer was accepted.

The following morning, Monday, March 23, Mr. Dunn called a school assembly. He had divided the town into twenty-two sections, one for each faculty member. Students were instructed to go to the teacher for their neighborhood when they left the hall. Teachers gave further instructions, and then each group elected a student leader.

After a second assembly when they received identifying badges and receipt forms for monetary contributions, students were released from classes, some to collect and others to sort donations. Radio broadcasts must have alerted listeners about the drive because the volume of gifts was staggering. Some people even took blankets from their own beds to give to the student collectors. No refusals were reported.

Barbara Reagan Lawrence remembers somewhat unhappily that her mother gave a collection of her dolls. When Barbara protested, her mother told her firmly, "There are children who need these a lot more than you do."

The high school gymnasium was the collection center. At one point thirty automobiles were backed up in the schoolyard waiting to be unloaded. While one line of students ran down the fire escape to the cars, another ran up to the gym with arms full of donated goods. Signs designated areas on the floor for the different types of clothes, toys, food, bedding, etc. By 4:30 there were sufficient mountains of articles to fill 450 large crates.

The next morning, Tuesday, March 24, Mr. Dunn led a small convoy of seven automobiles and a well-filled truck to Lowell. Ivan Smith, Charlotte Porter Richardson, Eliot Duncan, Charles Vye, and Walter Oakman of the faculty went along. Allan Lord, who was an underclassman, went on one delivery trip, and he can still describe vividly the scene at one flooded bridge connecting Bradford and Haverhill, with the tremendous force of the current surging through the bridge and the great cakes of ice and heavy debris smashing against it.

That first delivery was directed to the St. Louis School, where six hundred women, elderly men, and children were being sheltered. The toys, soap, and clothing were gratefully received. After it was learned that the women had not had a change of hosiery in a week, new stockings were purchased and sent up with the next shipment.

When the weekend came, some students continued to assist in flood work. Bill Lyons and Connie Creeden, Arthur Lavin, and Francis Nimblett went to Andover and spent the weekend rowing people from their flooded homes to dry ground.

Dr. Walter Creese described the 1930s in an appreciation he wrote for this volume in this manner:

My family would occasionally travel to Lowell, where my father's grandfather had first settled. Its huge textile mills, representing thousands of jobs and millions in investment, were empty and silent. . . . At other times we would journey to the Shoe City of Lynn where my mother first came from. Again, the derelict factories and long, empty streets of Lynn would haunt me. On holiday we drove to Lake Winnipesaukee, progressing through smaller mill towns like Newmarket; New Hampshire, . . . but there, too, in the Depression days there was silence and decay everywhere.

Concerned not only about the characters of his students but also about their careers during the Depression, Mr. Dunn recommended that the school committee in 1933 add a new course to the high school program, one in vocational guidance that would be offered on the postgraduate level. By this time, teachers had had their salaries cut ten percent, and the committee, in order to make positions available to unemployed teachers, had voted to fire several married instructors, like Mildred McGinley in the high school, whose husbands were working.

When he was asked to pick a student for a job opening, Mr. Dunn almost always made the correct choice. Constantine Papamechail was a young man with a perpetual grin on his face. His sister Vasiliea (Vaso) wrote to tell me about the time Police Chief John McDewell came to the school and asked Mr. Dunn if he could recommend a young man to assist in his office. I would guess that the Chief was an assembly speaker that day because Mr. Dunn said to him as they undoubtedly sat on the stage, "The young man who comes through the door with the biggest grin on his face is your man." Of course, it was Constantine. Vaso reports, "Mr. McDewell was the greatest boss and friend my brother ever had."

I'm reminded here of a wonderful line from Chapter One of Graham Greene's *The Power and the Glory*: "There is always one moment in childhood when the door opens and lets the future in." It refers to a character's finding his adult vocation in boyhood. It is a special person who can cause that door to open, and it is often a teacher who does so. That's what made Cornelius Dunn so much appreciated.

Rules of behavior and dress were closely observed. As Dean of Women, Margaret Wood saw that the latter were strictly enforced. One day when she caught Ruth Kimball with bright red nail polish on, she made her remove it, Even though it was the Depression, girls had to wear long stockings. One hot spring day, Ruth Hutchinson told me my aunt Audrey had friends draw a seam line down the backs of her legs with an eyebrow pencil so she could go without stockings. Mary Slade recorded for her fifty-fifth class reunion booklet in 1992 that the girls finally received permission to wear newly fashionable ankle socks after they had presented a petition for the change. They would not have been successful had Mr. Dunn not been sympathetic to their cause.

Mr. Dunn had the great asset of knowing when to make exceptions and thus, open doors. For example, when she was still in high school, June Ferris, an attractive and ambitious girl, was soloist for the Boston Society Band, a swing band playing at coming-out parties, country clubs, and banquets around Boston. On Saturday nights they performed at Salem's Hotel Hawthorne, where curious dowagers, long-time guests at the hotel, watched the dancing from the small balconies overlooking the ballroom.

At this time, June was preparing to become a dance instructor by traveling regularly to New York City, where she took lessons in ballet, acrobatic, tap, and ballroom dancing. Her mother, Myrtle, and her father, Chester, were unusually supportive of their daughter and not without sacrifice. Myrtle usually accompanied June whenever she sang with the band or went to New York.

Before June was even out of high school, she had her own school of the dance. Because her youngest pupils, those of three and four years of age, had to meet before her school day was over, Mr. Dunn arranged things so it was possible for her to leave around 12:30. Her teachers did not object, probably because they asked her to dance so often at their assemblies that Miss Crocker would call on her first in geometry to determine if she had done her homework.

At one time, June taught five hundred students in Danvers. She had various studios around the Square—the old Grange Hall, the Masonic Temple, and then the top floor of the National Bank Building. Since there is only a five-year difference in our ages, I must have been in one of her first ballroom classes. Her mother played the piano, and we boys were instructed in all the traditional amenities—bowing, presenting our arms, placing our gloved hands correctly on a girl's back, etc.

I was a cut-up during classes because I did not dance well. One night Ruth Tibbetts, my partner, and I were observing the demonstration of an intricate step by an older couple. Ruth made what I considered a belittling remark about the girl's dancing, and I reminded her, "You're no Ginger Rogers." She gave me the type of glance that sent my argyles plummeting and hissed, "Well, you certainly are not Fred Astaire."

Mr. Dunn's flexibility sometimes led to improvisation. Marston Busineau, later a successful local businessman operating a small chain of office supply stores, didn't graduate with his class because he had failed a semester of English. Mr. Dunn scheduled his make-up classes the next fall during the noon hour so that Marston wouldn't lose time at work. When he had successfully completed the course, it was still months away from graduation time, so Mr. Dunn and Mr. Duncan concocted a special graduation ceremony in the principal's office with brief remarks and congratulations from these two administrators.

Being flexible never meant being a pushover with Cornelius Dunn. He never shrank from punishing a student. He just did it in his own way. Those of us who were sent to his office for some infraction of rules remember best his eyes which could express good humor, tolerance, or total disgust. Like an arrested felon, we had first to sit on the long, hard wooden bench in the outer office. And sit and sit and sit. He was giving us sufficient time to dwell on our transgressions and make silent resolutions to mend our sorry pasts. It was almost a relief to stand in front of his desk and be asked to recite our delinquencies. "What's that?" he would snap "Speak up. I can't hear you." We would mutter the reason for our being there "Is that something you're proud of?" he would ask. We would answer that we didn't think so now. "All right," he concluded the session. "Now suppose you collect your books and get back to class. And remember I don't expect to see you back here again. That wasn't worthy of you."

Atonement came in the number of afternoons back that we were assigned. Seldom during those uncomfortable times did we students doubt that Mr. Dunn appreciated and genuinely liked us. He gave us the type of attention that young people have always needed and without which they turn bitter and grow rebellious.

In 1943, I had sent for an application for entrance into Bowdoin College, a school I had wanted to attend from the time I was in junior high school, although I had never even seen the campus. Intimidated at the thought of studying in Brunswick, I put off filling out the application form and assembling the necessary records until one day I was passing Mr. Dunn's office. He stopped me and asked, "Dick, have you sent in your college application yet?" I admitted that I hadn't, that it was still in my locker. "Go and get it," he instructed me, "and come back to the office." When I returned, he sat me down at his desk and told me not to leave until I had completed the form. The materials were sent to the college's admissions office the next day, and in February of 1944, I left Danvers to commence my freshman year at Bowdoin.

There was never a time when Mr. Dunn didn't care about his students. When he was nearing retirement and couldn't get around the school so well as he once had, he would stop a few students and ask them to drop into his office and tell him how things were going.

In addition to having Mr. Dunn, Holten High School was fortunate in the quality of its teachers. Some, like Frances Wadleigh Scott, were outstanding. Mathematics had an unusual number of women chairmen, probably because of the difficulties confronting them in the male-dominated fields of science and technology. Education was the gainer. We had instructors like Eloise Crocker, Frances Everett, Dorothy Kraft Kimball, Elsa Brown, and Myrtle Root. This is not to say that all instructors were superior ones. Even some of the best had odd character traits. During the time of this chapter, for example, racial and religious bigotry was common. One faculty member always wore an orange scarf on St. Patrick's Day. Her opening remark for a school year was, "You know there are many different religions in this country. Let's just go around the room and see how many are represented in this classroom." Thus, from the first day, she had separated the sheep from the goats. And as excellent as she was, Charlotte Porter Richardson employed a motivational device of negative value. Her opening remark to freshmen was, "I can tell just by looking around the class who is going to fail Latin."

Back in the 1930s when she was still Miss Porter and an accomplished equestrian, she suffered a bad fall from a horse. She was away from her classes for several months recuperating. When she returned, she was extremely nervous. Finding the concentration necessary for correcting tests too upsetting, she paid one of her best students, Virginia Sherry, to do this work. For objective tests, she made out answer keys and for translations, she would provide the same passage in English. However, Virginia, or Winkie as she was called, still had to make many decisions on word choice and syntax on her own, but she did well.

At that time, leather workers like Winkie's father were frequently out on strike or faced lay-offs. That Christmas, Miss Porter appeared at the Sherry home with several gifts. To Betty, the youngest child, she gave a colorfully illustrated *Mother Goose*, and for her student she had selected a pink evening gown and silver slippers.

A later student, Sally Tomlinson, credits the teacher she knew as Mrs. C. P. Richardson with instructing her in more than just Latin: "She also taught me English grammar, ancient history, and geography. She was one of my five best teachers."

When, her pupils got to know her better, they discovered that she was not a towering ogress but a perceptive woman of considerable good humor. As her hearing became less acute, she once chided Sally, "Sarah. Sarah. Speak up! Only the freshmen are afraid of me, and that's only for the first three weeks."

Miss Frances G. Wadleigh in 1956 at the time of her retirement.

Some of the best of Holten High's administrators and faculty would occasionally make insensitive statements about problems adults regarded as minor ones. Marie Lynch told me that whenever her choristers fretted, Rachel Kerans would let out the stops of her Wurlitzer voice and say, "Worry never solved a problem or paid a bill." And whenever a senior, unhappy over the graduation pictures that he or she was going to give friends, complained to Mr. Dunn, he would say, "If nothing else, the camera is a clearinghouse of all our pet vanities."

Because Mr. Dunn almost always had an appropriate word for all events, it's something of a relief to recount the day a girl left him absolutely speechless. He had just finished his routine of passing the bench and staring down at her. Finally, he said to this young lady, "I'm very disappointed in you. You are going to have to be punished." She stood up, put an arm around his shoulder and said in a consoling, motherly tone, "There, Mr. Dunn I don't blame you one bit." He spun on his heels and returned to his office.

Finally, even with superior teachers, not all students became eager ones. An example of those who found themselves later is famed ornithologist Olin Sewall Pettingill, Jr., who perhaps more than anyone else in America popularized the avocation of bird watching. Most famous for his manual *Ornithology in Laboratory and Field*, published in 1939 and now in its fifth edition, he has written numerous books and articles, especially for the Audubon Society, like *The Audubon Illustrated Handbook of American Birds* (1968). Many bird watchers in this part of the country invariably carry his *A Guide to Bird Finding East of the Mississippi* with them on their birding expeditions.

However, at Holten High School he told a *Salem Evening News* reporter when his autobiography, *My Way to Ornithology*, was published in 1993, "I was not a good student in school. I had my mind on a lot of things, including Eleanor." Those other things, besides his future wife Eleanor Rice, included a chicken business and photography. At the Essex County Fair in 1924 his birds took two first prizes and four other awards. They also earned money for photography by the sale of their eggs. He spent a great deal of time in his basement darkroom, developing and printing his own photographs. This hobby led to the superior quality of illustrations in his books.

It was Pettingill's good fortune that, when it came to college, he had determined parents with the persistence and means to send him first to a year of postgraduate work at Kent's Hill before he went to Bowdoin.

In 1935, Mr. Dunn reported that thirty-five percent of Holten High School graduates were pursuing studies in institutions of higher learning. For those who could not expect financial assistance from their families, sports—football, especially—was a way to gain further education. That support, however, was not always sufficient to keep an athlete in college. That was the case with Tony Morose, a brilliant scholar in his high school class and its president. He received a scholarship to Holy Cross, but he was forced to drop out because of a lack of funds.

There were others who never attended college yet gained a degree of expertise in sometimes esoteric areas. That was the case with Ervin Conley, captain of the 1931 football team. He learned the tree business in the Civilian Conservation Corps. In 1946, Erv went to Maine and began, with his wife Jane, Conley's Garden Center in Boothbay Harbor. Through self-study, he became an expert in the life of the prehistoric Red Paint People, whose campsites he examined firsthand. Besides being a two-year president of the Maine Nurserymen's Association and an officer in other business-related organizations, Erv was the first president of the Maine Archaeological Society. In the 1950s, he was appointed a liaison person between the Penobscot Indians and the State of Maine.

If a poll were conducted of her students, most of them would name Frances Wadleigh Scott their outstanding teacher. As head of the English Department, she taught the college-bound seniors and juniors. She was an intelligent, well-educated woman, with a great sensitivity to the needs of her students.

The words of some of her students attest to their affection for her. Whenever Eleanor Roberts thinks of her alma mater, she told her classmates in a reunion booklet, "My first thought is always of Miss Wadleigh. She did not let you get close, but was always there when you needed something." Norma Silvernail, on the other hand, loved Miss Wadleigh for her "genuine warmth." Norma admits, however, that there was work aplenty in Miss Wadleigh's classes—precis and paraphrase exercises, the memorization of poetry, and a great deal of writing. No matter how difficult the lesson, to work with her in Room 26 was to experience the joy of learning. Perhaps Ernest DiPaolo summed up Miss Wadleigh best when he said, "She was a very special person." She was indeed.

Two present-day authors who recall her with appreciation are Pettingill and a distinguished professor of architecture and art, Dr. Walter Creese. Pettingill has written in his autobiography:

Room 26 was the room for the head of the English department. An English class sits in that spartan chamber under a large framed photograph of Stratford on Avon, which may well have hung in the town hall/high school.

> *Miss Wadleigh cited books that I should read and encouraged me to write compositions emulating their style. She took time in class and out to criticize my efforts, showing me where I could improve by varying my sentence structure, avoiding wordiness, and expressing myself in a concise manner. So inspired was I that I wrote five pieces for the literary section of* The Holten, *the school magazine.*

Pettingill noted that his Aunt Millie was so impressed with his writing success while he was still in high school that she changed her will leaving half her estate to him "in order that its income might give me an independent means of support for my ambition." Few authors have so immediately benefited from their labors.

About the teaching of varied sentences, it was with Miss Wadleigh that we studied *The Sir Roger Coverley Papers* for the content, humor and Neo-Classical style with those linchpins of the literary essay—the loose, periodic, and balanced sentences. One spring morning in the early 1930s when she asked an overly romantic coed to give an example of the last, the girl stood up and dreamily answered, "To err is human; to love, divine," sighed deeply and sat down amid the hooting of her classmates. But no one got embarrassed for long in Miss Wadleigh's classes. "That's right, class," she broke in "To love means to forgive."

Walter Creese recalls, "(In Frances Wadleigh) we had a first-class teacher and a subject with which to learn, but it was incongruous to me that we were acting out the epic events of Shakespeare's plays like *Macbeth* or *Julius Caesar* in that rectilinear classroom WPA-fresh and Spartan, with standard blackboards uniformly illuminated by white, hanging globes."

Of her skill in reaching "the thirty or forty student personalities sitting along the neat desk rows," Walter wrote,

To teach is to deal with improbabilities, the X power of extended linkage, hoping something positive will eventually come together. What she did for my individuality was to move right in to channel its youthful impetus. She not only identified my character quickly, but decided to try to harness its rampant imagination for some good purpose by appointing me chief editor of the Holten High School magazine. . . . She was, in our lives, the El Supremo of beneficial purpose. [Because of the Depression] our parents, out of necessity, had much less self-confidence to share with us. I felt that if she had put her wager on me in that sort of on-sight way, the least I could do was to start believing in myself and try hard not to let her down.

Walter's first two books—*The Legacy of Raymond Unwin* and *Search for Environment*—dealt with "the root system of the Industrial Revolution in its seed bed of northern England" because industry had been two hundred years a "constituent part of the everyday environment." Several books later, he turned to Nature in *The Crowning of the American Landscape.* Of that 1985 volume, he wrote me:

Miss Wadleigh's positive speaking about New England literary figures like Frost, Dickinson, Thoreau and Emerson, helped bring me eventually to read more about Transcendentalism, and the regional dialogue with unspoiled nature, as a sign and form of spiritual guidance other than that by transport, technology and material manufacture. I wanted to reach the open shores of the lakes away from Boston (or Newmarket, or Union, New Hampshire) at last. . . . A democracy could be crowned with the glory of totally coordinated beauty, just as a monarchy, with its aristocracy educated in the arts, was from the fifteenth to the eighteenth century, if enough comprehension, thought and planning were generated. The intellectual ought to have a definite role. The introduction of The Crowning says that my imagination was fired up when I discovered that Frederick Law Olmstead had laid out the urban Fens of Boston to remind everyone of the salt marshes of Byfield and Newbury (and even Danvers), to which the first Puritans had resorted for food and building materials. Wasteland had once been nurturing land. The latter spread of the shore, with its redeeming green and gold inlets of first landscape, was very different from that of the later improvised factory cities. We had once been able to look at an original tidal inlet out of the big windows of Miss Wood's French class.

In appearance Miss Wadleigh would not be called attractive. Pettingill describes her accurately as "tall, gaunt, with a long, narrow face exaggerated by hair drawn tightly back in a low pug." Yes, she was tall and straight like the pines of her beloved New Hampshire. She favored plain dresses over which she draped a cardigan sweater. She wore sensible, laced-up black shoes. All in all, she had one of those characterful English faces that made her a natural to play roles like David Cooperfield's Aunt Betsey Trotwood or that addled, rejected bride, Miss Havisham, in *Great Expectations.* She was not, however, an actress, but a great teacher. In Pettingill's words, she was "a teacher in the truest sense."

One trait that aided her was an even temper. Never raising her voice, she could quiet us with just two words, "Now, Class." Dorothy Hart, another of her students, remembered the day she asked if anyone had lost the four-year honor pin she had just picked up in the hall. Much to the class's amusement a boy noted for his good

The great appeal of joining The Holten *staff, besides Miss Wadleigh's relaxed and perceptive presence, was the chance to see oneself in print either in writing, art, or photography. Seated, left to right, Edward Dow, Helen Horgan, Stacia Zuk, Geraldine Tremblay, Edith Turenne, Virginia Bennett, Ruth Williams, E. Leonard Kane (editor), Merle Bradstreet, Marjorie Watters, Barbara Ferris, Mary Batchelder, and Alton Jones. Standing: Richard Ingalls, Donald Horgan, Gloria Welch, Lucy Belle White, Nancy Erickson, Sally Budgell, Alma Miller, Audrey Reid, Ralph Raynard, Kevin Gaffney, Robert Parsons, and Robert Feindle.*

looks rather than his scholarship held up his hand. Without a word or change of expression, she walked up and placed the pin on his desk. With the laughter turned on him now, he squirmed uncomfortably in his seat and muttered, "Oh, Miss Wadleigh, act your age." She quietly replied, "Why, sir, I always believe what a gentleman tells me." It was at once the soft answer that turns away anger and a put-down.

Miss Wadleigh helped us students gain an appreciation of literature that remained with us for the rest of our lives. Besides the novels of Dickens, she loved best the plays of Shakespeare and J. M. Barrie, and the poetry of the Romantics Byron, Shelley, and Keats. It would be an exaggeration to say her voice was liquid melody (and trite). Say that when she read, she read extremely well. She became our daytime "Lux Radio Theater," our Mr. First Nighter, who took us in our imaginations to that little theater just off Times Square. From the moment she began the opening line of *A Tale of Two Cities* ("It was the best of times, it was the worst of times,") to her reading of Sidney Carton's final words spoken in the shadow of the guillotine ("It's a far, far better thing I do. . . ."), she had our complete attention. Of course, she didn't read the whole novel, but she certainly knew how to pick the best parts.

She was dedicated to the proposition that all her students should develop a love of literature, even those who would complain about having to read some of it. Tom Shehan, as we've seen, was led by Sally Dow, but also Frances Wadleigh, to become an unusually avid reader. How many of us, like Tom, keep a log of our weekly reading? These women helped him see that the world of the mind,of the literate person, could be as stimulating as any of the other attractions of the outside world.

One morning in Miss Wadleigh's class, he groused aloud that he hated poetry and saw no good reason for studying it. Outwardly unperturbed by his outburst, she calmly asked, "Mr. Shehan, you like the verses of Rudyard Kipling and Robert Service, don't you?" Tom admitted that he did. "Well, then," she pointed out, "you don't dislike poetry, you just don't like certain kinds of poetry."

In such ways she built up our trust and loyalty. The best proof of that came the day her slip dropped down around her ankles faster than the sails on the Ancient Mariner's doomed ship. No one even snickered. She kicked the garment into a desk drawer and went right on with the lesson.

Before her vocabulary tests, she often provided mnemonic devices to form unforgettable associations. Cynthia Hawkes recalls the one for the word *tenacious*: "Just think of a bulldog clinging to the seat of someone's trousers and not letting go," When she gave a test, she never patrolled the aisles. Instead, she sat at the end of the golden-oak table in front of the class where our copies of *Senior Scholastic Magazine* were piled, glancing up occasionally to ask if there were any questions. Although she challenged the brightest students, she never stooped to asking trick questions.

For all she gave of herself professionally, she was remarkably silent about her personal life. Almost no one knew that her nick-name was Dot; that she coached girls' basketball for two years at the high school in North Easton before coming to Danvers in 1920; or that she once led a week's mountain hike over the Presidential Range of the White Mountains in 1924. The party consisted of Eleanor Rice, Sewall Pettingill, Roger Berry, and Lawrence Kinney, all of Middleton. In her later years, no one knew that the diamond ring she wore before her retirement signified her engagement to Ernest Scott, whom she later married. Perhaps love metamorphosed her. In any case, her picture in the June 1956 *The Holten*, for which she had served for so many years as literary advisor, shows her a lovely, dignified woman, stylishly dressed with her hair arranged in a soft wave.

Frances Wadleigh taught us much about subject matter and more about life—good literature can enrich and give meaning to our daily lives, love extends beyond romance, and trust given is returned without demanding it. Also, we are responsible for our own failings ("It is not in our stars, dear Brutus,/But in ourselves that we are underlings."). Every day that passes finds us still recalling those mental hooks she provided to fix forever an elusive concept or definition. Who's to say that a good teacher does not affect eternity?

In the last *Holten* of her teaching career there is a poem, "Miss Wadleigh Muses," that is otherwise unsigned. I think it could be hers:

Year after year they come to me
These pupils with questioning looks,
Year after year they leave me
As they leave their outgrown books;
And I wonder sometimes if I've taught them
Just some of the worthwhile things,
Just some of the things they'll need in life,
Be they peasants or poets or kings.

Have I taught them the joy of clean living?
That Honor is better than Fame?
That good friends are the greatest of treasures?
Wealth, less than an untarnished name?
Have I taught them respect to the aged?
Protection to those who are weak?
That silence always is golden
When gossip bids them speak?

Have I taught them that Fear is a coward
Who is beaten when they say, "I can?"
That Courtesy ranks with Courage
In the heart of the real gentleman?
Have I taught them these things and the others
That will help make them brave, kind and good?
If I have, then I care not if they tell me,
That Julius Caesar was killed by Robin Hood.

The 1941 championship football team back from New York City. In the front row, left to right, are Vincent Picillo, Jack Murphy, Joe Shabowich, Peter Louvaris, Dick Morrissey, Connie Papamechail, Allen Spofford, and Christ Spiliotis. Second row: James Lynch, Don Meagher, John DeCotis, Mr. Dunn, Emile Mercier, Allie Pydynkowski, Coach Vye, Walter Kornachuk, Jack Zollo, "Babe" Dempsey, and Mingo Citroni. Third row: George Spears, Bill Bellows, Eddie Dzierzak, George Michallyszyn, William Cashman, Peter Kusek, Fred Wennerberg, Philip Evans, William Gongas, George Mackel, Earl Clay, Arthur Thibodeau, Lloyd Blute, Al Lyons, Jack King, and William Colligan.

CHAPTER VII

Holten High School—War Years
1940–1946

Throughout our history, public schools have been seen as integral to the acculturation of the latest influx of immigrants. By the 1940s, many first and second generation Americans were in Holten High School. John Eaton Jr., U.S. Commissioner of Education, declared in 1872, "Education, the great process of assimilation . . . should receive more attention than any other function of our civil life. It should be conducted more intelligently." Citizens during World War II took seriously the country's motto, "E Pluribus Unum." America was proudly the melting pot.

A privilege of full citizenship is that of defending one's country. Danvers lost over sixty men and one woman, Bertha Grady, a nurse from the Danvers State Hospital, in World War II as contrasted to fifteen lost in World War I, the majority of whom died from illness, mainly pulmonary in nature, rather than wounds.

Two of the greatest consequences of World War II that affected schools were the entrance of mothers into the work force in great numbers and the federal government's funding of programs to prepare more and better-trained scientists and engineers, a practice that continues to this day. One result of such downgrading of the humanities has been that colleges and secondary schools no longer produce the number of graduates who become published poets and novelists like those in the 1920s and 1930s at Holten High School.

Although the Depression did not end until the war effort intensified following the bombing of Pearl Harbor, economically the country was better off than it had been in the 1930s. Politically, however, there existed polarization in the nation between those anxious to aid Great Britain fighting alone against the Fascist powers and those who spoke out for neutrality and America first.

While President Franklin D. Roosevelt had signed the United States Neutrality Act in 1937, he was then drawing the country close to war. Under his administration's initiatives, obsolete World War I destroyers were taken out of mothballs in 1940 and exchanged for military bases in British-held territories in Newfoundland and the Caribbean. In the same year, the Selective Service and Training Act was passed. On March 11, 1941, Congress enacted the Lend-Lease Bill. Despite a well-publicized, emotional Mothers' Crusade against it, war materials were soon sent to those combatants whose defense was seen as vital to the protection of America.

Citizens opposed to such measures regarded the 1823 Monroe Doctrine as sufficient warning to keep Allied and Axis powers alike out of Latin America. Since Nazi bunds were being formed even within the United States, that conviction was naive. So effective was Nazi propaganda in disguising its evil intentions that a college professor, S. I. Hayakawa, developed his 1941 textbook, *Language in Thought and Action*, to instruct college and secondary school students how propaganda and advertising affect us.

In those days, the Monroe Doctrine and Latin America were frequent topics in the United States news media. We read or heard about the Pan American Union, Pan American Conferences, Pan American Airlines, and the Pan American Highway. Pan American Games were set for 1942, but had to be postponed until after World War II. As a foreign-language course, Spanish had been added to the high school curriculum because of these ties. And in 1944, Commercial Spanish, taught by Gladys Damon, became a new course at Holten High.

In music, dance, and film, teenagers were made aware of Hispanic culture. Rio de Janeiro and Buenos Aires were favorite settings for Hollywood musicals. The diminutive Brazilian Bombshell, Carmen Miranda, with her five-inch platform soles, ruffled skirts, and towering fruit-basket headdresses delighted movie audiences. Dressed like her, a hairy chested football player became a familiar sight in Sweater Benefits. At proms and senior receptions, the Snake Dance and the Bunny Hop were supplanted by the Conga Line. As they wound around the dance floor, carefree revelers sang, "Boogie-Woogie Conga."

When war broke out in 1941, not because of the President's British assistance programs, but the Japanese sneak attack, the nation became united as never before. Besides his New Deal programs to create jobs, FDR and his wife, Eleanor, had previously taken the lead in promoting racial harmony. In 1938, in an address to the Daughters of the Revolution, he greeted his audience with the reminder that he and they were all descended from immigrants and revolutionists. His conservative listeners were resentful, not so much at the former term as at the latter.

Jane Porter's graduation party guests: Nancy Porter, Joan Cook, Mary Sillars, Jane Porter, Patricia Reynolds, and Barbara Shannehan; and Charles Morse, Arthur Vaillancourt, Alden Goodnow, Gordon LeFavour, Robert Caliga, and Francis Caskin.

Then when the Black opera singer Marian Anderson and her manager said that she had been banned from giving a concert at the DAR's Constitution Hall, Mrs. Roosevelt resigned from the organization, and Interior Secretary Harold Ickes invited Miss Anderson to give her concert on the steps of the Lincoln Memorial.

Not all New England first families were as chauvinistic as the leaders of the DAR. Jane Porter's mother arranged a pre-senior reception dinner for Jane and her friends in 1942. The girls wore the same white dresses they wore on the evening previous to their graduation exercises in the lyceum hall of the Peabody Institute Library:

I remember [Jane wrote me about getting ready for the dinner] I helped mother clean and vacuum and dust, plus polish silver. My mother made sure she served chicken a la king, that way she could use the same sauce and prepare it with tuna fish for the Catholic kids who had to eat fish on Friday. It all looked the same. I'm sure she had spoken with each [Catholic] mother to assure her that everything would be O.K.

Their parents drove the young guests to the dance that evening. The exceptions were Arthur Vaillancourt and his date, Joan Cook, Wallace's daughter. After Arthur had spread a white sheet over the front seat of his car so Joan wouldn't soil her dress, he drove them to the high school. During the dance, many parents spent all or part of the evening in the gym balcony watching the sometimes sedately waltzing, sometimes exuberantly jitterbugging couples. Afterwards Arthur and Joan went to Howard Johnson's at Beverly Bridge. Midnight snacks of this type were not common until after World War II when access to automobiles was easier for young people.

Throughout his tenure as principal, Cornelius Dunn scrupulously avoided, directly or indirectly, reflecting ethnic or religious judgments. For the 1948 yearbook dedication he gave expression to his feelings:

May you realize that we as United States citizens can do whatever future assignment falls to us if we meet it with courage and faith. More than all else we must stand together: no questioning creeds of our comrades nor the race of their forebears. We may expect to promote the ideals of our great homeland by working together for her honor, greatness, and glory. To that end let us dedicate ourselves.

Where race was concerned, a definite contrast can be seen between the narrow range of different ethnic names on the 1932 championship team and that of the 1941 team when more boys of southern and eastern European ancestry played: Dominic Citroni, John DeCotis, Walter Kornachuk, Peter Louvaris, John Zollo, Alphonse Pydynkowski, Joseph Shabowich, and Peter Kusek.

Those of Polish and Russian extraction were sons of parents who had moved out of Salem around 1914 to buy homes on Liberty Street or in East Danvers, where there was land enough for backyard gardens and a few farm animals. Northern Italians a decade or two earlier had done the same thing. Before my grandparents developed Lummus Avenue, they (or more accurately, my grandmother) had had a mini-farm there, just off Danvers Square.

If the 1932 teams had brought pride and relief from the worries of the Depression, the 1941 team did the same in the season just before hostilities began for the United States. This second Northeastern Conference championship team was led by Captain Emile Mercier. The first game against Beverly was a disappointment since it is agreed that the Danvers eleven outplayed their traditional rival. In the third quarter Jack Murphy scored the only Danvers touchdown on a pass from Bill Bellows. The effort to score the extra point failed. Then in the fourth quarter, Beverly scored its only touchdown and successfully rushed for the point. The game ended 7-6.

The other seven games against Winthrop, Punchard, Winchester, Reading, Marblehead, Swampscott, and Newburyport had less tension. The Royal Blues defeated previously undefeated, untied Winchester, 14-6. Whenever the team was scoring too many points, Coach Vye rubbed it in to a few losing teams by sending in not only his second team but one or two small freshmen players. The star athlete for Danvers was Allie Pydynkowski, a quiet and unassuming young man.

To celebrate their victory that happy fall, the team was treated to a weekend trip to New York City. Much of the money was raised by a post-season game that pitted brother against brother. It was played at St. John's Prep on Thanksgiving Day between the Royal Blues and a team made up of alumni like Wade Blute, Pat Begin, Bob Gaffney, Ray Blute, and Cyrus Newbegin. Frank Callahan was their coach. While the champs were urged on by their pertly clad cheerleaders—Eileen Eastman, Constance Duncan, Nancy Mae Wiley, Arline Hiltonen, Joan McLaughlin, Shirley Mello, and Helen Bates—the alumnae cheerleaders—Henrietta Newbegin, Kay Zollo, Nadja Melta, Hazel Mello, Dorothy Moreau, and Dot Stone—were dressed in brown coats, the only garment they each owned that was similar in appearance.

Readying the entrance parade for the post-season game between the1941 championship team and the alumni is Claude Phillips (dark suit). Flag bearers are Bruce Bryer and Hugh Wheelwright. Head cheerleader is Constance Duncan.

Drum major Don Ingraham of the improvised alumni band sported a coonskin cap.

For three periods the champs were held to a scoreless tie. The alumni had made a safety in the previous period, but Hardy Wallace, acting as lineman, recalled the ball because both sides, he claimed, were offside. Then in the final quarter, Wade Blute, attempting to take the ball out of the safety zone, was tackled, giving the Royal Blues a two-point lead. A long pass from Bill Bellows to Allie Pydynkowski gave their team the only touchdown of the game. Whenever the Northeastern champions had forced the game near the alumni goal line, they were penalized—or so they claim today. So the game ended as 8-0 victory for the Class C Division winners.

Another source of money was the "On to New York"dance held at the Richmond Junior High School auditorium on the evening of November 19. The blue-covered program containing 122 ads—ranging from Nesson's department stores' full-pager to Mrs. Page's eighth-pager for her Sip & Bite restaurant at 25 Maple Street—was, by itself, profitable. Dick Putman's orchestra provided the music.

The individual dances that night were dedicated to the players; "The Indian Love Call," to Pete Louvaris; "Me and My Shadow," to Mingo Citroni; "The Jitterbug," to Babe Dempsey; "When Irish Eyes Are Smiling," to Jack King; etc. The coaches were honored with "We Three," and the fans with "Thanks a Million."

The boys went to New York that weekend, accompanied by Coach Vye and his assistants, Charles Pelonzi and Jack MacDonald, and a contingent of families and friends. They sailed overnight on the Eastern Steamship Line's *New York* with its fancy ballroom and deluxe cabins through the Cape Cod Canal to their destination. On the way, they got a full tour of the boat because the brother of Duke Wallace, no relation to Hardy, was the ship's steward. Dick Morrissey, who supplied much of this material, had luck playing the slot machines:

For a dime I hit the jack-pot for $15.00! And fifteen dollars in 1941 was something else! I think my mother and father had scraped up a dollar for me on the trip! Anyway, a lady (?) had tried to take half of my winnings which had spilled to the floor of the salon, and Jack MacDonald, Coach Vye, and Juney (Clarence) Lyons knuckled her to turn it over to them and they to me, although they gave me five dollars, keeping the rest for me to give to my mother and father upon return. (The parents of 12 kids at the time.)

As for the activities in the city, Thurl "Boppo" Brown provided this montage for hometown readers of the *Herald*:

Charlie Blute, police officer who went on the trip as an escort, now realizes he will have to check on his marksmanship after the shooting scene he was in in Hellzapoppin (an Olsen and Johnson revue)—Alex (Allie) Pydynkowski had a chance to see what he looked like to others when at RCA he gazed into the television set—get the boys to tell how they went aboard the fireboat—souvenirs, souvenirs, souvenirs, now won't the coeds flash in their new bracelets, earrings, pins, and powder boxes—we hope JoJo Shabowich found the guy who insulted him in the football stands at the Fordham game—'Dinty' (Edward) Doyle, former Danvers boy, who has made good over radio and in the newspaper world, was on hand to do all he could to make the team feel at home in the land of tall buildings—Taxi, taxi, almost became a byword when anyone wanted to go anywhere.

When some of the boys were heading for the elevator to go down to the lobby of the Governor Clinton Hotel for checkout, Dick wrote, "Someone came up to our floor as we were leaving and told some of the guys to return the towels and silverware they had stashed in their suitcases because they were checking them down in the lobby! It was a total lie, but you should have seen some of them scramble back to the rooms to repack!!!"

Their return on the *New York* was that ship's next-to-the-last civilian cruise. After that, it was taken over by the government and converted into a school for servicemen. The ballroom was partitioned off into classrooms, the dining room became a cafeteria, and the deluxe cabins were turned into barracks with bunks and desks. Then in September of 1942 both Eastern steamships, the *Boston* and the *New York*, and six other coastal vessels were turned over to the British Ministry of Transport, under lend-lease terms, to act as hospital ships or troop carriers on D-Day. These boats were part of what was known as the Honeymoon Convoy, a reference to the ships' former popularity with newlyweds. Both Eastern ships were sunk on the way to Britain by German U-boats.

The team returned to school on the morning of November 24, and Miss Damon, the school's unofficial photographer for years, took their picture.

Ask anyone where he was when the news came that Pearl Harbor had been bombed, and he can tell you. I remember that I was leaving the Sunday matinee at the Orpheum Theater when my pleasant thoughts of getting a new beagle hound were interrupted by people excitedly rushing into the lobby with the news.

The next day we were all assembled in the school gymnasium to hear President Roosevelt's declaration of war against the Axis powers. We sophomores stood nervously together in the balcony. When Mr. Roosevelt's familiar voice began, there was no need for a teacher's telling us to be quiet: "Yesterday, December 7, 1941, a date which will live in infamy, the United States of America was suddenly and deliberately attacked by the naval and air forces of the Empire of

A perennial feature of the football season was the team cartoon that appeared in the Boston Herald.

With a wartime shortage of gasoline for snowplows and men to work for the street department, high school boys were hired to shovel off Danvers Square in 1942. Pictured here are Philip Evans, Roger LeVasseur, Tony Galipin, George Spears, Albert Mozejko, Edward Dzierzak, Peter Kusek, Christopher Daley, and Dick Zollo. Kings of the mountain are Richard Haskell and Leland Martin. Photographer was Frank Cooke Jr.

Japan." Following that speech, Mr. Dunn urged the boys to stay in school to complete their educations so that they could be of more service to their country. But almost immediately they began to enlist. The school committee passed a ruling that any junior or senior boy who joined up would receive his diploma, if he was passing in all courses.

As to other school matters after the outbreak of the war, the Glee Club had to change its Spring concert segment featuring songs from Gilbert and Sullivan's operetta *The Mikado*, which had been in rehearsal. The opening selection beginning, "If you want to know who we are, we are gentlemen of Japan,"was, under the circumstances, painfully ironic.

Therefore, the previous year's medley from *H.M.S. Pinafore* was performed again with great success. Jack Dresser, already a professional singer and dancer, sang "I Am the Captain of the *Pinafore*." The sight of short, boyish John Linehan intoning "When I Was a Lad" drew good natured laughs, as did his duet with his tall classmate, Tom Meakin, about the merry maiden and the tar. The two played off each other with, we all thought, great comedic skill. It wasn't until 1947 that feelings against the Japanese abated enough to include *The Mikado* in a spring concert. This time soloists were Philip Hopkins and William Hazen. The three little maids from school were Margaret and Barbara Creeden and Muriel Thomas.

The war altered school life. Air raid precaution drills were held regularly. Boys in manual training classes constructed airplane models for various service schools, giving instruction in the identification of friendly and enemy planes. Physical education classes were doubled for junior and senior boys. After one or two blizzards, upperclassmen were released from classes to shovel off Danvers Square. During summer vacations, some of the football team were given work by the Public Works Department digging ditches. And in autumn, students were also let out of school early to help local farmers harvest their crops. While one of the few jobs available to boys and some girls in the 1930s had been weeding, a greater variety of after-school work now opened up, like clerking at the First National, the town's first supermarket.

History and social studies classes studied the progress of battles and the geography of the countries involved on large maps. Previously unfamiliar names of foreign places came into common usage—Corregidor, El Alamein, Palermo, Anzio, Murmansk, Saipan, Okinawa, Hiroshima, and Nagasaki. One of Mr. Coates's chemistry students, David Knowlton, was impressed at how this man grew agitated when we studied dyes because, Mr. Coates said, Great Britain had handed the manufacture of coal tar dyes over to Germany before the war because of heavy English investments in the Indian indigo dye industry, thereby giving the enemy a greater capacity to produce munitions.

When the war was on, David became a machinist for Smith and Winchester at the end of Warren Street. The result of keeping up with work and studies was that he, like others, was always tired:

I was then working many hours in a machine shop after school and on weekends and so [I] would often put my head down on my desk and go to sleep. The teacher who usually monitored the [study hall] period did not like to see me sleeping and would wake me up with the promise of dire consequences if I did not stay awake. A couple of times Connie came around the back of the room on one of his little "tours." He knew I was working and that my grades were OK so he would only smile and occasionally remind me not to snore. What a guy!

Teachers who had not left for military service volunteered to assist with the setting up and administration of rationing programs for sugar, home fuel oil, and gasoline; selective service registration; Red Cross blood drives; and the sale of war bonds and stamps. They completed special first-aid courses to help the injured in case of air raids. Some took second jobs on the night shift of factories producing war materials. The last was a departure from the professional standards of American education. But much was excused because of the war emergency. No longer, for example, did mothers have to remain in the home taking care of their children. They could now wrap their hair in a bandanna, don overalls, and work beside Rosie, the riveter, doing what was formerly considered a man's job.

Several area universities offered women crash courses in mathematics and the sciences to prepare them for positions in engineering and technology. Following one such course at Boston University, Dorothy Cooley found work in the Sylvania plant on Sylvan Street in its engineering department.

Corinne Wilkins was the first young woman allowed to take mechanical drawing at Holten High, thanks to Mr. Low. She proved to be an adept pupil, so skilled, in fact, that when Sylvania contacted the school for a senior to work as an engineering draftsman, Mr. Low recommended her. Later, following her graduation from LaSalle, Corinne worked for several small engineering firms around Boston. When the John Hancock building was being constructed in Copley Square, she began working for Hickson Engineering as a lighting engineer. As the most recently hired employee there, she was sent to the construction site to revise the designer's blue prints for the electrical lines as the actual process of building necessitated changes.

When her sister Pauline transferred from Middlebury College to study at MIT, Corinne got Pauline a job working alongside her. These two may have been the first hard-hat female workers graduated from Holten High.

Back at the school, math teacher Frances Everett taught a new course in 1942 that would in peacetime have gone to a man, a course in aeronautics, described by Mr. Smith as "a study of mathematics and science needed as basic training for airplane pilots." It was open to both sexes. Miss Everett's prototype class the year before was made up of volunteers who met after school. Among them were John Murphy, Priscilla Amnott, Lawson Weinburg, Charles Russell, and Jack Zollo. To learn something of what it was like to be a flyer, the last three named built a simplified

Richard Crosby, English teacher, had just returned from basic training in 1942. He is seen here with students, left to right, Harold Proctor, Ernest Armand, and Bruce Bryer.

Jack Zollo was always a scholar. He was also the family daredevil.

model of an airplane cockpit with a control stick and pedals for controlling wing flaps, etc. In simple terms, it was an oversized box in which the students sat.

Miss Everett could never conceive how valuable this class was to be to one of those young people in her class. He was Jack Zollo, and his World War II adventure became known publicly during President Carter's administration when Jack was serving on the federal energy commission and doing a great deal of flying between his home in Rumford, Maine, and Washington. On one flight, he left behind a copy of the *Rumford Falls Times* on the seat, for which he had written an article.

The man who next occupied the seat was General W. E. Wicks, USA Retired, who subsequently wrote a letter to the editor of the *Times.* The letter was given a title, "The Devil in Baggy Pants."Part of it is quoted below:

For many years I have thought about writing a book about interesting people that I have come in contact with over the years.

I have a footlocker full of notes, but no book. A little while back, I boarded a plane at Kennedy Airport and in the seat was a copy of the Times *newspaper of Rumford, Maine, which I decided to glance over. In this issue was an article on energy by a Jack Zollo. Zollo not being a common name, I thought that I would do a little investigating and I discovered that this Jack Zollo was the same fellow that was to be one of the characters in my unpublished book.*

My first meeting with this fellow, alias John "The Prof" and "The Devil in Baggy Pants," was in Italy during World War II. The Allied troops in this one particular sector were pinned down by heavy German artillery fire.

These troops were incurring a high casualty rate and were unable to advance because of it. At the Command Post people were feverishly trying to locate a forward observer plane to enable our artillery, which up to this point was very ineffectual, to zero in on the enemy.

As may happen in war, where there was a plane there was no pilot available and vice versa. Suddenly there was a plane up in the air and radioing coordinates to our artillery headquarters. I was dispatched to find out who this "hot shot" pilot was, as the plane appeared to be on acrobatic maneuvers, and to congratulate him for providing the information that silenced the German artillery.

Arriving at a small field I found two young First Lieutenants emerging from an L-4 that had its nose between two trees and its wings folded back. I asked who had piloted the plane and where he came from.

The pilot said that his name was Zollo and that he came from "the front." The plane was one he had located back a mile or two. It had been shot up and it took him a few hours to get the motor to run. Then with a few pieces of wire, etc. he patched up some of the controls.

I found that his pilot training consisted of a text book course that he had taken in high school and this was not only his first experience in flying, but the first time that he had ever been in the cockpit of an airplane.

I then asked him why in hell he had attempted such a crazy thing and his answer was— "It seemed to be better to do something than to just sit around and either bitch or get killed." His men called him "The Prof" because he was bright and had helped them out of many "jams" with innovative ideas.

Not surprisingly, Jack emerged from World War II with a Silver Star. When the young officer who had volunteered to serve as his radioman heard the good news that he had been on Jack's maiden flight, he fainted. Jack had landed the plane between two trees because he didn't know how otherwise to brake it.

Thanks to Frances Everett he was later exempt from taking differential calculus at the University of Maine. Not all her students, of course, were intrigued with mathematics. In any case, few found word problems in the textbooks gripping, emotion-laden struggles. In writing of the advantages of Latin over math, Barbara Clark observed in a *Holten* essay, "The thrilling adventures of Aeneas surely put to shame the flimsy exploits of A, B, and C (sometimes known as X, Y, and Z), who fill tubs with leaks or row upstream against the current with the tide going out at ten miles per hour." To counter this attitude, Miss Everett used a variety of methods to get us to think like mathematicians. She would pose questions about everyday experiences to get us to see the practical applications for her abstract subject. Many of them placed us in automobiles; one, for example, forced us to think how it would be possible to figure without a speedometer how fast the car was traveling. (Part of the solution had to do with the fact that telephone poles were spaced 100 feet apart.) When gas rationing forced most automobiles off the road for long periods of time, she showed us how we, as front seat passengers, could play simple or complex computational games with the license-plate number on the car ahead of us.

If Jack Zollo's experience had been exhilarating in the vein of an Errol Flynn wartime film, the suddenness of World War II's start precluded many of those romantic sentiments that Col. Thomas Wentworth Higginson had once thrilled to on rereading an old Latin text—sentiments like, "It is sweet and glorious to die for one's country." Beginning in 1942, some of the small red, white, and blue banners families hung in their front room windows to tell passersby how many men and women they had sent to war began bearing gold stars.

There were many firsts in World War II. Two of them for Danvers and other communities were the number of airmen who lost their lives and the number of women who entered the service. Consider the second. No real accounting has been made of the Danvers women who took part in World War II. Among the nurses were Eileen O'Connor, Pauline Hill, Helen Harrigan, Louise Kimball,

Wilma Kirwin, Louise Pitman, Dorothy Welch, and Audrey Zollo. The majority of those in a military branch were in the Army: Wilma Eldridge, Laura Flynn, Mary Hitchcock, Olive Fothergill, Mary Meagher, Eileen Sutherland, and Sarah Wilkins. Constance Duncan was in the Coast Guard. There were others, but this is a start for whoever wants to assemble a complete list. It would be a service to local history.

Of the airmen who were lost, Howard Lewis was killed in a plane crash in Beeville, Texas; and James Bailey, in a crash in England. Fred M. Cogswell, Jr., and J. Francis McDermott lost their lives in bombing missions over Germany; Robert Gaffney lost his life over Japan. Frank W. Leach, Francis M. Monahan, Jr., Frederick Smith, and Donald Webber were killed in the fight for New Guinea and Indo China.

In the fall of 1943, Gordon Hansen was on furlough before being shipped overseas. His sister, Virginia, wrote me on November 11, 1993, how he saw her distress as he was packing to return to his base. "He hugged me and kissed me good-bye," she told me, "and I was trying not to cry. The last thing he said to me was, 'Don't worry, Sis. We're going to win this one. God bless you.'"

Gordon's parents learned later that he had volunteered to help destroy a German machine gun post around Venefro, Italy. After the mission was successfully completed, he sat down on the protective parapet of the implacement and was in the act of lighting up a cigarette when a sniper's bullet ended his young life. At least three men who played on the 1941 football squad were killed—Edward Dzierzak, Lawson Weinburg, and Jack Murphy, who was Tess Creeden's nephew. Both Eddie and Jack were members of Danvers sports dynasties like Steve Hawkes and Jim Gaffney before them. Eddie lost his life in the South Pacific on November 10, 1944. Jack was killed in April of 1945 in the fighting for control of Okinawa, but since he was listed as missing in action, he was not officially declared dead until a year later. Lawson Weinburg was killed at Campoleone, Italy, on May 31, 1944.

Pvt. Gordon Hansen, 1922–1943

Others who may have been present in the gymnasium on December 8, 1941, and later lost their lives were William Silva, Joseph Ouimette, Roy Nickerson, Rene Cyr, Clayton Belben, and Herman T. Kennedy, Jr. Anastasia Zollo was one of six members of her family who wrote for *The Holten*. When her oldest son, Louis, was killed at Cisterna, Italy, on February 2, 1944, she wrote to Archbishop Francis J. Spellman, the New York prelate who visited American fighting men on every front, of her feelings after she lost Lou. The Archbishop quoted part of it in his *No Greater Love: The Story of Our Soldiers* as a source of courage and consolation to other gold-star mothers. While it is still difficult after all these years for me to reread her words, I quote them because one theme of this chapter has to do with the assimilation of first and second generation Americans:

Mothers' hearts are laid wide open these days by the fear and anxiety for the safety of their sons. I am not proud of the fact that my son had to give up his very young life for greed and avarice, but I am proud that he was a good soldier. If this was his mission in life, I know he did it well. Day by day I grow more grateful, thinking God must have loved Louis very much to have lifted him out of the horror and cruelty of war. It is my greatest consolation.

Another consoling thought is that he died in Italy. If it was in one of those small old Italian towns with the cobbled stone streets, where the donkey carts go up and down led by a singing peasant, where the skies are bluer than anywhere else in the world, then he is right back where his roots came from. The sod may be blood-soaked now, but one day God will make it verdant and fruitful again. If he gave up his life to help my father's beloved Italy, perhaps this is as it should be. How strangely He weaves the patterns of our lives!

Now I know why Louis wrote, "As I get closer to things, I don't think I'll make the boat home," and another time he said, "Some one has to do this job, and remember, Mom, you taught me many are called but few are chosen, and if we follow that thought we can't go wrong!"

Knowing that he volunteered to go on patrols, I feel humbly proud of this lad of mine, for I know he must have had a very special sort of courage, realizing full well the uncertainty of his return.

Unfortunately, more and more townspeople learned of the loss of one of their loved ones. Few families were untouched. Out of her distress for the happy lads she would never see again, Margaret Proctor Wood, who by virtue of the number of her poems centered on life in Danvers comes closest to being our poet laureate, commemorated all of them in the elegy, "In Memoriam, Holten High School Servicemen":

Gone are the boys to answer strange new calls.
Gone are the laughing lads who roamed our halls.
Gone to old, sad lands, in khaki new.
Gone with uplifted hearts, in sailor blue,
Gone to a bitter war, and prison walls.

Home are the lads, and drawn, the last quick breath.
Home from their planes and jeeps, their tanks and ships.
Home from each far horizon, where it slips
Into Eternal Love, that knows no death.

The high school float for the June 3, 1950, centennial anniversary of Holten High School. The teacher is Maria Grey Kimball, a long-time member of the Danvers School Committee.

CHAPTER VIII

Holten High School— The Concluding Years 1947–1962

In the 1950s a series of tensions was changing our lives. The close community that was America in World War II was disintegrating. There was now an assertion of the rights of the individual. Despite programs on television like "Ozzie and Harriet" and "Father Knows Best," family togetherness was less cohesive. For one thing, in those prosperous years, many young people owned automobiles and that gave them greater independence from home and school.

The baby boom and housing developments in suburbs like Danvers made extensive school and interstate highway construction imperative. Burdened by increased taxes, both parents felt it necessary to work in order to maintain their standard of living. The onset of criticism of our schools created another strain that led to an erosion of the former cooperation between parents and teachers. Even before their retirement, many older teachers were told by mothers or fathers, "You just stick to your teaching; I'll teach my children their manners." On the first or second sunny June morning, seniors would play hookey and drive off to distant beaches for parties. The next day, smiling and sunburned, they would present their excuses from home at the principal's office.

A practice that continued from the war was that of federal subsidy of instruction in mathematics and sciences. Is that bad? Those unknowingly used as human guinea pigs in radiation experiments where no follow-up studies were performed, or those today who see the need for more philosophy or ethics courses for individuals engaged in genetic experimentation might answer, "Yes."

However, whenever school reform was proposed with, for example, the addition of developmental, remedial, or guidance programs and additional supervisory personnel, it was almost always with the purpose of strengthening existing programs of study. There also remained a close rapport between teachers and students. The counterculture and social rebellion of the 1960s had not yet made adolescents distrustful of anyone over thirty-five.

All these pressures have dimmed an understanding of the basic purpose of public school education. In a November 1993 article for *Harper's* Benjamin R. Barber states, "The *public* in public schools means not just paid for by the public but procreative of the very idea of a public. Public schools are how a public—a citizenry—is forged and how young, selfish individuals turn into conscientious, community minded citizens."

One of the conditions created by World War II was a shortage of teachers. Before this, as noted, it was the practice of the Danvers School Committee to have local young people teach elsewhere before hiring them. Starting in 1947, however, several of us were employed with little or no experience: Joseph Albanese, Virginia Carey Grondin, Doris King Hughes, and I. At the same time, following the customary route, Georgia Williams and Virginia Sherry returned to their alma mater from teaching at Winthrop High School.

I was twenty-one when I joined the faculty although I had never had an education course or done student teaching. It didn't take Mr. Dunn long to realize that I was in trouble, and despite a busy schedule, he undertook to become all the pedagogical courses I had not studied at Bowdoin. My history and philosophy of education, my tests and measurements, and my English methods, all became one heavy cram course of on-the-job training.

One day each week he came into my classroom for a full period's observation. Each of those hours seemed an eon. At two-thirty the same day, I had to go to his office to hear his evaluation. I can still remember some of his suggestions: "Don't stand in front of the windows when you speak; it hurts your students' eyes." "Pay attention to the physical condition of your room." "Don't sit down when you teach; your students will relax mentally if you do." "'Repeat that again' is redundant."

By the time April rolled around I was ten pounds lighter. Finally my second graduation from Holten High School came the day he said to me, "Dick, I hope you're not planning to teach somewhere else next year." I was still learning, but thanks to him, I was a much better instructor than I had been in September. I shall always be grateful to Mr. Dunn for his understanding and kindness. Seeing a young man anxious to succeed in his chosen profession, he had taken the time to make his goal possible.

During the war, army and navy personnel were sent to college campuses to study meteorology and other subjects of military importance. Even before enemy-held territories were liberated, recruits were enrolled in centers giving intensive courses in foreign languages. These institutions featured language laboratories and stressed the spoken word. In the 1950s, such laboratories entered the nation's secondary schools, including Holten High School when Mr. Richard Jordan and Miss Jeannette Bonville taught Spanish and French respectively. To better facilitate language acquisition among Danvers school children, French and Latin were taught in the eighth grade.

With this emphasis on change in foreign languages, instruction in the old traditional, proscriptive rules of grammar and usage also shifted to a linguistic approach in English classes. Distinctions between *shall* and *will*, *I* and *me*, *who* and *whom*, etc. grew dim in students' minds because of a lack of instruction during this transitional period. Another reason was that rote learning was considered passe.

Mr. Dunn was quoted at the time by a *Danvers Herald* reporter, whose main interest was sports writing, as having said, "Me and the faculty agree. . . ." Considerably nonplused, Mr. Dunn called to complain. Far from being apologetic, the reporter said casually, "Oh, I thought all that *I*, *you* and *me* stuff went out the window long ago."

For aspiring writers in nonfiction and poetry, a lack of knowledge here has often meant uncertainty about how to express themselves when, for example, it comes to the principal parts of verbs. Such younger authors now turn to language pundits like William Safire, Edwin Newman, and the Random House dictionaries, all of whom place value on good usage. There is little unhappiness for those educated prior to World War II. Note the contrast in this regard between two excellent Danvers writers, Jean Pedrick and Richard B. Trask.

Miss Pedrick was graduated from Holten High in 1939. She is the author of a novel, *The Fascination* (1947), and five volumes of poetry—*Wolf Moon, Pride and Splendor, The Gaudy Book, Greenfellow,* and *Saints.* In addition to several published chapbooks as well, Miss Pedrick is a feature writer for the *Beacon Hill News* in Boston, where she lives. She has taught and lectured at Northeastern, the Boston Center for Continuing Education, and the New Hampshire Center for the Arts.

Jean Pedrick was poetry editor of *The Holten* in 1938 and the magazine's editor-in-chief in 1939. Among her many poems is one, "Agricola," which she has given me permission to print here because of its connection with Holten High:

Agricola
On the first day, on the first page:
Agricola. Thrilled because
I instantly saw the agriculture in it
I sat straight up in my chair.

Wally drowsy behind me, a milker
of cows, manure in his boot treads;
dosing, too, in the back row, Steve
who plays the horn like Bix
in Buddy Batistini's father's band
into the small hours at the roadhouse
made of a long, old barn. . . .

"La-tin," I say it thoroughly to myself,
"This year I'm taking La-tin,"
as one would say *I'm taking liberties.*

Outside the wide-flung windows, bees,
seemingly aimless, give off small fuzzed
sounds like sleeping boys. In a field,
brown, a man turns hacked stalks under.
The next field, green and slubbed with gold,
sews itself to the sky reflected,
just now, just for this hour, in the tiny
tidal river. At the edge his woman,
wearing yellow, dips up and down
like finest linen the piggies of baby
number three. (Her first two
think they're fishing.) *Agricola,*
the farmer. *Agricolae,* of the farmer,
the farmer's. His.

As well known as she is, the reason Miss Pedrick is not a household name whose poems appear in anthologies with the words "Familiar" or "Favorite" in their titles is due to the narrower appeal of contemporary literature for the reader. In our leisure time we are oriented now to image and sound more than print. The result has been for us in Danvers, the cessation of that marvelous rush of published creative writers from Holten High School in the 1920s and 1930s, Jean Pedrick being the last of that set.

She has written an appreciation of Frances Wadleigh Scott that explains the confidence of an older Danvers writer with grammar and the mechanics of expression:

(Miss Wadleigh's) influence was both profound and magical. I seem to know things about writing—the uses of like and as, for example, or that strange, necessary shift, sometimes from I was to I were, things that confound some of my contemporaries. When pinned down, I've always answered, "I had a superb English teacher in high school." The magic lay in how painless it was. It was a joy to do work for Miss Wadleigh, because she honored one's thinking, one's effort, even one's willingness to take risks. As editor of The Holten, *I enjoyed with her a more adult working relationship. She never imposed her judgment. We were the editors. But she was there like a rock when we turned to her with doubts. Where can it have come from, that unfailing respect for the half-risen, half-baked creatures that inhabited her sunny days?*

I learned quite a lot about history from Miss Porter, from Miss Wood, the price of ennui and desespoir—and two French folk-songs. But when I think of those days, it is Miss Wadleigh who comes back whole, her forthrightness, her lovely manner and mien, her infinite interests—a tall, plain Erato, an enabler, a part of my life I have always kept and cherished.

How lucky we were, and we knew *how lucky we were!*

Danvers has never had a more capable or more widely respected historian nationally than its present amiable town archivist, Richard B. Trask, an authority on an unusually broad range of subjects—witchcraft, social and military life in Colonial days, early house construction, and photography among them. It also should be added, an executive of impressive ability. Who else could have more effectively directed and coordinated the diverse activities of the 1992 witchcraft tercentenary observances than Dick? Like Miss Pedrick, he has published articles and books on his interests—*The Devil Hath Been Raised, As the Century Turned* (co-author), *The Meetinghouse at Salem Village*, and the current *Pictures of the Pain.*

He remembers his English teacher, Mrs. Gertrude Kirby O'Connell, explaining to her students why she would work hard with them, "I'm going to be the last teacher here who will teach you grammar and usage." Dick's mental response was, "GREAT!" Today, this writer, who credits his freshman social studies teacher, Edward Gwin, with stimulating his interest in American history, says, "I wish I had paid more attention, but the future was a mere speck on my horizon." Richard Trask writes very well. What he has experienced is the lack of confidence about considerations like correct case or tense, annoying gnats to concentration, that can interrupt the flow of ideas when there are so many more important matters involved in composition.

It is mainly in nonfiction that Holten High School graduates are published today. A few of them even have an international readership. Has any other Danvers writer produced a more attractive volume than Carl Crossman in his definitive *The Decorative Arts of the China Trade*? It is based on his earlier *The China Trade*, published by Salem's Peabody Museum in 1972. Its colored illustrations of Chinese paintings, furniture, silk embroideries, and "exotic curiosities" with their detailed captions attest to this well-traveled author's quest for the best examples to accompany his text. It is a volume that deserves its critical praise.

It was in adolescence that Carl discovered his interest in this field. Following Wesleyan, he began working as an assistant curator of maritime history at the Peabody. Encouraged by its then director, Ernest Dodge, he examined the unseen treasures of the museum stored in barrels and on shelves in the basement. This hands-on experience and a great deal of study made him the respected expert that he is. After the Peabody, Carl became the president and manager for two decades of Childs Gallery on Newbury Street in Boston. Semi-retired now, he is a knowledgeable and entertaining lecturer on luxury cruises to the Orient.

Writers in science and mathematics often present papers or publish articles as a source of information to others working on the same or similar problems in their fields. In other words, their writings are more in-house and less well-known to the public than those of the fiction writer who strives for universal appeal.

Warwick Millar, now a professor of statistics at the University of California in Berkeley, is one of three Ph. D.'s in Holten High's Class 1957, the other two being Roger Hubbard and the late David Leach. Through articles like "The Asymptotic Minimax Principle of Statistical Theory," Millar has gained a reputation in his field far beyond his campus. In 1989, for instance, he traveled to Germany as the guest of the applied mathematics department of the University of Heidelberg.

An earlier alumnus than either of these men, Crossman or Millar, was Cecil Peterson, now Patterson, who is the author of a dozen college texts. After earning his Ph. D., he taught at the University of Illinois' College of Education. In all, Patterson has contributed, according to the fortieth edition of *Who's Who in America*, 150 articles to various learned journals on the subjects of counseling, rehabilitation, and psychology.

For the progressive educator, the joint facilities shared by the students in both Conant Street schools, created a community-like environment. These larger spaces—the gymnasium, assembly hall, shops, and cafeteria—permitted more diverse activities than had the cramped, limited quarters of the old town hall/high school. The new gymnasium, as we have seen, meant that the girls would no longer have to walk up to the old armory building at 128 Maple Street nor did the boys have to hike down to the Pillsbury Block on High Street for the same game.

Over the years, the well-lighted Holten High gymnasium took on the heady ambiance of sour sweat and gamey sneakers. Among its many uses were physical education classes for grades 7–12, medical check-ups, basketball and volley games, cheerleading practice, pep rallies, emergency assembly hall, freshman girls' orientation "parties," and school dances. During the war years, annual spring gymnastics evenings were held under the direction of Coach Vye and girls' physical education instructor Charlotte Parrot. These programs drew enthusiastic audiences.

On the evening of the last event, the heavy mats that hung along the walls furnishing some protection for ricocheting basketball players were laid out on the floor for tumbling and other exercises. The girls alternated with the boys in these and other demonstrations throughout the program. Stout ropes were let down from the ceiling for climbing races between a team made up of senior and freshman boys and one of junior and sophomore boys. Girls wove in and out around a Maypole until they had created a colorful braid. At other times, the floor was a bustling six-ring circus with boys and then girls alternating to play a variety of games like circle dodge ball, jump the snake, and swat your neighbor. Both sexes performed gymnastic routines on the buck, horse, and parallel bars, but only the boys worked on the rings. Still, it was a great advance for the young women who, at the turn of the century, did little more than swing Indian clubs.

The special part of these programs was the sports tableaux of gilded varsity athletes posing under bright spotlights. The program that began with marching drills ended when these golden living statues saluted the flag.

School dances were held in either the gymnasium or the auditorium. They were the Sophomore Hop, the Junior and Senior Proms, and the Senior Reception, the last being a by-invitation-only affair. For a time there were also costumed Sadie Hawkins Day dances based on cartoonist Al Capp's hillbilly characters. This dance depicted an annual event in Dog Patch when a girl could chase a boy and marry the one she caught.

The most popular band over the years was Manuel's Black and White. Formed in Beverly in 1916, it took its name from the original four members: David and Otis

Attillo Capra and Faith-Anne Coley take a turn around the dance floor.

Cynthia Hawkes leads the Bunny Hop.

(Ote) Manuel, the two black musicians, and Walter Piccard and George Janotta, the two whites. Other musicians who joined the band after 1916 were Al Mitchell and Charles Manuel, Sr. Today, those in the group are in their seventies and eighties, but still entertaining at North Shore functions.

In an article, "An 'Unforgettable' Band," Alexander Stevens, writing for *North Shore Sunday,* told how in the 1940s this band played in one room of the Savoy ballroom in Boston while Tommy Dorsey, Duke Ellington, Count Basie, or Louie Armstrong played in the main room. On more than one occasion, Manuel's outdrew the featured musicians. One night, Louie Armstrong, wondering where his audience had gone, went into the smaller room to discover Ote Manuel putting on his impression of the Satchmo.

Since the Manuels could play swing or sweet equally well, it provided a full evening of dancing. Its sweet (slow) sets included the standard waltz and the fox trot. If a young man was lucky, either dance ended in a low dip. But the most popular dance of the war years was the jitterbug, an acrobatic jazz version of the old two-step. While it became a tamer dance in later years, in the beginning it was uninhibited with hips swinging, skirts flying, and the lady being passed between her partner's legs or flipped over his back. One movement had the girl locking her legs around her date's waist and her arms around his neck. Then the two began an exaggerated pecking motion as if they were trying to pluck corn from their partner's ears.

An evening of fun, rather than romance, was the informal Sophomore Hop. The 1948 sophomores advertised their dance in this bit of verse:

> It's going to be good. It's going to be great.
> So come on, fellows, get your date.
> Get permission from her Pop.
> Take her to the Sophomore Hop.

To encourage large attendance, two deans of women told girls that they could go without dates. Most girls were reluctant to do this, and those who did felt like wallflowers, even though there were tag and elimination dances. The favorite dance for this unsophisticated collection of young people was not a slow fox trot but an energetic Bunny Hop with the dancers in single file, clutching the waist of the person in front of them, the whole line weaving in and out of the auditorium or gym doors.

Some of the bands that played on these evenings were made up of local high school musicians. Newell Griffin had a band in the 1930s with everyone playing the saxophone, an instrument popularized by big-band leaders like Rudy Vallee or Jimmy Dorsey. Other school groups were led by Sol Levenson, Tom Meakin, Roger LeVasseur, Priscilla Benvy, and Dick Putnam Jr.

For all these dances, yards of crepe paper streamers and masses of balloons in the school colors of blue and white or class colors festooned the walls and ceiling. A prosperous class might even rent props like a many-faceted mirrored ball, similar to the one at the Totem Pole in Norembega Park or the Crystal Ball in Shawsheen Village, where we danced to the music of Baron Hugo. Rotating high above the floor, the tiny mirrors sent shards of reflected light like whirling flakes of snow around an otherwise low-lit hall while couples clung close (never too close) and shuffled slowly around their crystal wonderland to such "Hit Parade" tunes as Hoagy Carmichael's "Stardust."

During this era, school dances were well

Always the center of admiring students, Mr. Dunn talks to one of the couples at the Senior Dance in 1956. In the foreground are Andrea Hurd and Sandra Boardman.

Queen Sylvia Newbury and her court at the Senior Dance in 1957: Phyllis DiVincenzo, Priscilla Deschenes, Sandra Storm, Andrea Dabose, Mary Duffill, and Marcia Wilt.

These couples have gone to the Golden Anchor in 1953 for an after-the-dance supper: Merle O'Donal, Rae Milbury, Irene Yonge, and Gary Couhig.

chaperoned affairs. Rituals were still important. A dance officially got underway with a grand march led by the class president, invariably the football captain, and his date. This ceremony concluded with everyone's going through a reception line to greet their chaperons and class officers and dates. Almost always chaperons included Mr. and Mrs. Dunn, Mr. and Mrs. Smith, Mr. and Mrs. Duncan, Margaret Wood or Charlotte Parrot, and a member or two of the school committee and their spouses.

Gradually, over the years, dance cards were eliminated as swapping partners became less popular. All the young men wore suits, slacks and jackets, or tuxedos, and the young women wore gowns with gardenia or orchid corsages pinned to the shoulder or worn around their wrists. Gallant young gentlemen made a point of asking unescorted female teachers to dance. When Miss Parrot once thanked a visiting escort for their dance, he replied, "Hey, pretty or ugly, six to sixty, I ask them all."

Another social event, other than dances, held in the gymnasium was the celebration banquet for the school's centennial celebration on June 3, 1950. Registration and class reunions were held on Friday, the day before. That first night, couples danced to the music of Ruby Newman and his orchestra. On Saturday afternoon there was a baseball game between alumni and the school team. There were seven hundred in attendance at the banquet. At that time, there were four thousand alumni of the school. Chairman for the weekend was Guy T. Creese. Dinner festivities began when Lucy Belle White sang the national anthem. Throughout the dinner, the Danvers Rotary Club orches-

JoAnne Wilkins leads a cheer during a rally in the gym on September 21, 1956.

Priscilla Deschenes and Gerry Donahue participate in the three-legged race during Senior Day activities. Denise Harmony looks on from the sidelines.

tra played. Their soloists were Geraldine Turenne and Stacia Zuk.

James Gaffney, Sr., who was the master of ceremonies, introduced the speakers. Both Ivan G. Smith and Cornelius Dunn spoke briefly. Charles S. Tapley provided a history of the school, and Maria Grey Kimball, former school committee woman, gave further information on the school's past. She was, in fact, descended from Judge Samuel Holten. Then an announcement was made of the generous Paris S. McCutcheon Foundation Memorial Scholarships by his widow Grace McCutcheon of the Ideal Baby Shoe. Each year since, a graduating young man and woman have received all-expense-paid, four-year scholarships to the colleges of their choice.

All these speeches took so long that it was ten-thirty by the time the evening's principal speaker, alumnus George C. Brainard, rose to speak. A successful banker and industrialist in Cleveland, he had the good sense to abandon his fourteen-page address. Instead, he spoke extemporaneously on "upholding the American way." The program concluded with Father Alexander Szypko's benediction.

The sport that neither the gym nor the fields of the park could accommodate was ice hockey. When an arena opened in Lynn in the 1950s, Ray Funchion who had captained the hockey team when the game was played on frozen ponds in the 1920s, revived the game then. This man also founded the North Shore Hockey League. Among his outstanding players was Barry Urbanski, who led both the hockey and baseball teams in 1957. An All-American at Boston University, Barry became the hockey coach at Salem State College, where he was later joined by Mr. Funchion. Other excellent players in hockey were Peter Duncan and Walter Gustavsen.

For a game with an earned reputation for roughness, these modern teams were gentlemen compared to those in Ray Funchion's own day as a player. In a recruitment article for the game in the February, 1922 issue of *The Holten,* the "Athletics" editor wrote:

> Say, fellows, how would you like to see a fight? Pretty nice, eh! But then you see lots of them in the movies, and if you've got a brother, you're probably more than a spectator quite often. Wouldn't you like to see another kind of fight for a change? Come out, then, and see the hockey team fight—you'll be surprised.

Joseph Devarenne, the team's captain, was described as a gentleman fighter, but when Ed Moriarty grew angry and the opponent's goal tender saw him coming, "He yells for a six-man defense." Norman Brown was described as a "human trip-hammer."

At the same time the fifties hockey team was playing well, the baseball team, which, as always, shared some of the same athletes, ended the 1956 season in the semifinals of the Eastern Massachusetts tournament. A number of the players in this sport hit over .300: William Morin, Richard Morse, John Quimby, Robert Hawkes, Donald Talbot, William Clark, Robert Peachey, and Robert Dowdell.

Another shared area of the two schools was the cafeteria, which served between 1,000 to 1,600 students a day. It was far superior to the old town hall/high school's. No longer did students have to walk the plank to reach its limited fare of a sandwich or a bowl of soup or chowder. Now, the cooks—Gertrude Banks, Mildred Johnson, or Beatrice Welch—and assistants Mary Thomas, Elizabeth Mugridge, and Frances Melcher prepared three different kinds of sandwiches; either soup or chowder with salted crackers; a salad with a hot muffin; a main dish generally with mashed potatoes, gravy, a vegetable, and a bread and butter sandwich; a second hot plate like spaghetti or American chop suey, if there was enough left over from the previous day's lunch. With a sufficient number of stoves, Ruth Ouimette, the pastry chef, could bake large batches of brownies or butterscotch squares or puddings for dessert. In the ovens of those stoves, Mrs. Banks, the first of the three cooks, placed as many as twenty frozen turkeys at 2:30, P.M. to be taken out fully cooked the next morning at 6:00 by Mr. Caron, the night custodian.

In the early 1950s, these cheerful, hard-working cooks posed for the camera: Gertrude Banks, Mildred Johnson, Louise Rivers, Beatrice Welch, and Mary Thomas.

At one time chocolate milk, candy bars, packaged cupcakes, doughnuts, and potato chips ("They are so Day-licious," according to the local manufacturer) were also offered. However, since much of the food was heavily subsidized by the federal government, its nutritionists made the cafeteria discontinue serving these.

The different cooks and their assistants were all part-time workers. A dedicated lot of women, they had the help of students who manned the cash registers and helped with the cleaning up. The hardest working of those young people were two boys who had the unpleasant task of cleaning off the returned trays. The man responsible for managing all this productivity was Eliot Duncan, originally from Rockland, Maine, From there he and his Owl's Head bride Pat had "gone down" to Bangor, where Ivan G. Smith, then principal of Holten High, observed Duncan in the classroom and hired him in 1923 for Danvers.

Humor and storytelling were important in his life. Say, "See you later," to someone from Maine like Bing Knight, Stafford and Roland Knights' father, and he's apt to reply, "Thanks for the warning." Dunc's wit ran from that type to broad, country-boy practical jokes. When Virginia Sherry taught in the commercial department, he impishly placed a realistic plastic lizard, which he had probably temporarily confiscated from a student, on the back of her chair. Then he waited in the rear of the room while her class filed in. Just as he had anticipated, as soon as she felt and then saw the apparently live reptile, she gasped in terror and went into something resembling the mating dance of the whooping crane. Dunc left the room, tears of delight running down his cheeks.

Surprisingly, one seldom got angry with him. There was never any malice in him. When he spoke to students, he tried always to compliment them on some accomplishment. One of the strengths of Holten High was this close personal relationship between administrators and students. Whenever he saw me in the corridor, Dunc invariably asked me if he had told me about the day my uncle Germano had climbed up the side of the town hall a day after a man billing himself as the Human Fly had performed that feat by means of the heavy quoining on one corner of the building. I had heard about it often from him and others like Thurl Brown, who had also been there, but like well-brought up young people in those days, I lied and politely said, "No, Mr. Duncan, you haven't."

(Poor Germano never forgot the day either—or its discomfort. He had scaled the building with two umbrellas tucked in his belt. when he got to the top, he didn't take into account the weight of his stout frame. He jumped, and the umbrellas immediately inverted like fragile parasols, hurtling him to the ground where he later told his daughters, Jacqueline and JoAnne, "I thought my feet had gone straight up through my body and stopped at my throat.")

This narrative trait of Mr. Duncan's was best brought out when the faculty was recording grades at the end of a term. Two teachers in a team used to read off the marks from the teachers' grade sheets, while two others wrote them down on either the report cards or the office record cards. Dunc's team in the fifties consisted of Frances Wadleigh, Virginia Sherry, and Ernest W. April, who succeeded Mr. Dunn as principal.

They were not a speedy group. Nor did they want to be. Dunc always turned over an office card to see the picture attached to the back. "Say, Dot," he'd comment to Miss Wadleigh, "this must be the child of. . ." and then they'd reminisce about the student's parents they'd had a quarter of a century before. By the time the rest of the faculty had exhausted themselves rushing to complete this chore and get outside for a smoke, his team would be enjoying a half time break with ice cream sandwiches he brought them from the cafeteria.

Between teaching, being assistant principal, managing the cafeteria and the magazine drives in the fall, Eliot Duncan worked long, extra hours for the school.

The magazine drive was always launched in the auditorium, another of the shared spaces. The program began when the tall magazine agent Del Obert, as bald as Mr. Dunn, rushed out on stage. The upperclassmen were already chuckling before Obert spoke his familiar opening line, "I got up late this morning and just had time to dress and brush the hair out of my eyes in order to get here on time." (Actually, he had spent the night just up the street with Eliot and Pat Duncan.)

Then he and Mr. Dunn engaged in a brief exchange:

Obert, explaining his lack of hair, "Grass doesn't grow on a busy highway."
Mr. Dunn, dryly, "It can't grow up through concrete either."

Whatever profit the school received from student sales of periodicals like *The Saturday Evening Post, Collier's, Liberty, Look, American Home,* etc. went into such projects as illuminating the individual Holy Grail pictures. For a few years, the company gave out individual prizes to the best salespeople. Then, to stimulate competition, daily high homerooms were treated to ice cream parties or received five-pound boxes of chocolates. The homeroom that had collected the most money at the end of the drive was allowed to go first to the cafeteria for a month.

While it is obvious that the Sweater Benefit was put on to buy heavy, woolen varsity football sweaters it was instituted, as we've read, by Mr. Dunn when he first came to town. Miss Damon of the commercial department was, for most of its years, the director. No sports teams ever had a more loyal fan than Gladys Damon.

Roger Budgell, Gladys Damon, and Mr. Dunn pose with sweaters earned from student efforts in 1953.

This program was first held at night for the public, and then, in an abbreviated form, at an assembly the following morning. Since there was a diversity of acts, it was necessary to find a suitable frame for each year's performance. Effective, but unobtrusive sets were built by David Humphreys' advanced shop students. In 1940, it was a crossroads diner with Jack Dresser and Robert Burnham as customers commenting on the acts and Nancy Moulton as the cashier. Once it was a group of entertainers bound for radio's "Major Bowes' Amateur Hour." I don't know who had the Major's famous opening line, "The wheel of fortune spins 'round and 'round, and where she stops, nobody knows." In 1942, it was the "Hawthorne" Post Office, where the entertainers came in to claim their mail. The clerks were Ernest Armand and Leonard Potter. In 1944, it was the lobby of the Chateau de Holten. In 1946, Clifford Bean and Sumner Burns, theatrical agents, held auditions backstage at the Orpheum theater. Sometimes it was just a variety show like "The Flip-Flops of '50."

David Humphreys in the shop. His students built the sets for senior plays and sweater benefits.

During the acts, dancers tapped, waltz-clogged, hula'd, backflipped, shuffled, glided, pirouetted, and toe-tapped across the boards. Trained singers or those with naturally pleasing voices sang everything from Puccini arias to Norma LaBelle's yodeling and James Karolides' raspy imitation of Louie Armstrong. Once the five man quartet of Neal McLaughlin, Richard Seavy, Richard Powers, George Vaillancourt, and Harry Ventre sang barbershop harmony. Some performers lip-synced lyrics by Bing Crosby, Elvis Presley, or Carol Channing. Over the years, one or two skits drew on someone's knowledge of the comic routines at the Old Howard Burlesque Theatre, especially the courtroom scene:

Judge: "In here, I'm justice."
Drunken Defendant: "Oh yeah! Well, I'm justice good as you are."

The finale of every Sweater Benefit was the chorus of football players led by Mr. Dunn. Their medley always included "Stout-Hearted Men." The applause following was so raucously enthusiastic that it set the glum portraits of those stern old-time heroes Governor John Endicott, John Greenleaf Whittier, and General Francis Dodge to rattling on the walls.

Thanks to Sandi Masi's collection of high school memorabilia, we have preserved for us the "Park Scene" from her Sweater Benefit:

Eight bars of SWINGING DOWN THE LANE is played by the orchestra.

As the Curtain goes up, four couples walk across stage in different directions. Lights go dim. Thunder and lightning sound effects, etc.

Couples stop and put up their umbrellas.

Introduction to SINGIN' IN THE RAIN and then couples begin song with routine.

After song—Lights come up slowly.

Jane W.: "Oh look, it's stopped raining!"

Couples put down umbrellas.

Alex.: "Let's go down to the Sweet Shop."

All: "Come on, kids. Let's go. . ."

All hurry out. Lights come on brighter. Sillars, Partridge, Hilton, Masi come on stage.

Judy H.: "Gee, isn't the sun bright now!"

Girls go to center stage and begin song HELLO, SUNSHINE.

After song—

Janet S.: "Where's your boy friend, Ruth?"

Ruth: "I don't know. He'll probably be late as usual."

Sandi: "Look, here he comes—"

Ruth: "I'll see you kids later."

Ruth goes and sits on park bench. Bruce walks over to her.

Bruce: "I'm sorry I'm late. You're not angry, are you?"

Ruth: "No—but (goes into song) WHEN I GET YOU ALONE TONIGHT.

After song—

Policeman walks on stage. Ruth and Bruce get up and leave. Ky Deschenes comes skipping on stage with beach ball.

Policeman : "Where are you going, my pretty young maid?"

Ky: "Why I'm going" (goes into song) BY THE SEA.

While Ky is singing, policeman stands with puzzled look. Then a boy walks on stage and goes to policeman to ask for directions. Both look at Ky. Just as song is about over the boy goes off stage.

After song—

Ky: "Well, I'm off." she goes skipping off.

Policeman: "You certainly are!"

After, policeman strolls toward one side of stage. On the opposite side, Jane Willet comes in, bends down at flower garden and starts to pick a flower. Policeman comes up behind her. He coughs. Jane straightens up quickly and looks guilty. Jack Fedas comes on stage at this point. Policeman leaves and Fedas begins song STROLLING THROUGH THE PARK ONE DAY. He goes over to Jane as he sings song. Couples come strolling on stage again. Towards the end of the song the couples drift off slowly.

After songs———

Irene Yonge walks on stage with Bob Barbin. She is chattering and smiling at him. She pulls him along beside her towards park bench. Bob appears to be bored. Janet Sillars comes rushing on stage and goes over to bench.

Janet: "What are you doing with her? You were meant for me—."

Donald Gorman struts across the stage in this skit from a Sweater Benefit. Takeji Matsubara's handsome, five-panel screen is in the background.

Irene looks very huffy and gets up and leaves. Janet goes to center stage looking very hurt. Bob gets up from bench and picks flowers while Janet begins the verse of YOU WERE MEANT FOR ME. When she gets to chorus, Bob comes over to her and presents her with the flowers as she goes into chorus of song.

After song—Janet and Bob go and sit on park bench. Light on stage becomes very weak.

The lamplighter comes on stage and puts on lamp (all other lights go out completely.) Four couples drift on singing THE OLD LAMPLIGHTER .

After song—Couples keep as quiet as possible and stay towards back of stage. Grandmother and grandfather come out (stroblite) singing "I'LL SEE YOU IN MY DREAMS and MOONLIGHT BAY. The whole cast comes on stage quietly.

After two songs—

Lights go on and whole cast sings TILL WE MEET AGAIN.

CURTAIN

Senior plays were most often performed on the same stage as the Sweater Benefits. It was a bare, shallow, inadequate one. For regular assemblies and town meeting nights that were held here, it was suitable, the only decoration being Takeji Matsubara's handsome, gessoed screen with the town seal in the arch of the central panel. Whenever a play demanded a larger setting, the stage at the Peabody Institute Library was utilized.

In the 1920s, Miss Dow directed a few classics, but by the 1950s light comedies prevailed. In 1955, the play was "You Can't Kiss Caroline"; its setting was a drug store, "the favorite hangout for the high school gang." Only one play ever made headlines. When Mr. Roger Barry, English teacher, directed "Curtain Going Up" in 1957, one of the actors in a pretended altercation hit the stage so violently that he had to receive medical attention. Only the presence of the cast of the same play from Peabody High School saved the evening. The Peabody senior who was to portray the same character stepped into the role, and the play went on.

My own vivid memory of that high school stage was co-directing the senior play, "Oh, Kay," for the class of 1954 with Miss Virginia Sherry. Neither Wink nor I had the least desire to volunteer for this duty, since we both were advisors for other extracurricular activities but primarily because we had never done any directing before. However, Mr. Dunn was desperate, and what he did next revealed another side of his nature.

He first went to Wink and said, "Dick Zollo says he'll direct the senior play if you'll assist him." He hadn't seen me at all. Once he got her OK, he said to me, "Wink Sherry will direct the senior play, but she'd like you to help her." Despite this deception, when we became engaged, he and Helena were the first two, outside of our families, that we told.

Plays aside, for regular assemblies each Wednesday morning, teachers most often had charge of the programs, which, not surprisingly, were appropriate for their subjects. Foreign language clubs like Jeannette Bonville's *Le Cercle Entre Nous*, Peter Abidian's *El Club Panamericano*, and Richard Jordan's *El Club de Español* some times gave their performances in French or Spanish. Students in after-school activities like J. Casey Olds' Future Teachers of America or John Ellery's Radio Guild put on programs to recruit new members. So did *The Holten* staff, except that it also used to distribute awards for the best selections by non-board members. Other awards assemblies included the announcement of sweater recipients and the distribution of Peabody Honor Society pins. Graduation honor parts were announced on Senior Day on April 1. During that assembly, Mr. Dunn, the perennial senior class advisor, would often exhort the class to "Let the rest

Commercial students and their teacher Henry Derouin observe IBM procedures at the Ideal Baby Shoe in 1959 previous to similar equipment being installed at Holten High.

of the school know the seniors are still alive." The remainder of that day, they spent frolicking in the gymnasium.

In the area of science, a very popular nature program was given each year by alumnus Gilbert Merrill. "As a young man," he once wrote back to his alma mater, "I spent most of my time in the fields and woods along the Danvers River with a pair of binoculars and a collecting net." Gib was always accompanied by Spooky, the great horned owl, who could swivel his head almost all the way around. Spooky sat disdainfully on a perch throughout the performance, occasionally blinking in an imperious manner. Gib once let a large timber rattlesnake loose. Perhaps because he had been bitten more than once, Gib was a little slow in retrieving it. The snake slithered close to the edge of the stage looking angrier than a teacher about to dispense afternoon session slips. Both the young men and women in the front row let out a few frightened screams before the snake was safely bagged up.

Another alumnus, Dr. Stewart Duncan, who has taught biology and ornithology at Boston University on the undergraduate level and parasitology at the University's medical school, once drove to Boston with Gib when Spooky was a nestling. Spooky sat on Stewart's lap with disastrous results. With a poet's unerring ear, Stewart recalls that he got doused with a bounteous supply of "gooky."

Like others interested in biology and ornithology, Dr. Duncan credits Miss Lois Curtis and her enthusiasm for her subject as the one who encouraged him and "gave everything" for him and others. While still in high school, several students—Hollis Hayden, Gib Merrill, Robert Nappe, Bennett Keenan, and Stewart—were members of the Essex County Ornithology Club that met around a large wooden table in the Peabody Museum in Salem. Both Bob Nappe and Stewart served as presidents of the club. From 1949 to 1986, Stewart made canoe trips down the Ipswich River with some of the others identifying and counting the migratory land birds.

For several years, General Electric Company in Lynn sent out engineers with a kind of simplified Century of Progress exhibition to interest young men in its apprenticeship program. We were given our first demonstrations of cryogenics at this time. Either John Sloan or Raymond Swinnerton, the demonstrators, would bounce a tennis ball to show its elasticity, then dramatically donning a pair of thick, protective gloves, one or the other would grasp the ball in a long set of tongs and immerse it in a steaming cauldron of liquefied gas. We all watched fascinated at what ensued. The ball was dropped to the floor again, only this time it didn't rebound. Instead it shattered into hundreds of tiny, brittle fragments.

A scientist more interested in heat than extreme cold is Dr. Roger Hubbard, Class of 1957, another Middleton author and the nephew of Ervin Conley. Roger determined on a career in science while still in high school. Today, thirty-seven years later, he is the writer of over two hundred publications on the subject of environmental medicine. He is the director of Environmental Pathophysiology at the U.S. Army Research Institute of Environmental Medicine in Natick and as such he is recognized as a leading authority on the effect of heat on the human body and heat-related illnesses. His writings on the subject extend far beyond military journals; they have appeared in encyclopedias, medical journals, and sports magazines. Most impressive about his work to the general public is the fact that Dr. Roger Hubbard prepared the survival manual carried by our troops in Desert Storm.

In another type of assembly program, state officials from the registry of motor vehicles brought in films to shock students into sensible highway safety habits. *Carefully We Roll Along, Spinning Wheels,* and *Driven to Kill* were some of the titles. These came before a drivers' education course, taught by men like David Humphreys and Coach George Radulski, entered the course of study.

Before the school had a guidance department, career-oriented assemblies were held. Among these was a Burdett College film, *I Want a Job.* Once or twice, a representative from the state's department of health gave girls advice on how to dress and conduct themselves in a business office. This department's agent delivered a talk of dubious humor, "How Attractive Is Your Personality?" She saved her biggest ho-ho for the conclusion, "Women in slacks should never turn their backs."

In the beginning, of course, individual teachers had a great deal of influence in advising students on college choices. Mr. Coates sometimes used reverse psychology on a senior who, he felt, had unrealistic ambitions. When Robert Southworth, now a prominent physician heading a large private clinic in Ohio, told him he planned to go to Harvard to study medicine, Mr. Coates looked at him a few minutes before asking him quite bluntly if this was just a pipe dream of Bob's or if he really were serious. When Bob convinced him of his sincerity, Mr. Coates gave him whatever help and encouragement he could. Mr. Dunn and the Dean of Women did most of the advising. Both of their offices had college catalogs that students could sign out.

Assemblies aside, in the auditorium on Fridays, Rachel Kerans conducted her music classes. Like art teacher Maude H. Denton, Miss Kerans was responsible for giving instruction to all students in the Danvers school system. Her favorite tunes in the outsized high school songbook were international folk songs—"Bendemeer's Stream," "Flow Gently, Sweet Afton," and Stephen Foster's "I Dream of Jeannie" and "My Old Kentucky Home." As the class sang, she would walk up and down the aisle leaning over to listen to individuals, hoping to find a candidate for the glee club. She always had a student pianist like Elizabeth Rider, Marie Cook, or Elizabeth Wells to accompany the singing.

Rachel Kerans was a woman of infectious good humor. She often wore expensive antique jewelry, which she and Florence Leavitt, a teacher in the Richmond, bought at Daniel Low's estate sales in Salem. Whenever she announced near the final five or ten minutes of each class that students could choose their own favorite songs, the boys would shout out, "Rachel, Rachel" (I've been thinking what a queer world this would be, if the girls were all transported far beyond the Northern Sea).

Her enthusiasm for music originated in her family home, a Victorian mansion at 24 Conant Street, now the site of St. Mary's of the Annunciation Church. Her father, Charles Kerans, was a wealthy leather manufacturer from Canada, who had made his fortune by concocting a formula for a russet-colored dye, the worldwide standard color for luggage and harnesses that had previously been a European monopoly. American manufacturers of these items rapidly transferred their business to his Danversport factory beside Porter's River on Liberty Street.

Band director Attilio Capra sits proudly with his musicians in 1953. First row: Theodore St. Pierre, John Martin, Julie Bailey, Roger Farrin, Maureen Ford, Philip Hooper, Francine LeBlond, Kay Williams, and Jeannette Perrault. Second row: Donald Birnie, Pauline Perrault, Sandra Masi, Cynthia Hawkes, Kathleen Lynch, Gail Matsubara, and James McNiff. Third row: Richard Wessell, Lois Underwood, Nancy Cunningham, Jane Humphreys, and Richard Martyn. Fourth row: Jan Peterson, Joan Hearn, Priscilla Wheeler, Mary Riley, and Donald Bolduc. Fifth row: Richard Putnam, Barbara Damon, Gary Couhig, Barbara Strojny, Betty Spakas, and Grace Cunningham. Sixth row: Chester Twiss, Robert Churchill, Jon Humphreys, Robert Sigman, Philip Wood, Harry Lear, and William Webb.

Kerans and his wife Elizabeth, encouraged their children to invite classmates in for amateur musicales, poetry readings, and games like charades. As a result, Rachel studied music and her sister Rebecca, dancing. Miss Kerans was the only modern teacher hired, who in lieu of college had been prepared by tutors.

The culmination of her year's instruction and that of the director of instrumental music, Claude Phillips, was the ambitious Spring Concerts. Take, for example, the 1938 program. The orchestra played the "Light Cavalry Overture" by Von Suppe; "The Sleeping Beauty Overture" by Tchaikovsky; "Poem" by Fibich; a selection from "Bohemian Girl" by Balfe. George Batchelder played a cornet solo, "Showers of Gold," by Clarke. The Glee Club sang eight songs from Bizet's "Carmen." The accompanist was Ruth Janes. The band played "The Scarlet Mask Overture" by Zamecnik; "Simplicity" by Lee; a clarinet trio "Allegro, Opus 55" by Beethoven and played by William Joyce, John Moffette, and Maurice Frye; "Sparklets" by Mileo; "Nola," a xylophone solo played by Hollis Hayden accompanied by the band; and "Patriotic Patrol" by Zamecnik. All in all, it was a full and satisfying evening of classical music.

Miss Kerans and Mr. Phillips had outstanding student musicians on whom they devoted a great amount of time. Elizavetha Sokoloski, a prodigy of Rachel Kerans, had a career on the concert stage. Violinist Olive Dragon, cellist Aldene Eaton, and clarinetist Sally Ann Budgell, became members of the Salem Philharmonic that gave Sunday concerts at Ames Hall in the Salem YMCA. Claude Phillips was the conductor. Louis Stella became a concert pianist, and Richard Twardzik, who once gave an inspired performance of "The Golliwog's Cakewalk" at an assembly, transferred his affection from classical compositions to progressive jazz.

Claude Phillips, a man of mercurial moods, rehearsed his band in the small room abutting the principal's office. Over the years this space became lined with long, black-framed pictures of each graduating class. Mr. Dunn and Mr. Duncan would go in there frequently to refresh their recollections of classes or individuals. It was in this manner that Mr. Dunn honed his remarkable memory of our names. During football season, Mr. Phillips would have the band practice the selections they would play on Saturday afternoons. Then he took the musicians out to the field behind the school for marching drills. Although it was not especially difficult to form the letter D or the initial letter of the opposing team's school, reversing direction, a maneuver that required the members to about-face and proceed down through the ranks of those still marching forward, was daunting. Eventually the band became adept enough to accomplish this and play at the same time. Before then, Mr. Phillips' frustration would have turned into footstamping tantrums.

On the other hand, he could be surprisingly patient with an earnest young musician of slight skill. Sally Ann Budgell, who like Bruce Eaton, David Knowlton, and Richard Jackson, joined the band when she was in the fifth grade, admired Claude Phillips for another trait, "He let kids try things." Sally became Mr. Phillips' best clarinetist. When she expressed an early desire to direct the band, he allowed her to try it. Bruce Eaton, as an adult, a chairman of the Danvers School Committee, directed the band for the 1942 Sweater Benefit.

One of Mr. Phillips' successors in the early 1950s was described in a *Danvers Herald* article as "genial, modest, and unassuming." Indeed, they provide an accurate characterization of probably the most capable and appreciated director of instrumental music in the high school. His name was Attilio A. Capra, but to his band members he was Uncle Tilly. In the Army, he had been a Special Services trumpet player in musical groups providing the music for USO productions like "Anything Goes" and the Radio City Rockettes. Before coming to Danvers, he had earned his bachelor's degree from the Boston Conservatory of Music, and while he was in Danvers, he received his master's degree from Boston University. In his second year in Danvers, he took the band into the Northeastern Massachusetts

Music Festival on May 2, 1953, where they were awarded an upper division rating in their first competition. As far as Mr. Dunn was concerned, the only negative thing that Bud Capra did was to marry the principal's secretary, Mary Nowak, and end her working career.

As mathematical progressions are part of music so is inversion. As rock music increased in popularity, classical music declined until Holten High no longer had an orchestra. For a brief time, Mr. Capra resurrected a small one, but then he could no longer find violinists. The most frequently heard instruments became those equipped with electrical umbilical cords. In the 1959 school report, Mr. Good informed taxpayers, "[In order to] add some vitality to the ever diminishing interest in strings in our community, we have inaugurated a new program. Youngsters who are interested in studying strings are now provided one year of class instruction without charge. At the end of one year, if they are successful, they continue their study with a private teacher." In that year, Danvers was conducting the most ambitious musical program on the North Shore. Director then for all music in the system was Alphonse M. Tatarunis.

The need for counseling and guidance services in the public schools had been recognized at the turn of the century by John Dewey. *The Holten's* "Alumni" columns had always utilized former students to inform readers about college life and printed lists of the college choices of the previous year's graduates. In 1947, James Lynch and Paul Dow wrote what life was like during their first two years at West Point. In the same year, Robert Perry described a year spent at the University of Stockholm as an exchange student.

By the 1950s, Ivan G. Smith's earlier charge to teachers to produce happy scholars had expanded to well-adjusted ones. It was a responsibility of American education underscored by authorities like Arthur Jones. In a very popular textbook *Principles of Guidance* (fourth edition, 1951), he noted the rearing of children by "permissive" parents, an adjective that became the catchword for parenting in that decade.

According to Jones, seventy-five percent of American mothers were not at home when their children returned from school. The start of the day was also of concern. In the 1950s, breakfasts were served in Danvers schools since many pupils were arriving for classes without having eaten an adequate meal. Because job opportunities were plentiful, the dropout rate from the secondary level was another concern. With the promise of more complex machines to come, machines that would impact on all kinds of employment, there was a need for trained professionals to explain the diversity of career fields and their requirements.

Despite the necessity of professional guidance counselors, the establishment of state-mandated laws dictating the number of personnel, one generally for every 250 students, was resented by the tax paying public. In Danvers, the guidance department rose from one director at the commencement of the decade to a director, three counselors, and a secretary at the end. Other kinds of supervisors and directors were added to the system in this decade of growth.

By far, the greatest causes of rising taxes were baby boom and land development. Woodvale, North Street, Whipple Hill, Forest and Summer Street housing projects all came about then. The resultant overcrowding of schools led to double sessions and the setting up of emergency classrooms in cafeterias and the town hall. In 1951, the Great Oak School was opened; in 1956, the Riverside and Highlands Schools received their first pupils; and in 1962, Danvers High School came into being. In 1955, increased population also required a new Hunt Memorial Hospital.

Considering the work performed to open Holten High School in 1931, it will come as a surprise to some readers that as early as 1938 the school suffered from overcrowding. In that year, the Danvers School Committee had been warned that

Holten High exceeded the state limit of thirty pupils per teacher. Of ninety-seven classes, only thirty-two had enrollments of thirty or fewer. The drain of boys from the school during World War II had kept the town from receiving more warnings.

Annoying to local taxpayers, too, was the formation of the Danvers Teachers' Union led by returning war veterans who loved teaching but were tired of working two jobs to support their families. A post-war challenge to traditional teacher preparation was the demand from liberal arts colleges and professors for more academic and fewer methods courses. Younger teachers found ritual formalities in fraternal organizations and what previous generations had regarded as "sacred duties" as without much relevance to them.

As stressful as all these factors were, the worst blow of all to America's pride came on October 4, 1957, when the Soviet Union launched Sputnik I, thereby winning the Cold War race to be the first to send an object into orbit. It can be said that before this event, the nation's public schools could do no wrong; after, that they could do nothing right.

At that time, two major efforts were made to improve American secondary education by modifying existing programs. The first came in 1958. James B. Conant, a former chemistry professor and retired president of Harvard working on a grant from the Carnegie Corporation, presented recommendations for improving the high schools in a report, *The American High School Today.* His visits to schools of recognized excellence convinced him that guidance services should be extended, small high schools (those graduating fewer than 100 seniors) should be replaced by large, regional high schools, and ability grouping for required courses should have the addition of advanced placement courses for the academically talented. There were other recommendations as well.

Contemporaneous with the Conant report, the Congress passed the National Defense Education Act to improve the teaching of the sciences, mathematics, foreign languages, and guidance. Later, English was included. These NDEA grants were generous in the manner of the GI Bill for veterans following the second world war. Candidates for the new grants were carefully screened to identify leaders among them who were expected to return to their schools and pass on what they had learned. At the various colleges and universities offering approved courses, they had their tuition, board and room, and textbooks paid for, and received a stipend as well.

To expand and update the three main tracks—college, commercial, and general—at Holten High, advanced placement courses were first taught by John Logan in biology, Myrtle Root in mathematics, and Lawrence Leistinger in chemistry. Henry Derouin was hired as an instructor of IBM procedures and modern office machines in 1959 for the commercial department. And the first efforts were made to involve general students in local businesses as motivation for them to complete their educations.

Blocking the success of such programs in the 1960s was the rise of the counterculture and the struggle of minorities to gain recognition and of individuals to gain their rights, *rights* (often devoid of responsibilities) being the catchword of that decade.

By then, however, the Danvers school system had a new superintendent, Clifford J. Good in 1954. And after the retirement of Mr. Dunn, Ernest W. April, who had taught English at Holten High School for fourteen years, became the new high school principal in 1958. There was also a new administrator at this level, a director of secondary education, Eugene C. Crowell, in 1961.

As for Cornelius F. Dunn, after his wonderful retirement party, he settled down to enjoy his remaining years. A quiet person, he remained close to home. But when, for example, he went down to a Danvers Square supermarket to shop, everyone stopped to talk with him. The checkout girls and the stock boys were solicitous of him as they joked and bagged his purchases. He made regular appearances in some elementary-school classrooms at the invitations of the teachers.

Then Helena Dunn suffered a long final illness. Mr. Dunn himself became ill and infirm. Fortunately, he had his son Neil to help him. And we alumni made regular visits to him at the Heritage House Nursing Home on Sylvan Street. After class reunions, we brought him some of the refreshments and showed him pictures of the parties. At other times we stopped to talk with him as he sat in a chair or on the steps of the nursing home sunning himself. He always knew us.

Perhaps not so surprising was that apparently inexhaustible source of faith and courage that helped him bring comfort to his fellow patients. Frail though he had become, he inspired in them the same love and devotion we felt for him, He passed away on May 7, 1977. His name is preserved today in the Dunn Middle School and the Dunn Scholarship.

In August 1991, Attorney David A. Mills wrote the editor of the *Danvers Herald* about the North Shore Community College and its coming to town. In it, he gave an assessment of his secondary-schooling that sums up the feeling of most of us, "We in Danvers had the best—no question—the best. At Holten High and at the Richmond, we had the best. Phillips Exeter, Governor Dummer, they had it good—but so did we. What a gift we had. Teachers who loved us and respected us. . . . It was Holten. It was Richmond. Ask about 10,000 of us. We still live around here."

Mr. Dunn was the sum of what he taught us. He may not have been King Arthur's perfect knight, but he came as close to being one as most of us shall ever know. The success Holten High School had was, in great measure, due to him.

BIBLIOGRAPHY

Note: Bibliographical information for *The Holten* issues, Danvers town records, town reports, and school committee annuals, articles in the Danvers Historical Collections, newspaper articles, interviews, and letters is given in the text. In addition to information from *Who's Who in America*, further material about authors came from the *Directory of American Scholars, Contemporary Authors, Current Biography* and the like was located by researchers at the Maine State Library in Augusta. Most of the material about Charles Vye came from articles about him at the time of his death.

History, Biography, and Literature

Abbe, Charles. *Hill Wind.* Ed. by George Abbe, New York, 1936.

Abbe, George. *Voices in the Square.* New York, 1938.

Adams, James Truslow. *The March of Democracy.* New York, 1932.

Archer, Charles. "Danvers," pp. 96–114. *Standard History of Essex County, Massachusetts.* Boston, 1898.

Bay Psalm Book of 1640. Reprint edition. Chicago, 1956.

Bean, Douglas. *Danvers Honor Roll.* Danvers, n.d.

Boas, Ralph and Louise. *Cotton Mather: Keeper of the Puritan Conscience.* New York, 1928.

Brown, Thurl. "Danvers Town Halls." *Danvers Historical Collections.* Volume XLII, 1924, pp. 99–115.

Centennial Celebration of Danvers, Mass., June 16, 1852. Boston, 1852 (Contains John Proctor's address.)

Crossman, Carl. *The China Trade.* Salem, 1972.

———. *The Decorative Arts of the China Trade.* Princeton, 1991.

Earle, Alice M. *Child Life in Colonial Days.* New York, 1899.

Ford, Paul Leicester. *The New England Primer.* New York, 1899.

Handlin, Oscar. *Boston's Immigrants.* New York, 1970.

Hansen, J. W. *History of the Town of Danvers from Its Earliest Settlement.* Danvers, 1848.

Jedrey, Christopher M. *The World of John Cleaveland.* New York, 1970.

Lerner, Max. *America as a Civilization.* 2 vols. New York, 1961.

Mather, Cotton. *Magnalia Christi Americana.* 2 vols. Hartford, 1853.

May, Samuel J. *Life of.* Boston, 1873.

Messages of the President of the United States. Washington, 1872.

Morgan, Edmund S. *The Puritan Family.* New York, 1966.

Morison, Samuel Eliot. *Builders of the Bay Colony.* Boston, 1930, and Henry Steele Commager. *The Growth of the American Republic.* New York, 1942.

Moynahan, Frank E. *Danvers, Massachusetts.* Danvers, 1899.

Palmer, George H. *The Life of Alice Freeman Palmer.* Boston, 1908.

Pedrick, Jean. *Bos, Bovis.* Pleasant Hill, 1993.

Perley, Sidney. *The History of Salem, Massachusetts.* 3 vols. Salem, 1924.

Pettingill, Olin Sewall, R. *My Way to Ornithology.* Norman, Okla., 1992.

Proceedings at the Reception and Dinner in Honor of George Peabody. Boston, 1856.

Rice, Charles B. *Proceedings at the Celebration of the 200th Anniversary of the First Parish of Salem Village.* Boston, 1874.

Shehan, Thomas. "A Tribute to Cornelius F. Dunn," *Danvers Historical Collections.* Volume XLIII, 1967, pp. 80–88.

Smith, Helen S. *Colonial Days and Ways.* New York, 1900.

Spellman, Francis Cardinal. *No Greater Love: The Story of Our Soldiers.* New York, 1945.

Starkey, Marion. *The Devil in Massachusetts.* New York, 1950.

Sullivan, William B. *Danvers' Welcome Home to Her Sons from World War I.* Address delivered June 28, 1919.

Tapley, Harriet S. *Chronicles of Danvers.* Danvers, 1923.

Tharp, Louise H. *Until Victory: Horace Mann and Mary Peabody.* Boston, 1953.

Watkins, Lura. *Middleton, Massachusetts: A Colorful History.* Salem, 1970.

Wells, John. *The Peabody Story.* Salem, 1972.

Wertenbaker, Thomas Jefferson. *The Puritan Oligarchy.* New York, 1947.

Winthrop, John. *Journal (The History of New England).* 2 vols. Boston, 1853.

Zollo, Richard P. Portions of "Danvers Yesterday" columns written for the *Danvers Herald* from 1980 to 1984.

Education

Barber, Benjamin R. "America Skips School." *Harper's.* November, 1993, pp. 39–46.

Burnett, Charles T. *Hyde of Bowdoin.* Boston, 1931.

Butts, R. Freeman and Lawrence A. Cremin. *A History of Education in American Culture.* New York, 1953.

Chauncey, Henry, ed. *Talks on American Education.* New York, 1962.

Colburn, Warren. *Intellectual Arithmetic.* Boston, 1826.

Conant, James B. *The American High School Today.* New York, 1959.

Cremin, Lawrence A. *The Transformation of the School.* New York, 1968.

Dunton, John. *Life and Errors.* Nineteenth century copy of the London edition, 1686.

Dunton, Larkin. *A Memorial of the Life and Services of John D. Philbrick.* Boston, 1887.

Eliot, Charles. *Late Harvest.* Boston, 1924.

Hyde, William DeWitt. *God's Education of Man.* Boston, 1899.

Jones, Arthur. *Principles of Guidance.* Fourth edition. New York, 1951.

James, William. *Talks to Teachers.* New York, 1924.

Locke, John. *Some Thoughts Concerning Education.* New York, 1938.

Marr, Harriet Webster. *Old New England Academies.* New York, 1959.

Monroe, Paul. *Founding of the American Public School System.* New York, 1940.

Palmer, George H. and Alice Freeman Palmer. *The Teacher.* Cambridge, 1908.

Third Annual Catalogue of the People's Literary Institute and Gymnasium at Pembroke, N.H. for the Year Ending November 9, 1842. Concord, 1842.

Danvers High School Band, March 1929.

CHAPTER NOTES

Chapter I

First Schoolmaster

On April 8, 1629, the ministers Samuel Skelton and Francis Higginson signed an agreement with the Dorchester Company, which settled Salem, "to doe their endeavor in their places of the ministery as well as in preaching, catechizing as also in teaching, or causing to bee taught, the Companyes servants and their children. . . ."

After their arrival in America, a day of fasting was declared on July 20 for the founding of the church in Salem. The fasting was felt necessary because of the solemnity of the decisions to be made. The Reverend Higginson was elected the teacher; and the Reverend Skelton, the minister. The latter's name appears on early maps of Danvers as one of our first grantees of land. Skelton's Neck is the point of land down which River Street runs today. (See Perley's *History of Salem*, v.1.)

Language Acquisition

The first principle of language laboratories was introduced in 1692, the year Cheever's *Accidence* was published. At that time, John Locke's *Some Thoughts Concerning Education* appeared. It consisted of a series of letters written to Edward Clarke concerning the instruction of Clarke's son. In it, Locke proposed that a "living language"—French—be taught first, but not by "master, rule, or grammar," rather "by talking it into children in constant conversation, and not by grammatical rules."

Seventeenth-century scholars could learn by Latin study, according to Locke, "geography, astronomy, chronology, anatomy, besides some parts of history." However, Latin would be taught only to those going on to professions that required it.

Not every graduate of a grammar school was proud of his study of Latin. New England orator Edward Everett Hale in *A New England Boyhood* tells us that in his first year in Boston Latin in 1831, he found that the time-honored study of that subject consisted of the memorization of long lists of words so dull an exercise that "half the boys were driven from the school before they had been there two years." And he further observed that these dropouts were the boys of "quick and bright minds, who went off into business." (Just the boys Locke said did not need to study Latin.)

Even by the time of graduation with so many classics read, such was the emphasis on memorization and the lack of explanation that Boston businessman Joseph Gardner told Hale, "I can remember (as an adult) the block on which I was standing in the Place Vendôme in Paris, when, as by a revelation, it occurred to me that Andrews and Skoddard's *Latin Grammar* was made from the Latin language, and that the Latin language was not made from Andrews and Stoddard's grammar as up to that moment I had always supposed."

"Where Andrews and Stoddard enter," wrote the author and clergyman Thomas Wentworth Higginson (1823–1911), "it is inevitable that all joys should flee." Nevertheless, in an essay, "On an Old Latin Text-book," written for *The Atlantic Monthly*, Higginson later thought better of his Latin school grammar book, "What great thoughts were found within (its) pages, what a Roman vigor was in these maxims! 'It is Roman to do and to suffer bravely.' 'It is sweet and glorious to die for one's country.' 'He that gives himself up to pleasure is not worthy the name of a man.' 'It is the part of a brave and unshaken spirit not to be disturbed in adverse affairs.' 'At how much is virtue to be esteemed, which can never be taken away by force, nor purloined; is neither lost by shipwreck, nor by fire, nor is it changed by the alterations of seasons and times.'"

Some bright twentieth-century Danvers college course students, by way of contrast, took a great degree of pleasure in showing off their Latin acquirements, even if it was in doggerel form. Note the following poem that appeared twice in *The Holten* over the years:

Boyibus kissibus
Sweeti girlorum.
Girlibus likibus,
Wanti somorum.
Pater puellibus
Enter parlorum
Kickibus boyibus
Exibus dorum.
Nightibus darkibus.
Nonus lamporum.
Climbibus fencibus;
Breechibus torum.

Better to enjoy the above than to parse it.

Memorization

The mention of memorization in Chapters I, II, and III prompts some further comments on the subject. New England's first seventeenth-century best seller, as noted, was written by a Malden clergyman, the Rev. Michael Wigglesworth, in 1622, "The Day of Doom." Ill for years and unable to perform his clerical duties, Wigglesworth composed his long narrative poem as a means of supporting himself. Sales far exceeded his hopes. Of the 1800 copies first printed almost all were sold in a single year. Numerous editions followed. One out of every twenty people in New England, it has been said, or about one in every four families owned a copy. It had the popularity here that John Bunyan's *Pilgrim's Progress*, published in 1678, had in England.

The entire action of Wigglesworth's poem transpires on Judgment Day, the day of doom. Christ is the arbiter, and like His Father, a deity of exquisite justice. He places the martyred saints and the Elect on his right and reprobates (hypocrites, Sabbath-polluters, whoremongers, etc.) on his left. In Biblical terms he is separating the sheep from the goats. All the types of sinners have a chance to defend their behavior in life, after which Christ shows them the errors that they as people of free will had made. Even infants who "from the womb into the tomb were straitway carried" to death are not excluded since as Adam's descendants they are tainted by his sin. They are all to be cast into a fiery lake of burning brimstone, and

There must they ly, and never dy,
Though dying every day.
There must they dying ever ly,
And not consume away.

Difficult as it may be to believe, children memorized some of the most dramatic scenes, and others learned all 224 verses by heart. If the types of sinners depicted seem to be too mature for little minds to comprehend, the reason is that childhood as we appreciate it today did not exist as a separate age group during the Colonial era. From a tender age, eighteenth-century children of wealthy parents, for example, were dressed in the identical clothes that their parents wore—tight corsets for little girls and embroidered vests under heavy velvet waistcoats for little boys. Both wore wigs on formal occasions.

When, in the eighteenth century, children began to be bribed to memorize passages, oftentimes from the Bible, a weakening of Puritan fervor is quite evident.

It was for, example, the custom for planters on British-held Caribbean islands to send their children north to be educated. Alice Morse Earle's *Child Life in Colonial Days* cites a letter written in 1718 by Lydia Coleman of Boston to her grandson, the Honorable Hugh Hall, Judge of the Admiralty in Barbados, about his young brother and ward Richard, who was attending Boston Latin. "He loves his books and his play too," she wrote. "I hired him to get a Chapter of ye Proverbs & give him a penny every Sabbath day, & promised him 5 shillings when he can say them all by heart. I would do my duty by his soule as well as his body. . . ."

Corporal Punishment

Even a frail and gentle art teacher like Mabel Spofford resorted to physical punishment to keep order in the one-room country schools in which she first taught. In 1906, she recorded in her diary that during her initial teaching assignment in Vermont, she whipped three boys and had a tussle with a fourth. She ended that entry, "Otherwise a good day."

Here, as pointed out in the text, was a lady of most tender sensibilities. In addition to the story of her iris "disposal," I would add that she also kept her food scraps neatly wrapped in the refrigerator so that the garbageman's pigs would have unspoiled food.

So ingrained in the minds of school administrators and instructors was their belief in the efficacy of whippings that I can recall as a young teacher at Holten High School in the late 1940s going into a large educational supply house in Boston where I found a cardboard barrel in the back of the store filled with limber, dowel-shaped rods. I asked a clerk what they were for. After looking at me closely to be sure I was naive enough to ask such a question, he told me they were rattans. He advised me if I planned to use one to be sure I had a janitor present to confirm that the beating given to a student had not been so severe as to break the skin. I never thought I had passed up the opportunity of a lifetime that day when I left the store with just a package of bulletin-board pictures to illustrate scenes from Sir Walter Scott's *Ivanhoe*.

Today there are many states of the Union in which corporal punishment in schools is still legal.

Chapter II

Schoolmaster Epes' Grandson Samuel

Samuel Epes, a Captain in Colonel Pickering's Essex County regiment, commanded one of the Danvers companies at the Battle of Lexington and Concord. A good military leader, Samuel became a pathetic character in old age. Salem's famous diarist, the Rev. William Bentley, finding in his tragedy material for a tsk-tsk-how-the-mighty-have-fallen moral tale, recorded on December 24, 1804: "Yesterday was buried in this Town, Major Samuel Epes, aet. 56. . . . (He) possessed a very handsome landed interest in Danvers, the same estate which now makes such an appearance under the name of the Derby gardens & barns. The house is the same the Major possessed. The Major without much economy, less judgment in his affairs, sold his estate to Mr. (Elias Hasket) Derby for paper money at the time of the most rapid depreciation, & actually trifled the whole away."

The doctor's account of Samuel Epes's death may have been colored by a transaction Bentley apparently had had with Epes in 1792. In the diary on May 11 of that year, Bentley wrote, "Rode up to Danvers, settled for Minister's Pasture, & left my right in Mr. Holt's hand. Viewed the Pasture & observed the situation. Thought of separating my part. Major Epes has had the improvement by taking advantages."

On the property that Derby bought from Epes and his uncle John, he had the Salem architect Samuel McIntire design a handsome, two-story Federal gazebo, the same structure Ellen Endicott had moved to Glen Magna at the beginning of this century. Today, proudly set among beautifully restored gardens, it sits "an architectural gem" that claims nationwide admiration.

Schoolmaster Epes's Son Daniel

Owning such an extensive farm in Danvers, the Epes's utilized slave labor. Danvers historian Harriet S. Tapley reports that this Daniel in 1754 sold a Negro boy, Primus, to Ebenezer Jacobs for five pounds, six shillings, and eight pence. During the Revolution when, in 1777, there was a shortage of men for the army, Primus Jacobs enlisted just a year and a day after his marriage to Dinah Smith and served six years in the Continental Army. His first enlistment was under Captain Samuel Page, Jeremiah's son. This meant that Primus spent the winter of 1777–1778 in Valley Forge, a period of service that sunshine patriots avoided.

Chapter III

Lucy Larcom's Dame School

The best and probably most complete account of an Essex County dame school is given to us by Lucy Larcom, the poet, in her autobiography (still in print) *A New England Girlhood.* Best known for her religious verse, Miss Larcom edited John Greenleaf Whittier's literary anthology, *Poems of Three Centuries*, and she compiled two collections of children's literature, *Child Life in Poetry* and *Child Life in Prose.*

In 1826 at two years of age, Lucy was sent to a school conducted by "Aunt Hannah," who lived above the Larcoms' West India goods shop in Beverly. If a child in their neighborhood could walk, talk, and was considered educable, he or she was sent to Aunt Hannah to learn to read. (Aunt and uncle were terms of respect for old people.)

This teacher utilized both her kitchen and her parlor for her classroom. When a tiny one grew tired, she let it take a nap on a comforter laid out on the floor. One of the children's favorite scenes was of this woman spinning on her flax wheel, "wetting her thumb and forefinger at her lips to twist the thread, keeping time, meanwhile, to some quaint old tune with her foot on the treadle."

Housework aside, Aunt Hannah was conscientious about giving instruction. Her main goal was to teach a child to read the opening chapter of the Bible, a traditional goal. "The proudest Scriptural conquest in school" was Miss Larcom's assessment of that attainment. Also traditional was the lack of explanation. Little Lucy wondered long about the "four fathers"—Adam, Eve, Cain, and Abel—and whether or not she was a Jew or a Gentile.

Aunt Hannah was also traditional where punishment was concerned. She was not afraid to beat a child's open palms with her ferrule. Girls sometimes received a rap on the head from her silver thimble. It's difficult to believe that Lucy got punished often. She was too good a student.

"But I learned my lessons in a few days," she reported, "standing at Aunt Hannah's knee while she pointed them (words) out in the spelling book with a pin, skipping over the 'a b abs' into words of one and two syllables, thence taking a flying leap into the New Testament, in which there is concurrent family testimony that I was reading at the age of two years and a half."

As this paragraph continued in the *Girlhood*, it is clear that while a New England schoolmistress might act stern and was dutyfilled about her work, she could still be compassionate. "Certain it is," Miss Larcom continued, "that a few passages in the Bible, whenever I read them now, do not fail to bring before me a vision of Aunt Hannah's somewhat sternly smiling lips, with her spectacles just above them, far down on her nose, encouraging me to pronounce the hard words. I think she tried to choose for me the least difficult verses, or perhaps those (like the Beatitudes) of which she was herself especially fond."

Chapter IV

Local Attitude Toward Learning

On June 16, 1852, at the town's centennial observance, Judge John Proctor, the exceptionally capable crusader for free high schools, attributed the dearth of college graduates here to the fact that "the people of Danvers have been anxious to realize a more speedy income on their investments than is ordinarily found by trimming the midnight lamp. As a general thing, they value objects in possession more than those in expectancy; their faith is not strong enough to sustain the hope of distinction by means of literary efforts."

Chapter V

Miss Sally Dow's Generosity

Miss Dow gave the first major bequest received by the Penobscot Marine Museum in her hometown of Searsport, Maine–$150,000 and her home and its contents. Later her sister Kate Dow Nichols contributed an additional generous gift. The Dow family acquired its wealth, not from the sea, but from the steel industry in the Midwest. (See *Down-East,* July 1994.)

Chapter VI

Writing Dynasties

So much has been made of athletic dynasties that it should be pointed out that where *The Holten* was concerned, families were equally well represented. First, there were the sisters Grace and Helen Kirby, both of whom were editors. So were Dorothy and Helen Cooley. Leonard Nolan was business manager, but his son Leonard followed in his uncle Kenneth's footsteps and served as editor. Norman Brown was the editor in his generation, and his daughter Debbie was in hers. Wink Sherry, her brother James and her sisters Barbara and Elizabeth were all department editors. I had two aunts—Anastasia and Audrey—and three cousins—Audrey Reid, Jacquelyn and JoAnne Zollo—who were on the staff. My cousins and I were department editors. Later Wink and I were both faculty advisors. There were other families as well.

Chapter VII

Racial Matters

Dr. Alfred Stearns, former headmaster of Phillips Andover Academy addressed an assembly on the subject: "We should not feel superior to anybody of different race, creed, or color."

In *More Rhymes of a Lifetime*, Miss Wood included a poem of hers previously published in the *Boston Herald*:

Color

What does God do
With the human race,
With the black and white,
The yellow and brown,
When they go to Heaven

And see His face?
Does He say, "Now black men
You go down;
The yellow men can't mix
With the brown?"
The Son of God called all men
Kin, (and)
Ignored the color of their skin.

Maine Sports Hall of Fame

On June 10, 1994, Jack Zollo was inducted into the Maine Sports Hall Fame in the Bangor Civic Center. According to the *Maine Sunday Telegram*: "At 5-foot-8 and 180 pounds, Zollo was consistently outweighed but just as consistently outplayed his opponents as he sparked a series of strong Black Bear teams—1946, '47, '48."

Other Danvers athletes previously inducted there were Dana Dougherty, John Flynn, Robert Hawkes, and Tom Shehan.

Chapter VIII

Teacher-Student Relations

In characterizing teachers in the 1950s, one alumnus, Allen R. Wylie, wrote me from Vermont on February 7, 1994, "They were, in my opinion, examples of a rare and perhaps lost breed. They expected your best, and they were able to get it. Similarly. . . . They *expected* you to behave. They did not attempt to win your friendship, but rather your respect. Having garnered the latter, the former came as appropriate. I have maintained a relationship with Mrs. Root for these 36 years and have found her always to be the archetype of a teacher."

Mr. Dunn's Retirement

On January 20, 1958, the anniversary of Mr. Dunn's arrival in Danvers, he was presented a bouquet of forty red roses by Gladys Damon and Eliot Duncan at a special assembly in the gymnasium.

INDEX

M

N

O

P

ABOUT THE AUTHOR

Virginia Sherry Zollo has had a wide range of experience in education from kindergarten and high school teaching to instructing on the college level. For almost a decade she was a commercial teacher at Holten High School, where she was financial adviser of The Holten and adviser to several of the school's classes. When she and Dick were married on December 25, 1956, many of her students referred to her new spouse as Mr. Sherry.

Richard P. Zollo is professor emeritus from Salem State College and Honorary Historian of the Danvers Historical Society. In addition to serving as editor of the Danvers Historical Collections for several years, he was the faculty advisor for *The Holten* and the school yearbook, *The Onion*, when he taught at Holten High. Since retirement, he has written three volumes on local history: *As the Century Turned: Photographic Glimpses of Danvers, Massachusetts, 1880–1910* (Co-author): *On the Sands of Time: The Biography of Charles Sutherland Tapley*; and now *Ladies and Gentlemen Always: The Illustrated Story of Holten High School.*

Richard and Virginia Zollo are pictured here at Bunratty Castle, Ireland, on a recent tour with members of their church in Boothbay Harbor.